Lecture Notes in Computer Science   14368

Founding Editors

Gerhard Goos
Juris Hartmanis

Editorial Board Members

The series Lecture Notes in Computer Science (LNCS), including its subseries Lecture Notes in Artificial Intelligence (LNAI) and Lecture Notes in Bioinformatics (LNBI), has established itself as a medium for the publication of new developments in computer science and information technology research, teaching, and education.

LNCS enjoys close cooperation with the computer science R & D community, the series counts many renowned academics among its volume editors and paper authors, and collaborates with prestigious societies. Its mission is to serve this international community by providing an invaluable service, mainly focused on the publication of conference and workshop proceedings and postproceedings. LNCS commenced publication in 1973.

Belgacem Ben Hedia · Yassine Maleh ·
Moez Krichen

Editors

Verification and Evaluation of Computer and Communication Systems

16th International Conference, VECoS 2023
Marrakech, Morocco, October 18–20, 2023
Proceedings

 Springer

Editors
Belgacem Ben Hedia ⓘD
CEA LIST
Gif-sur-Yvette, France

Yassine Maleh ⓘD
Université Sultan Moulay Slimane
Beni Mellal, Morocco

Moez Krichen ⓘD
Al-Baha University
Al Baha, Saudi Arabia

ISSN 0302-9743   ISSN 1611-3349 (electronic)
Lecture Notes in Computer Science
ISBN 978-3-031-49736-0   ISBN 978-3-031-49737-7 (eBook)
https://doi.org/10.1007/978-3-031-49737-7

This Springer imprint is published by the registered company Springer Nature Switzerland AG
The registered company address is: Gewerbestrasse 11, 6330 Cham, Switzerland

Paper in this product is recyclable.

Preface

This volume contains the papers presented at the 16th International Conference on Verification and Evaluation of Computer and Communication Systems (VECoS 2023), held during October 18–20, 2023 in Marrakech, Morocco, and hosted by Cadi Ayyad University.

The event of this year continues the tradition of previous editions held 2007 in Algiers, 2008 in Leeds, 2009 in Rabat, 2010 in Paris, 2011 in Tunis, 2012 in Paris, 2013 in Florence, 2014 in Bejaïa, 2015 in Bucharest, 2016 in Tunis, 2017 in Montreal, 2018 in Grenoble, 2019 in Porto, 2020 in Xi'an (virtual), and 2021 in Beijing (virtual).

As in previous editions, VECoS provided a forum for researchers and practitioners in the areas of verification, control, performance, and dependability evaluation in order to discuss the state of the art and challenges in modern computer and communication systems in which functional and extra-functional properties are strongly interrelated. The main motivation was to encourage cross-fertilization between various formal verification and evaluation approaches, methods, and techniques, and especially those developed for concurrent and distributed hardware/software systems.

The Program Committee of VECoS 2023 was composed of 71 researchers from 21 countries. We received 36 full submissions from 17 countries. After a thorough and lively discussion phase, the committee decided to accept 12 regular papers. The topics presented covered a range of subjects, including approaches to improving the scalability and efficiency of formal verification and their applications to blockchain, smart contracts, and neural networks. The conference also included two invited talks, one on analysis of Petri nets and the other on verification of concurrent programs.

We are grateful to the Program and Organizing Committee members, to the reviewers for their cooperation, and to Springer for their professional support during the production phase of the proceedings. We are also thankful to all authors of submitted papers, to the invited speakers, and to all participants of the conference. Their interest in this conference and their contributions are greatly appreciated.

October 2023

Belgacem Ben Hedia
Yassine Maleh
Moez Krichen

Organization

Executive Committee

Program Chair

Yassine Maleh — Sultan Moulay Slimane University, Morroco

Program Co-chair

Moez Krichen — AlBaha University, KSA

General Chairs

Moha Taourirte — Cadi Ayyad University, Morroco
Said Rakrak — Cadi Ayyad University, Morroco

Publicity Co-chairs

Belgacem Ben Hedia — CEA-LIST, Université Paris-Saclay, France

Steering Committee

Djamil Aissani — Université de Bejaia, Algeria
Mohamed Faouzi Atig — Uppsala University, Sweden
Kamel Barkaoui (Chair) — CEDRIC CNAM, France
Hanifa Boucheneb — École Polytechnique de Montréal, Canada
Francesco Flammini — Ansaldo STS, Italy
Belgacem Ben Hedia — LIST CEA Université Paris-Saclay, France
Mohamed Kaâniche — LAAS-CNRS, France
Bruno Monsuez — ENSTA Paris, France
Nihal Pekergin — Université Paris Est Créteil, France
Tayssir Touili — LIPN, CNRS Université Paris Nord, France

Referees

Y. Abdeddaim	S. Dal Zilio	L. Ma
W. Adoni	I. Demongodin	Y. Maleh
D. Aissani	K. El-Fakih	R. Meyer
Y. Ait Ameur	M. Escheikh	A. Mili
R. Ammour	A. Fantechi	B. Monsuez
M. Asavoae	A. Geniet	M. Mosbah
M. Faouzi Atig	M. Ghazel	A. Muthanna
E. Badouel	S. Haddad	A. Nouri
K. Barkaoui	A. Harbaoui	M. Ouaissa
F. Belala	R. Iosif	M. Ouaissa
M. Belguidoum	A. Jemai	S. Ouchani
I. Ben Hafaiedh	M. Jmaiel	C. Palamidessi
B. Ben Hedia	J. Julvez	V. Paun
I. Ben Dhaou	B. Kerim	P. Poda
S. Bensalem	K. Klai	G. Pu
P. Bonhomme	M. Krichen	A. Rabéa
A. Bouajjani	L. Kristensen	R. Robbana
H. Boucheneb	A. Kucera	R. J. Rodríguez
A. Boudguiga	M. Lahami	O. H. Roux
Y. Chen	A. Legay	L. Sliman
Z. Chen	O. Lengal	T. Touili
F. Chu	A. Lisitsa	W. Wu
G. Ciobanu	D. Liu	X. Yin
J. Couvreur	G. Liu	

Additional Reviewers

C. Ding	N. Marir	M. Lahami
X. Wang	I. Garfatta	R. Maseli
G. Fersi	T. Joven	J. Wu
R. Reali	A. Oarga	M. Taha Bennani
M. Blicha	B. Lotfi Mediouni	F. Fakhfakh
M. Hruska	S. Ho	

Sponsoring Institutions

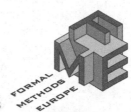

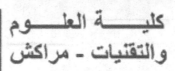

Keynote Speakers

On Verifying Concurrent Programs under Weakly Consistent Memory Models

Ahmed Bouajjani

Paris Cité University, France
abou@irif.fr

Abstract

Developing correct and performant concurrent systems is a major challenge. When programming an application over a memory/storage system, a natural expectation would be that each memory update is immediately visible to all concurrent threads, which means that the views of the different threads are (strongly) consistent. However, for performance reasons, only weaker guarantees can be ensured by memory systems, defined by what sets of updates can be made visible to each thread at any moment, and by the order in which these updates are made visible. The conditions on the visibility order guaranteed by a memory system corresponds to its consistency memory model. Weak consistency models admit complex and unintuitive behaviors where memory access operations (reads and writes) may be reordered in various ways w.r.t. the order in which they appear in programs. This makes the task of application programmers extremely hard. It is therefore important to determine an adequate level of consistency for each given application, i.e., a level that is weak enough to ensure high performance, but also strong enough to ensure correctness of the application w.r.t its specification. This leads to the consideration of several important verification problems:

- the correctness of an application program running over a weak consistency model;
- the robustness of an application program w.r.t. consistency weakening;
- the fact that an implementation of a system (memory, storage system) guarantees a given (weak) consistency model.

The talk gives a broad presentation of these issues and some results in this research area. The talk is based on several joint works with students and colleagues during the last few year.

How to Use Polyhedral Reduction for the Verification of Petri Nets

Silvano Dal Zilio

LAAS - CNRS, France
ali.mili@njit.edua

Abstract

I will describe a new concept, called polyhedral reduction, that takes advantage of structural reductions to accelerate the verification of reachability properties on Petri nets. This approach relies on a state space abstraction which involves sets of linear arithmetic constraints between the marking of places. We have been using polyhedral reductions to solve several problems. I will consider three of them. First, how to use reductions to efficiently compute the number of reachable markings of a net. Then how to use polyhedral reduction in combination with a SMT-based model checker. Finally, I will define a new data-structure, called Token Flow Graph (TFG), that captures the particular structure of constraints that we generate with our approach. I will show how we can leverage TFGs to efficiently compute the concurrency relation of a net, that is all pairs of places that can be marked together in some reachable marking.

Contents

Factorization of the State Space Construction for Cyclic Systems with Data

Johan Arcile[1]([⊠]), Raymond Devillers[2], and Hanna Klaudel[1]

[1] IBISC, Univ Evry, Université Paris-Saclay, 91025 Evry, France
{johan.arcile,hanna.klaudel}@univ-evry.fr
[2] ULB, Bruxelles, Belgium
rdevil@ulb.ac.be

Abstract. In the context of formal modeling and verification of complex systems composed of cycling entities, we propose a method allowing to speed up the construction of state spaces exploiting symmetries. The method is suitable for systems continuously updating large data but whose transitions do not depend on the particular data values. Using a judicious ordering of operations, the method avoids non-necessary multiple treatments thus allowing to factorize a part of the computations. We prove that the method is correct and complete, and illustrate its application on a case study composed of a network of cycling timed automata extended with data.

1 Introduction

The formal verification of real time systems is a topic of importance, with a lot of theoretical and practical works in various contexts (multi-core systems [21], security protocols [4], embedded systems [12], internet of things [2], etc.), and several tools that have proved their usefulness (Uppaal [18], Kronos [10], Imitator [3], Prism [17], Tina [9], Romeo [20], etc.). However, and despite all the efforts to make them as efficient and user-friendly as possible, these tools and techniques are still rarely used by system designers [7,23], partly due to a lack of support for complex data structures and the ability to cope with really big state spaces.

Our motivation is to verify temporal logic properties of systems with data, in particular multi-agent real time systems comprising agents having a cyclic behaviour and whose states are described by a large number of variables. The applications we have in mind are for example autonomous vehicles, flying drone squadrons, mobile robots completing tasks according to their own objectives, etc. The formal description of such systems often leads to huge state spaces, due to large value domains, compromising any verification using traditional techniques and tools. However, in some cases, these state spaces have symmetries which may be exploited. In this paper, we propose some improvements in the state space construction.

B. Ben Hedia et al. (Eds.): VECoS 2023, LNCS 14368, pp. 1–14, 2024.
https://doi.org/10.1007/978-3-031-49737-7_1

The idea of our approach is to start with a specification $\mathcal{M}$ of a system which may be expressed in terms of a labelled transition system. We do not need to specify the syntax at this stage (for example, it could be a network of timed automata). We consider an extension of $\mathcal{M}$ with data, denoted $\mathcal{M}^+$ satisfying that transition enabling does not depend on data values, and data updates are only possible through update functions associated to transitions. A state in $\mathcal{M}^+$ is then composed of a *control* part (for timed automata, that would be clocks and locations) and a *data* part. The usual way to compute the state space of $\mathcal{M}^+$ is to compute successor states with the semantics of $\mathcal{M}$ extended with data (for example, extended timed automata).

Since data does not impact the availability of transitions, the evolution of the control part of states does not depend on the evolution of data. If $\mathcal{M}$ contains cycles, these cycles generally disappear in $\mathcal{M}^+$ because of data, but the control part is still the same (cyclic) and may be factorized. Our idea is to compute the state space of $\mathcal{M}$, *i.e.* ignoring data, which is a labelled transition system and use it as a specification to be extended with data, leading to a state space that is equivalent to the one of $\mathcal{M}^+$ while being computed faster. For example, with timed automata, this factorization avoids to compute several times the same clock zones in successor states. In general, this method is all the more effective as the difference of the number of states between $\mathcal{M}$ and $\mathcal{M}^+$ is large. This is particularly interesting in the context of on-the-fly exploration methods, where the state space is built while verifying properties.

Contribution. In this paper, we define first a general way to extend a specification with data, then propose a method of factorization and prove its soundness and completeness. For finite systems, we propose a method allowing to reduce the size of the state space while preserving temporal logic properties of interest. Finally, we apply the method to examples of networks of timed automata of realistic size applications of systems of autonomous vehicles.

Outline. The paper is structured as follows. The next section introduces some related work. Then, Sect. 2 fixes the context, recalls main notions and defines our new approach, called factorization. First we define the data extension and its semantics; then, we introduce the factorization method for a faster computation of the state spaces and prove the equivalence of the state spaces obtained by traditional algorithms and using the factorization method. We end this section by discussing the theoretical gain of computation time of this approach. Based on factorizations, Sect. 3 proposes an abstraction for finite state spaces, leading to a construction of a reduced state space having interesting properties in terms of language equivalence and temporal logic properties. Section 4 illustrates the method on networks of timed automata and provides some experimental results. Section 5 concludes the paper.

1.1 Related Works

The formal verification of applications involving a large number of variables is challenging right from the modeling stage [24]. Most of the model checking tools do not allow to extend their formalism with data. Therefore, implementing such a specification would require some automated assistance, and would be impractical to use at best, and might even be impossible to handle for the tool. This issue has been addressed by the community, since the state of the art tool Uppaal supports timed automata extended with data structures. Yet, even while modeling is facilitated, such models give way to the usual state space explosion problem.

Model Checking with Large Data Structure. Statistical model checking [19] simulates runs of the system in order to provide a statistical estimation of the satisfaction of some property. This method can easily express complex cyber-physical systems with a large number of data variables. However, they do not allow to express non-determinism, and they do not provide formal guarantees of their results.

Real-Time Abstractions. Several abstractions, like the clock extrapolation [8, 14] or the calendar model [15, 22] have been devised over the years to deal with state space representation in the context of real time systems. Those methods focus on state space explosion due to the real time aspects of the system and ensure a finite state space even when dealing with dense time. As our work aims at facilitating the construction of state spaces in the context of real time systems extended with data structures, it is complementary to those abstractions.

In [13], the authors propose a timeless variant of the calendar model for quasi-periodic distributed systems ([11], cyber physical systems where each process owns a local clock). Although this work has analogies with ours by the way it abstracts real-time aspects based on cyclic behavior of components, it is syntactically restrictive with respect to real-time constraints and provides an over-approximation of the original calendar model.

2   Specifications, Data Extension and Factorization

In this section, we present the main concepts and ideas of our approach. We try to stay as general as possible and do not restrict ourselves to any specific formalism. Thus, we accept any specification whose semantics may be expressed in terms of a labelled transition system (LTS) and whose data extension does not impact transition enabling. Indeed, most formalisms used in the formal verification community, such as Petri nets or timed automata, can meet these criteria, with the syntactic constraint that data variables should not be used in guards, invariants or anything that could prevent transitions to be enabled.

Definition 1 (LTS). *A labelled transition system (LTS) is defined as a tuple* $(S, \Sigma, \rightarrow, s_0)$, *where S is a set of states, Σ is a set of actions (transition labels), $s_0 \in S$ is the initial state and $\rightarrow \subseteq S \times \Sigma \times S$ is the transition relation. A sequence of actions of the LTS is a word $w \in \Sigma^*$ such that there is a sequence of transitions starting in s_0 and ending at some state s whose labels form w.*

From now on, we will only consider specifications $\mathcal{M}$ whose semantics can be expressed as an LTS, and denote by $\mu(\mathcal{M})$ their semantics. We will of course assume that each state s may be reached from s_0 while following the arcs of $\rightarrow$.

Definition 2 (Data extension). *Given a specification $\mathcal{M}$, we define an extension of it with data and update functions by $\mathcal{M}^+ = (\mathcal{M}, \mathcal{V}, \mathcal{D}, \mathcal{F}, v_0)$, where*

- *$\mathcal{V}$ is a set of variables with domain $\mathcal{D}$;*
- *$\mathcal{F} = \{f_a \mid a \in \Sigma\}$ is a set of computable functions $f_a \colon \mathcal{D}^{\mathcal{V}} \to \mathcal{D}^{\mathcal{V}}$;*
- *$v_0 \in \mathcal{D}^{\mathcal{V}}$ is an initial valuation of variables.*

The semantics of such an extended specification is also an LTS. The states are pairs (s, v), where $s \in \mathcal{S}$ and $v \in \mathcal{D}^{\mathcal{V}}$.

Definition 3 (Semantics of an extended specification). *From a specification $\mathcal{M}^+$, we obtain the LTS $(\mathcal{S} \times \mathcal{D}^{\mathcal{V}}, \Sigma, \xrightarrow{\mathcal{F}}, (s_0, v_0))$, where $\xrightarrow{\mathcal{F}}$ is the set of transitions $\{((s, v), a, (s', f_a(v))) \mid (s, a, s') \in \rightarrow\}$. The semantics $\mu(\mathcal{M}^+)$ of $\mathcal{M}^+$ is defined as the part of this LTS that is reachable from its initial state (s_0, v_0).*

In order to simplify the presentation, we assumed that all the variables have the same domain. It is not a true restriction. Indeed, we may take $\mathcal{D} = \cup_{\nu \in \mathcal{V}} \mathcal{D}_\nu$, where each variable $\nu \in \mathcal{V}$ has its own domain $\mathcal{D}_\nu$, such that $\forall a \in \Sigma$, $f_a(\bigotimes_{\nu \in \mathcal{V}} \mathcal{D}_\nu) \subseteq \bigotimes_{\nu \in \mathcal{V}} \mathcal{D}_\nu$ and that $v_0 \in \bigotimes_{\nu \in \mathcal{V}} \mathcal{D}_\nu$. Then, for each reachable state (s, v), $v \in \bigotimes_{\nu \in \mathcal{V}} \mathcal{D}_\nu$.

An important property arising from this definition is that data does not impact the availability of transitions: the evolution of the control part of states does not depend on the evolution of data. This may be expressed in terms of the following lemma.

Lemma 1. *The sequences of actions of $\mu(\mathcal{M})$ and $\mu(\mathcal{M}^+)$ are identical.*

Proof. This Lemma is a direct consequence of Definition 3. The only difference is that, in the extension, the transitions have an impact on the data part of the states. □ 1

Let $\mathcal{M}^+ = (\mathcal{M}, \mathcal{V}, \mathcal{D}, \mathcal{F}, v_0))$ be a specification extended with data. The usual way to compute the state space of $\mathcal{M}^+$ is to start at the initial state and compute successor states with the extended semantics of $\mathcal{M}$. An alternative to compute $\mu(\mathcal{M}^+)$ is to first ignore the extension with data, consider its semantics $\mu(\mathcal{M})$ (*i.e.* a LTS) as a specification and then extend it with data. Formally, we note it as $[\mu(\mathcal{M})]^+ = (\mu(\mathcal{M}), \mathcal{V}, \mathcal{D}, \mathcal{F}, v_0))$.

Proposition 1. $\mu([\mu(\mathcal{M})]^+) = \mu(\mathcal{M}^+)$ *up to renaming of states.*

Proof. Given a state (s, v) of an extended specification, we refer to s as the control part of the state, and v as the data part. First, by Definition 3, extending a specification with data does not impact sequences of transitions with regard to the control part of states. Second, by Lemma 1, $\mu(\mathcal{M})$ and $\mu(\mathcal{M}^+)$ have the same sequences of actions. As the evolution of data part of states only depends on such sequences (by Definition 3), extending the LTS $\mu(\mathcal{M})$ with data results in the same sequences of transitions with regard to the data part of states than directly extending specification $\mathcal{M}$. Since the sequences of transitions in $\mu([\mu(\mathcal{M})]^+)$ and $\mu(\mathcal{M}^+)$ are identical both with regard to the control and data parts of states, those models are in fact identical.   □ 1

Intuitively, we shall consider that our specifications, as well as their semantics, result from some kind of "factorization" since we separated the control part from the data part. Indeed, whenever there are cycles in $\mu(\mathcal{M})$, computing $\mu([\mu(\mathcal{M})]^+)$ instead of $\mu(\mathcal{M}^+)$ allows to exhibit the cyclic control independently from the (non-necessarily cyclic) evolution of the data. The main observation is that a cycle in $\mathcal{M}$ does not necessarily correspond to a cycle in $\mu(\mathcal{M}^+)$ since data extension has a "multiplicative" effect on states. For example, a cyclic path

$$s_0 \xrightarrow{a_0} \ldots \xrightarrow{a_m} s \xrightarrow{a'_1} \ldots \xrightarrow{a'_n} s \xrightarrow{a'_1} \ldots \xrightarrow{a'_n} s \ldots$$

in $\mu(\mathcal{M})$, i.e., a path where a state s is reached infinitely often while following always the same path from this state, becomes

$$(s_0, v_0) \xrightarrow{a_0} \ldots \xrightarrow{a_m} (s, v') \xrightarrow{a'_1} \ldots \xrightarrow{a'_n} (s, v'') \xrightarrow{a'_1} \ldots \xrightarrow{a'_n} (s, v''') \ldots$$

in $\mu(\mathcal{M})^+$, which is unlikely to be cyclic around $a'_1 \ldots a'_n$ (unless $f_{a'_n}(\ldots(f_{a'_1}(v')) \ldots) = v')$. In such a case, the computation of $\mu([\mu(\mathcal{M})]^+)$ avoids to compute more than once the transitions and the control part (s) of the states from $(s, .)$ to $(s, .)$.

$$s \xrightarrow{a'_1} \ldots \xrightarrow{a'_n} s.$$

2.1   Gain Estimation

We can provide a theoretical estimation of the gain of computation time of building a state space with $\mu([\mu(\mathcal{M})]^+)$ instead of $\mu(\mathcal{M}^+)$. In the following, we will denote by

- $time(\omega)$ the computation time of the state space ω;
- $|\omega|$ the number of transitions in ω;
- t_{LTS} the average time needed to compute one successor state in the semantics of an LTS;
- $t_{\mathcal{M}}$ the average time needed to compute one successor state in the semantics of $\mathcal{M}$;

We then have

$$time(\mu(\mathcal{M})) = |\mu(\mathcal{M})| \cdot t_{\mathcal{M}},$$
$$time(\mu(\mathcal{M}^+)) = |\mu(\mathcal{M}^+)| \cdot t_{\mathcal{M}} \text{ and}$$
$$time(\mu([\mu(\mathcal{M})]^+)) = time(\mu(\mathcal{M})) + |\mu(\mathcal{M}^+)| \cdot t_{LTS}$$

since once $\mu(\mathcal{M})$ is computed, the semantics of $\mathcal{M}$ is no longer needed to extend with data.

Therefore, the gain of computation time can be expressed as

$$time(\mu(\mathcal{M}^+)) - time(\mu([\mu(\mathcal{M})]^+)) = |\mu(\mathcal{M}^+)| \cdot (t_\mathcal{M} - t_{LTS}) - |\mu(\mathcal{M})| \cdot t_\mathcal{M}$$

To summarize, the gain of computation time of building a state space with $\mu([\mu(\mathcal{M})]^+)$ depends on two factors: the difference in size (*i.e.*, number of states) between $\mu(\mathcal{M})$ and $\mu(\mathcal{M}^+)$, which directly depends on cyclicity; and the difference in time between t_{LTS} and $t_\mathcal{M}$, which directly depends on the complexity of the semantics of $\mathcal{M}$.

3   Reduced State Space

An interesting feature of our factorization is that we may apply classical reduction procedures to the control part of the system while preserving most of the temporal properties.

By definition, $\mu(\mathcal{M})$ is an LTS. If it is finite, it can be seen as a finite state machine (FSM) whose states are all accepting and that we will denote by $\mathcal{A}$. Thus, $\mathcal{A}$ can be determinized and then minimized using classical algorithms [16]. Below, we recall shortly these two notions.

Let $\mathcal{A} = (\mathcal{S}, \Sigma, \rightarrow, s_0)$ then $det(A) = (\mathcal{S}', \Sigma, \rightarrow', s_0)$ is its determinised version, where $s_0 \in \mathcal{S}' \subseteq 2^\mathcal{S}$ and $\rightarrow'$ are defined as smallest sets such that if $X \in \mathcal{S}', a \in \Sigma$, and if $Y \subseteq \mathcal{S}$ is the set of all states s' reachable from a state $s \in X$ by a transition labelled a, i.e., $\forall s \in X, (s, a, s') \in \rightarrow$, then $(X, a, Y) \in \rightarrow'$ and $Y \in \mathcal{S}'$.

Let $\mathcal{A} = (\mathcal{S}, \Sigma, \rightarrow, s_0)$ be a deterministic FSM and $\equiv \subseteq \mathcal{S} \times \mathcal{S}$ be the equivalence relation on states such that $\forall q, q' \in \mathcal{S} : q \equiv q'$ iff $\forall w \in \Sigma^*$ $q \xrightarrow{w} p \Leftrightarrow q' \xrightarrow{w} p'$, where $p, p' \in \mathcal{S}$. Then $min(A) = ([\mathcal{S}], \Sigma, [\rightarrow], [s_0])$ denotes its minimised version, where $[\mathcal{S}] = \mathcal{S}/_\equiv$ is the set of equivalence classes of $\mathcal{S}$ for $\equiv$, $[\rightarrow]$ is the set of transitions on those classes and $[s_0]$ the equivalence class of s_0.

This is illustrated on Fig. 1.

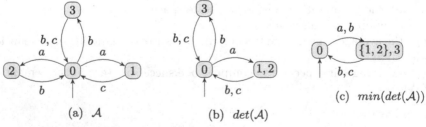

(a) $\mathcal{A}$ (b) $det(\mathcal{A})$ (c) $min(det(\mathcal{A}))$

Fig. 1. Example of determinisation and minimisation.

By definition, there is a language equivalence (*i.e.*, the sequences of actions are identical) between $\mu(\mathcal{M})$ and $min(det(\mu(\mathcal{M})))$. As a consequence all the properties based on sequences of actions stay valid. Since data is only impacted by such sequences, both systems are equivalent when ignoring the part of states that does not involve data. Extending $min(det(\mu(\mathcal{M})))$ with data results in $[min(det(\mu(\mathcal{M})))]^+ = (min(det(\mu(\mathcal{M}))), \mathcal{V}, \mathcal{D}, \mathcal{F}, v_0))$.

Definition 4 (bisimulation). *Let $\mathcal{A} = (\mathcal{S}, \Sigma, \rightarrow, s_0)$ and $\mathcal{A}' = (\mathcal{S}', \Sigma, \Rightarrow, s_0')$ be two LTS. A bisimulation is a binary relation $\approx \subseteq \mathcal{S} \times \mathcal{S}'$ such that $s_0 \approx s_0'$ and for all $p \approx q$:*

- *if $\exists p' \in \mathcal{S}$ s.t. $p \xrightarrow{a} p'$, then $\exists q' \in \mathcal{S}'$ s.t. $q \xRightarrow{a} q'$ and $p' \approx q'$, and*
- *if $\exists q' \in \mathcal{S}'$ s.t. $q \xRightarrow{a} q'$, then $\exists p' \in \mathcal{S}$ s.t. $p \xrightarrow{a} p'$ and $p' \approx q'$.*

Given $\mu(\mathcal{M}^+) = (\mathcal{S}, \Sigma, \rightarrow, s_0)$, we define its data projection (denoted $\overline{\mu(\mathcal{M}^+)}$) as the LTS $(\mathcal{S}', \Sigma, \Rightarrow, \overline{s_0})$ where $\mathcal{S}'$ and $\Rightarrow$ are the smallest sets such that, $\forall\, p \in \mathcal{S}, \exists\, \overline{p} \in \mathcal{S}'$ and $\forall\, p \xrightarrow{a} q, \exists\, \overline{p} \xRightarrow{a} \overline{q}$, where for any state $p = (s, v)$, $\overline{p}$ denotes its data part, i.e., $\overline{p} = v$.

Proposition 2. $\overline{\mu([min(det(\mu(\mathcal{M})))]^+)} \approx \overline{\mu([\mu(\mathcal{M})]^+)}$

Proof. By definition, $min(det(\mathcal{A}))$ preserves the sequences of actions of $\mathcal{A}$. As the value of the set of data variables v only depends on such sequences (see Definition 3), extending $min(det(\mu(\mathcal{M})))$ with data results in an LTS whose data projection is bisimilar to the data projection of the LTS obtained by directly extending $\mu(\mathcal{M})$ with data.   □ 2

As a consequence of Proposition 2, for any logic property ϕ (typically in a temporal logic for timed systems) built from the variable set $\mathcal{V}$ (typically from atomic formulas of the kind *variable = value*), we have

$$[\mu(\mathcal{M})^+, s_0) \models \phi] \Leftrightarrow [\mu([min(det(\mu(\mathcal{M})))]^+), [s_0] \models \phi].$$

This means that the semantics of the original specification extended with data satisfies ϕ, if and only if this is also the case for the semantics of its minimized and determinized state space extended with data. ϕ cannot rely on the control part of states (hence on clocks and locations in the context of timed automata) since some states may be merged in the determinization and minimization process (and hopefully will be, as this allows for shorter computation times).

4   Application to a Network of Timed Automata

In this section, we first illustrate our method on a toy example of a network of *timed automata* (TA). We then provide some experimental results based on an extended network of TA that models actual cyber-physical systems.

4.1   Timed Automata

First we shortly recall the definition of TA and their semantics. Syntactically, a TA is a finite state machine extended with *clocks*, real-valued variables that all evolve at the same rate. The domain of a clock x is $\mathbb{R}_{\geq 0}$. Given a set of clocks $\mathbb{X}$, we denote by *clock constraint* a Boolean formula over a set of inequalities of the form $x \bowtie c$, with $x \in \mathbb{X}$, $\bowtie \in \{<, \leq, =, \geq, >\}$ and $c \in \mathbb{N}$.

Definition 5 (Syntax of a network of TA). *A network $\mathcal{A}$ is a set of n timed automata $\mathcal{A}_i = (\Sigma_i, \mathcal{L}_i, \ell_i^0, \mathbb{X}_i, I_i, E_i)$, where:*

1. *Σ_i is a finite set of actions,*
2. *$\mathcal{L}_i$ is a finite set of locations,*
3. *$\ell_i^0 \in \mathcal{L}$ is the initial location,*
4. *$\mathbb{X}_i$ is a finite set of clocks,*
5. *for every $\ell \in \mathcal{L}_i$, $I_i(\ell)$ is a clock constraint,*
6. *E_i is a finite set of transitions $e = (\ell, g, a, R, \ell')$ where $\ell, \ell' \in \mathcal{L}_i$ are the source and target locations, $a \in \Sigma_i$, $R \subseteq \mathbb{X}_i$ is a set of clocks to be reset, and g is a clock constraint.*

Definition 6 (Semantics of a network of TA). *A state of a network of TA is a pair $(\vec{\ell}, \mathrm{v}(\mathbb{X}))$ where $\vec{\ell} = \ell_1 \ldots \ell_n$ where $\ell_i \in \mathcal{L}_i$, and $\mathrm{v}(\mathbb{X})$ is a valuation of each clock in $\mathbb{X} = \cup_{i=1}^n \mathbb{X}_i$. To simplify the notations, we write $I(\vec{\ell}) = \bigwedge_{i=1}^n I_i(\ell_i)$. The initial state is $(\vec{\ell^0}, \mathrm{v}_0(\mathbb{X}))$, where $\vec{\ell^0} = \ell_1^0 \ldots \ell_n^0$ and $\mathrm{v}_0(\mathbb{X})$ is such that each clock in $\mathbb{X}$ is valuated to 0 and $I(\vec{\ell^0})$ is true on $\mathrm{v}_0(\mathbb{X})$. The successors of a state $(\vec{\ell}, \mathrm{v}(\mathbb{X}))$ are:*

- *$(\vec{\ell}, \mathrm{v}(\mathbb{X}) + \delta)$ where $\delta \in \mathbb{R}_{\geq 0}$ and $I(\vec{\ell})$ is true on $\mathrm{v}(\mathbb{X}) + \delta$; or*
- *$(\vec{\ell'}, \mathrm{v}(\mathbb{X}))$ where there exists a transition $(\ell_i, g, a, R, \ell') \in E_i$ such that*
  - *g is true on $\mathrm{v}(\mathbb{X})$,*
  - *for any $x \in \mathbb{X}$, if $x \in R$ its valuation in $\mathrm{v}'(\mathbb{X})$ is 0, otherwise its valuation remains unchanged, and*
  - *$I(\vec{\ell'})$ is true on $\mathrm{v}'(\mathbb{X})$.*
  - *$\vec{\ell'} = \ell_1' \ldots \ell_n'$ where $\forall j \in [1, n]$ if $j = i$ then $\ell_j' = \ell'$, otherwise $\ell_j' = \ell_j$.*

In order to obtain the semantics of a TA extended with data we apply to TA Definitions 2 and 3. A state of an extended TA is a triple $(\ell, \mathrm{v}(\mathbb{X}), v)$. The successors of state $(\ell, \mathrm{v}(\mathbb{X}), v)$ are:

- $(\ell, \mathrm{v}(\mathbb{X}) + \delta, v)$ where $\delta \in \mathbb{R}_{\geq 0}$ and $I(\vec{\ell})$ is true on $\mathrm{v}(\mathbb{X}) + \delta$; or
- $(\ell', \mathrm{v}'(\mathbb{X}), v')$ where there exists an edge $(\ell, g, a, R, \ell') \in E$ such that
  - g is true on $v(\mathbb{X})$,
  - for any $x \in \mathbb{X}$, if $x \in R$ its valuation in $v'(\mathbb{X})$ is 0, otherwise its valuation remains unchanged, and
  - $I(\vec{\ell'})$ is true on $v'(\mathbb{X})$.
  - $\vec{\ell'} = \ell_1' \ldots \ell_n'$ where $\forall j \in [1, n]$ if $j = i$ then $\ell_j' = \ell'$, otherwise $\ell_j' = \ell_j$.
  - $v' = f_a(v)$;

4.2 A Toy Example

Let us illustrate the method on a simple network of TA extended with data $\mathcal{M}^+$ composed of two components with two clocks x and y and three actions a, b and c, represented in Fig. 2a. The data extension is very simple, it consists in a unique integer variable v, and three update functions $f_a(v) = v+2$, $f_b(v) = v-1$ and $f_c(v) = 2 \cdot v$. We assume that initially $v = 0$. Figure 2b depicts a small initial fragment of the state space of $\mathcal{M}^+$.

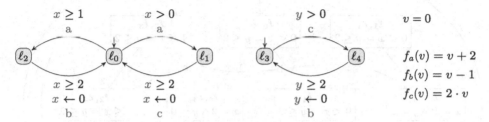

(a) A network of timed automata with data $\mathcal{M}^+$

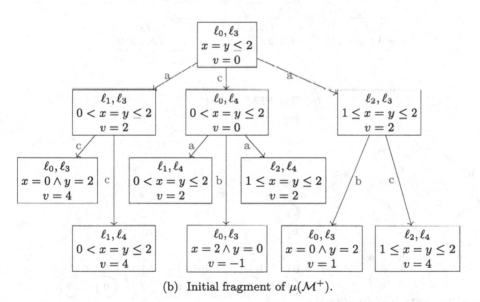

(b) Initial fragment of $\mu(\mathcal{M}^+)$.

Fig. 2. $\mathcal{M}^+$ and the initial fragment of its state space.

Figure 3 presents the consecutive stages of factorization and reduction methods applied to $\mathcal{M}^+$ defined above. First, Fig. 3a depicts the state space of $\mathcal{M}^+$ when ignoring data. One can observe that the obtained FSM is neither deterministic nor minimal. Next, if we want to obtain a reduced state space, we have to determinize and minimise this FSM. The resulting minimal FSM, where locations and clock values are removed, is depicted in Fig. 3b; it has 8 states and 13 transitions instead of 11 states and 20 transitions. Finally, this minimal FSM is used as a specification to be extended with data. The initial part of the obtained reduced state space of $\mathcal{M}^+$ is depicted in Fig. 3c, where the value of variable v is indicated inside the states.

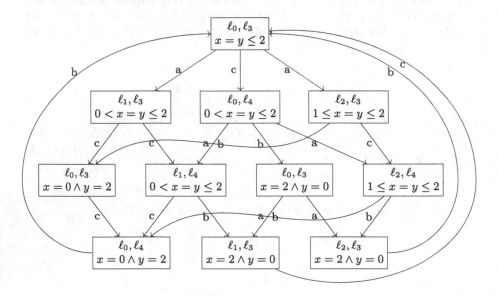

(a) The FSM of $\mu(\mathcal{M})$.

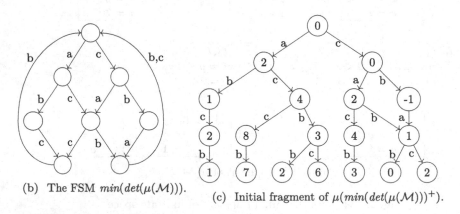

(b) The FSM $min(det(\mu(\mathcal{M})))$.

(c) Initial fragment of $\mu(min(det(\mu(\mathcal{M})))^+)$.

Fig. 3. The stages of construction of the reduced state space of $\mathcal{M}^+$.

4.3 Experiments on a Cyber-Physical System

The method has been experimented on models of communicating autonomous vehicles (CAVs) taken from [5]. The systems are modeled with networks of timed automata. They describe the behaviors of a few communicating autonomous vehicles on a portion of road. The knowledge and physical characteristics of each vehicle is stored in a data structure. Each vehicles alternatively computes some decision based on its knowledge, and communicates its intentions to surrounding vehicles.

We have taken three variants of a same scenario that differ with respect to the communication protocol between vehicles, denoted respectively as *Base*, *Infrastructure* and *Negotiation*, and whose models come from [1] and are implemented in the input format for UPPAAL.

Using UPPAAL, we measured the computation time of the state space of those models, then replaced the network of timed automata by the FSM obtained when ignoring data, and measured the computation time again. Table 1 presents those experimental results, showing the decrease in computation time for those models when using the factorization. Minimization was not applied since the obtained FSM where already minimized. The FSM obtained when ignoring data was composed of 10 states for models *Base* and *Negotiation*, and 62 states for model *Infrastructure*, and their computation time was negligible (< 0.1 s).

We also measured the computation time for the original state space, FSM and minimized FSM for our toy example of Fig. 2. In order to obtain a finite state space, we added an arbitrary minimum and maximum value for the data variable (respectively of -500000 and 500000), which is equivalent to introduce a finite horizon. The results are given in the column *Toy* of Table 1.

Table 1. Comparison of computation times on various models of CAVs taken from [5].

	Base	Infrastructure	Negotiation	Toy
Comp. time (s): $\mu(\mathcal{M}^+)$	8.2	24.2	261.7	56.4
Comp. time (s): $\mu([\mu(\mathcal{M})]^+)$	6.5	21.7	219.8	15.8
Comp. time (s): $\mu([min(det(\mu(\mathcal{M})))]^+)$	6.5	21.7	219.8	11.7
Ratio min/max	0.79	0.89	0.83	0.20

All in all, a significant gain is obtained with our method, although it is of a higher magnitude for our toy example. This can be explained mainly by the difference in complexity between the toy example, where a single operation is performed on each transition, and the CAV model, where hundreds of operations are performed on each transition. In this context, the gain of factorizing the control part of the states (*i.e.* locations and clock zones) has more impact in the toy example than in the CAV model.

5   Conclusion

Driven by the need for an efficient construction of the state spaces of multi-agent real-time systems with large data, we proposed a method which takes advantage of symmetries which are often present in such systems. The systems we focus on are transition systems extended with data variables, with the requirement that variable updates are only allowed on transitions but the enabling of transitions is independent from these variables. We then proposed a method to construct the state space of such models, by factorizing some computations.

In case of finite state spaces, we proposed a method to construct reduced state spaces that preserve some temporal logic properties focusing on the observation of data variables. This limitation has little impact since for cyber-physical systems, data variables correspond to the physical aspects of the system, on which the verification generally focuses.

As an illustration, we presented an application of the method on a network of timed automata extended with data. We also applied our method on specifications of complex cyber-physical systems of communicating autonomous vehicles. The results are promising and show a significant gain in state space construction times compared to classical approaches.

The method does not interfere with orthogonal approaches, such as abstractions designed to compute the state space of the specification with its original semantics, prior to the data extension (for instance, in the context of timed automata, the well known clock extrapolation guarantees a finite state space). The method can speed up the state space construction in general, but will be particularly useful when combined with exploration methods exploiting symmetries.

In the future, we plan to use the factorization described in this paper in conjunction with the *layer-based exploration* methods developed in [6] for a class of cyclic timed automata. The advantage of these methods is that they allow to generate the state space and check on-the-fly safety properties of cyber-physical systems having cyclic behaviors.

Acknowledgements. The authors appreciated the remarks and encouragements of the anonymous reviewers.

References

1. Verifcar models. https://forge.ibisc.univ-evry.fr/jarcile/VerifCar. Accessed 29 May 2023
2. Ahmad, S., Malik, S., Ullah, I., Park, D.-H., Kim, K., Kim, D.H.: Towards the design of a formal verification and evaluation tool of real-time tasks scheduling of IoT applications. Sustainability **11**(1), 204 (2019)
3. André, É., Fribourg, L., Kühne, U., Soulat, R.: IMITATOR 2.5: a tool for analyzing robustness in scheduling problems. In: Giannakopoulou, D., Méry, D. (eds.) FM 2012. LNCS, vol. 7436, pp. 33–36. Springer, Heidelberg (2012). https://doi.org/10.1007/978-3-642-32759-9_6
4. Arcile, J., André, É.: Timed automata as a formalism for expressing security: a survey on theory and practice. ACM Comput. Surv. **55**(6), 127:1–127:36 (2023)
5. Arcile, J., Devillers, R.R., Klaudel, H.: Verifcar: a framework for modeling and model checking communicating autonomous vehicles. Auton. Agents Multi Agent Syst. **33**(3), 353–381 (2019)

6. Arcile, J., Devillers, R.R., Klaudel, H.: Dynamic exploration of multi-agent systems with periodic timed tasks. Fundam. Informaticae **175**(1–4), 59–95 (2020)
7. Barnes, J.E.: Experiences in the industrial use of formal methods. Electron. Commun. Eur. Assoc. Softw. Sci. Technol. **46** (2011)
8. Behrmann, G., Bouyer, P., Fleury, E., Larsen, K.G.: Static guard analysis in timed automata verification. In: Garavel, H., Hatcliff, J. (eds.) TACAS 2003. LNCS, vol. 2619, pp. 254–270. Springer, Heidelberg (2003). https://doi.org/10.1007/3-540-36577-X_18
9. Berthomieu, B., Vernadat, F.: Time petri nets analysis with TINA. In: Third International Conference on the Quantitative Evaluation of Systems (QEST 2006), pp. 123–124. IEEE Computer Society. 11–14 September 2006, Riverside, California, USA (2006)
10. Bozga, M., Daws, C., Maler, O., Olivero, A., Tripakis, S., Yovine, S.: Kronos: a model-checking tool for real-time systems. In: Ravn, A.P., Rischel, H. (eds.) FTRTFT 1998. LNCS, vol. 1486, pp. 298–302. Springer, Heidelberg (1998). https://doi.org/10.1007/BFb0055357
11. Caspi, P., Mazuet, C., Paligot, N.R.: About the design of distributed control systems: the quasi-synchronous approach. In: Voges, U. (ed.) SAFECOMP 2001. LNCS, vol. 2187, pp. 215–226. Springer, Heidelberg (2001). https://doi.org/10.1007/3-540-45416-0_21
12. Cheng, A.M.K.: A survey of formal verification methods and tools for embedded and real-time systems. Int. J. Embed. Syst. **2**(3/4), 184–195 (2006)
13. Dabaghchian, M., Rakamaric, Z.: A timeless model for the verification of quasi-periodic distributed systems. In: Partha, S., Roop, Zhan, N., Gao, S., Nuzzo, P., (eds.) Proceedings of the 17th ACM-IEEE International Conference on Formal Methods and Models for System Design, MEMOCODE 2019, pp. 4:1 4:11. ACM. October 9–11 2019. La Jolla, CA, USA (2019)
14. Daws, C., Tripakis, S.: Model checking of real-time reachability properties using abstractions. In: Steffen, B. (ed.) TACAS 1998. LNCS, vol. 1384, pp. 313–329. Springer, Heidelberg (1998). https://doi.org/10.1007/BFb0054180
15. Dutertre, B., Sorea, M.: Modeling and verification of a fault-tolerant real-time startup protocol using calendar automata. In: Lakhnech, Y., Yovine, S. (eds.) FORMATS/FTRTFT -2004. LNCS, vol. 3253, pp. 199–214. Springer, Heidelberg (2004). https://doi.org/10.1007/978-3-540-30206-3_15
16. Hopcroft, J.E., Ullman, J.D.: Introduction to Automata Theory, Languages, and Computation. Addison-Wesley Publishing Company, Boston (1979)
17. Kwiatkowska, M.Z., Norman, G., Parker, D.: PRISM 2.0: a tool for probabilistic model checking. In: 1st International Conference on Quantitative Evaluation of Systems (QEST 2004), pp. 322–323. IEEE Computer Society. 27–30 September 2004, Enschede, The Netherlands (2004)
18. Larsen, K.G., Pettersson, P., Yi, W.: UPPAAL in a nutshell. Int. J. Softw. Tools Technol. Transf. **1**(1–2), 134–152 (1997)
19. Legay, A., Delahaye, B., Bensalem, S.: Statistical model checking: an overview. In: Barringer, H., et al. (eds.) RV 2010. LNCS, vol. 6418, pp. 122–135. Springer, Heidelberg (2010). https://doi.org/10.1007/978-3-642-16612-9_11
20. Lime, D., Roux, O.H., Seidner, C., Traonouez, L.-M.: Romeo: a parametric model-checker for petri nets with stopwatches. In: Kowalewski, S., Philippou, A. (eds.) TACAS 2009. LNCS, vol. 5505, pp. 54–57. Springer, Heidelberg (2009). https://doi.org/10.1007/978-3-642-00768-2_6

14   J. Arcile et al.

21. Maiza, C., Rihani, H., Rivas, J.M., Goossens, J., Altmeyer, S., Davis, R.I.: A survey of timing verification techniques for multi-core real-time systems. ACM Comput. Surv. **52**(3), 56:1–56:38 (2019)
22. Saha, I., Misra, J., Roy, S.: Timeout and calendar based finite state modeling and verification of real-time systems. In: Namjoshi, K.S., Yoneda, T., Higashino, T., Okamura, Y. (eds.) ATVA 2007. LNCS, vol. 4762, pp. 284–299. Springer, Heidelberg (2007). https://doi.org/10.1007/978-3-540-75596-8_21
23. Snook, C.F., Harrison, R.: Practitioners' views on the use of formal methods: an industrial survey by structured interview. Inf. Softw. Technol. **43**(4), 275–283 (2001)
24. Zheng, X., Julien, C., Kim, M., Khurshid, S.: Perceptions on the state of the art in verification and validation in cyber-physical systems. IEEE Syst. J. **11**(4), 2614–2627 (2017)

Verified High Performance Computing: The SyDPaCC Approach

Frédéric Loulergue(✉) [ID] and Ali Ed-Dbali [ID]

Univ. Orléans, INSA CVL, LIFO EA 4022, Orléans, France
{frederic.loulergue,ali.eddbali}@univ-orleans.fr

Abstract. The SYDPACC framework for the COQ proof assistant is based on a transformational approach to develop verified efficient scalable parallel functional programs from specifications. These specifications are written as inefficient (potentially with a high computational complexity) sequential programs. We obtain efficient parallel programs implemented using algorithmic skeletons that are higher-order functions implemented in parallel on distributed data structures. The output programs are constructed step-by-step by applying transformation theorems. Leveraging COQ type classes, the application of transformation theorems is partly automated. The current version of the framework is presented and exemplified on the development of a parallel program for the maximum segment sum problem. This program is experimented on a parallel machine.

Keywords: program transformation · scalable parallel computing · functional programming · interactive theorem proving

1 Introduction

Our everyday activities generate extremely large volume of data. Big data analytics offer opportunities in a variety of domains [4,13].

While there are many challenges in the design and implementation of big data analytics applications, we focus on the programming aspects. Due to the large scale, scalable parallel computing is a necessity. Most approaches either cite Bulk Synchronous Parallelism (BSP) [44] as an inspiration, that is the case of Pregel [32] and related frameworks such as Apache Giraph, or are related to, even if it is not often acknowledged, algorithmic skeletons [6]. This is the case of Hadoop MapReduce [9] and Spark [1].

Both BSP and algorithmic skeletons are structured and high-level approaches to parallelism which free the developers from tedious details of the implementation of parallel algorithms found for example in MPI programming, a de facto standard for writing HPC programs. While BSP is a general purpose parallel programming model, algorithmic skeletons approaches as well as the mentioned big data frameworks are limited to what is expressible by the building blocks they provide. This lack of generality is both a strength making them easier to use in the classes of applications they naturally cover, but also a weakness in

B. Ben Hedia et al. (Eds.): VECoS 2023, LNCS 14368, pp. 15–29, 2024.
https://doi.org/10.1007/978-3-031-49737-7_2

that expressing one's algorithm with these building blocks may become very convoluted or even impossible.

SYDPACC [27,28] is a framework for the CoQ proof assistant to systematically develop correct and efficient parallel programs from specifications. Currently, SYDPACC provides sequential program optimizations via transformations based on list homomorphism theorems [17] and the diffusion theorem [21]. It also provides automated parallelization via verified correspondences between sequential higher-order functions and algorithmic skeletons implemented using the parallel primitives of BSML [26] a library for scalable parallel programming with the multi-paradigm (including functional) programming language OCaml [24]. In this paper, we develop a new verified parallel algorithm for the maximum segment sum problem, which is for example a component of computer vision applications to detect the brightest area of an image.

The remaining of the paper is organized as follows. Functional bulk synchronous parallel programming with the BSML library is introduced in Sect. 2. Section 3 is devoted to an overview of the SYDPACC framework. In Sect. 4, we develop a verified scalable Bulk Synchronous Parallel algorithm of the maximum segment sum problem and experiment (Sect. 5) on a parallel machine the extracted code from the CoQ proof assistant. We compare our approach to related work in Sect. 6 and conclude in Sect. 7. The code presented in the paper is available in the SYDPACC distribution version 0.5 at https://sydpacc.github.io.

2   Functional Bulk Synchronous Parallelism

In the Bulk Synchronous Parallel model, the BSP computer is seen as a homogeneous distributed memory machine with a point-to-point communication network and a global synchronization unit. It runs BSP programs which are *sequences* of so-called *super-steps*. A super-step is composed of three phases. The computation phase is concerned with each processor-memory pair computing using only the data available locally. In the communication phase, each processor may request data from other processors and send requested data to other processors. Finally, during the synchronization phase, the communication exchanges are finalized and the super-step ends with a global synchronization of all the processors.

BSML offers a set of constants (giving access to the parameters of the BSP machine as they are discussed in [40] but omitted here) including `bsp_p` the number of processors in the BSP machine and a set of four functions which are expressive enough to express any BSP algorithm. BSML is implemented as a library for the multi-paradigm and functional language OCaml [24] ([34] is a short introduction to OCaml and its qualities). BSML is purely functional but using on each processor the imperative features of OCaml, it is possible to implement an imperative programming library [26] in the style of the BSPlib for C [19]. In this paper we are interested in the pure functional aspects of BSML as it is only possible to write pure functions within CoQ.

Given any type α and a function f from int to α (which is written f: int$\rightarrow\alpha$ in OCaml), the BSML primitive mkpar f (mkpar applied to f, application in OCaml and many other functional languages is simply denoted by a space) creates a *parallel vector* of type α par. Parallel vectors are therefore a polymorphic data-structure. In such a parallel vector, processor number i with $0 \le i$ <bsp_p, holds the value of f i. For example, mkpar(fun i$\rightarrow$i) is the parallel vector $\langle 0, \ldots, \text{bsp\_p}-1 \rangle$ of type int par. In the following, this parallel vector is denoted by this. The function replicate has type $\alpha \rightarrow \alpha$ par and can be defined as: let replicate = fun x $\rightarrow$ mkpar(fun i$\rightarrow$x). In expression replicate x, all the processors will contain the value of x.

(+)1 is the partial application of addition seen in prefix notation, it is equivalent to fun x$\rightarrow$1+x. Therefore replicate ((+)1) is a parallel vector of functions and its type is (int$\rightarrow$int)par. A parallel vector of functions is not a function and cannot be applied directly. That is why BSML provides the primitive apply that can apply a parallel vector of functions to a parallel vector of values. For example, apply (replicate ((+)1)) this is the parallel vector $\langle 1, \ldots, \text{bsp\_p} \rangle$. Using apply and replicate in such a way is common. The function parfun is also part of the BSML standard library and is defined as: let parfun f = apply(replicate f).

The primitive proj can be seen as a partial inverse of mkpar, its type is α par $\rightarrow$ (int $\rightarrow \alpha$). However, proj(mkpar f) is in general different from f. Indeed f may be defined on all the values of type int, but proj(mkpar f) is defined only on $\{0, \ldots, \text{bsp\_p} - 1\}$.

To transform a parallel vector into a list, one can define to_list as follows: let to_list v = List.map (proj v) processors where processors has type int list and contains the integers from 0 (included) to bsp_p (excluded).

```
module type SKELETONS = sig
  type α dislist (* A type for distributed lists *)

  val init :  int → (int → α) → α dislist
  val map :  (α → β) → α dislist → β dislist
  val filter :  (α → bool) → α dislist → α dislist
  val count :  α dislist → int
end
```

Fig. 1. A Signature for Algorithmic Skeletons on Distributed Lists

While mkpar and apply do not require any communication or synchronization to run, proj needs communications and a global synchronization. The value of each processor is sent to all the other processors (it is a total exchange). For a finer control over communications the primitive put should be used. It is the most complex operation of BSML and its type is (int$\rightarrow\alpha$)par $\rightarrow$ (int$\rightarrow\alpha$)par. The functions in the input vector contain the messages to be sent to other processors. The functions in the output vector contain the messages received from other processors. For example if the input vector contains function in_i at processor i, then the value $v = in_i$ i' will be sent to processor i'. After executing the put, processor i' contains a function $out_{i'}$ such that $out_{i'}$ $i = v$. Some OCaml values are considered to be empty messages so an application of put does mean that each processor communicates with every other processors. For the sake of conciseness we do not detail put further but we refer to [29].

```
type α dislist = { content : α list par; size : int }

let init (size : int) (f : int → α) : α dislist =
  let rem = size mod bsp_p in
  let ajust pid = if pid < rem then 1 else 0 in
  let local_size pid = (size / bsp_p) + ajust pid in
  let first_index pid =
    if pid < rem then pid * (local_size pid + 1)
      else (pid * local_size pid) + rem
  in
  {
    content =
      mkpar (fun pid →
          let lsize = local_size pid in
          let findex = first_index pid in
          List.init lsize (fun i → f (findex + i)));
    size;
  }

let map (f : α → β) (l : α dislist) : β dislist =
  { content = parfun (List.map f) l.content; size = l.size }

let filter (p : α → bool) (l : α dislist) : α dislist =
  let sum : int list → int = List.fold_left ( + ) 0 in
  let new_content = parfun (List.filter p) l.content in
  let local_sizes = parfun List.length new_content in
  let new_size = sum (to_list local_sizes) in
  { content = new_content; size = new_size }

let count (l : α dislist) = l.size
```

Fig. 2. A BSML Example

As an example, we implement in Fig. 2 the set of algorithmic skeletons on a data-structure of distributed lists whose module type is shown in Fig. 1.

We implement the distributed list type as a record type: its content is a parallel vector of lists and it also possesses a field for the global size of the distributed list. init is similar to mkpar, however for distributed lists the size is given by the user while it is always bsp_p for parallel vectors. We want the list to be distributed evenly: each processor contains `size/bsp_p` elements, or one more element than that.

   `map` is similar to the `List.map` function on sequential lists: it applies a function `f` to all the elements of the lists. Here each processor takes care of the sub-list it holds locally. `List.filter p l` uses a predicate `p` to keep only the elements of `l` that satisfy this predicate. Our `filter` skeleton does the same: the part about the content is easy to write. But we also need to update the global size of the distributed list and communications are required to do so. Note that after a filter, the distributed list may no longer be evenly distributed.

3   An Overview of SyDPaCC

We present the use of SyDPaCC through a very simple example. In this case the specification is already quite efficient, but often the specification has a higher complexity than the optimized program. This is for example the case of the maximum prefix sum problem presented in [28] and the maximum segment sum problem presented in the next section. For a short introduction to CoQ, see [2].

   Our goal is to obtain a parallel algorithm for computing the average of a list of natural numbers. To do so, we use SyDPaCC to parallelize a function that sums the elements of a list and counts the number of elements of this list. This specification can be written as:

```
Fixpoint sum (l: list nat) : nat :=
  match l with
  | [] → 0
  | n:: ns ⇒ n + sum ns
  end.
```

```
Definition count : list nat → nat := length (A:=nat).
```

```
Definition spec : list nat → nat * nat := (sum △ count).
```

`sum` is a recursive function defined by pattern matching on its list argument while `count` is just an alias for the pre-defined `length` function. The specification `spec` is defined as the tupling of these two functions.

   We then try to show that this function has some simple properties: it is leftwards, meaning it can be written as an application of `List.fold_right`, rightwards, meaning it can be written as an application of `List.fold_left`, and finally it has a right inverse, which is a weak form of inverse.

   For a list $l = [x_1; \ldots; x_n]$, binary operations $\oplus \otimes$, and values $e_l \ e_r$, we have:

$$\text{List.fold\_left} \oplus e_l \ l = (\ldots((e_l \oplus x_1) \oplus x_2) \ldots) \oplus x_n$$
$$\text{List.fold\_right} \otimes e_r \ l = x_1 \otimes (x_2 (\ldots(x_n \otimes e_r) \ldots))$$

spec is indeed leftwards, rightwards and has a right inverse:

Definition opr := fun n acc ⇒ (n + fst acc, 1 + snd acc).

Instance spec_leftwards: Leftwards spec opr (0,0).
Proof. *(* omitted *)* Defined.

Definition opl := fun acc n ⇒ (n + fst acc, 1 + snd acc).

Instance spec_rightwards: Rightwards spec opl (0,0).
Proof. *(* omitted *)* Defined.

Definition spec_inv (p: nat∗nat) : list nat :=
  let (s, c):= p in match c with 0 ⇒ [] | S c ⇒ s::(repeatv c 0) end.

Instance spec_inverse: Right_inverse spec spec_inv.

Each of these properties are expressed as instances of type-classes defined in SYDPACC. Basically type-classes are just record types (in these cases with only one field that holds a proof of the property of interest) and the values of these types are called instances. The difference with record types is that instances are recorded in a database. COQ functions can have implicit arguments: when such arguments have a type that is a type-class, each time the function is applied, COQ searches for an instance that fits the implicit argument. Instances may have other instances as parameters. In this situation to build an instance the system first needs to build instances for the parameters. Such parametrized instances can be seen as Prolog rules while non-parametrized instances can be seen as Prolog facts. COQ searches for an instance with a Prolog-like resolution algorithm.

For the inverse, we need to build a list l such that for a sum s and a number of elements c, we have spec $l = (s, c)$. One possible solution is to have $l = [s; 0; \ldots; 0]$. An application of function repeatv builds the list of zeros. If $c = 0$ then the list should be empty. The omitted proofs are short: from 3 to 9 lines with calls to a couple one-liner lemmas.

These instances are enough for the system to automatically parallelize the specification, as follows:

Definition par_average : par(list nat) → nat :=
  Eval sydpacc in
    (uncurry Nat.div) ∘ (parallel spec).

In this example, parallel spec will produce a composition of a parallel reduce and a parallel map. The automated sequential optimization of spec, then the automated parallelization, are triggered by the call to parallel that has several implicit arguments whose types are type-classes.

Two of them are notions of *correspondence*:

– A type T_{source} corresponds to a type T_{target} if there exists a *surjective* function join: T_{target} → T_{source}. We note $T_{source} ◄ T_{target}$ such a type correspondence.

Intuitively, the `join` function is surjective because we want the target type to have at least the same expressive power than the source type. If the source type is `list A` and target type is a distributed type such as `par(list A)`, there are many ways a sequential list could be distributed into a parallel vector of lists.

– A function `f`: $T^1_{source} \rightarrow T^2_{source}$ corresponds to f_{target}: $T^1_{target} \rightarrow T^2_{target}$ if $T^1_{source} \blacktriangleleft T^1_{target}$ and $T^2_{source} \blacktriangleleft T^2_{target}$ and the following property holds:

$$\forall(x : T^1_{target}), \texttt{join}^2(f_{target}\ x) = f_{source}(\texttt{join}^1\ x).$$

SYDPACC provides type correspondences such as `list A` ◄ `par(list A)` as well as several function correspondences including `List.map` corresponds to `par_map`. It also offers parametrized instances for the composition of functions with ∘, △ and × (pairing). Finally while looking for such instances, SYDPACC also checks if there are optimized versions of functions, captured by instances of type `Opt f f'` meaning `f'` is an optimized version of `f`.

These optimizations are based on transformation theorems expressed as instances. SYDPACC provides a variant of the third homomorphism theorem [17] that states that a function is a list homomorphism when it is leftwards, rightwards and has a right inverse. The first homomorphism theorem states that a list homomorphism can be implemented as a composition of `map` and **reduce**. The other transformation theorem available for lists is the diffusion theorem [21].

In the example, `parallel` looks for a correspondence of `spec` that triggers the optimization of `spec` which is done thanks to the two homomorphism theorems mentioned above. At the end of the Prolog-like search, it is established (and verified) than `spec` corresponds to a composition of a parallel reduce and a parallel map.

To obtain a very efficient program, the user can try to simplify the binary operation and the function given respectively as arguments of the parallel reduce and the parallel map. Indeed, by default the former is:

```
fun args ⇒ let (p1,p2) in spec(spec_inv p1 ++ spec_inv p2)
```

and the latter is `fun a ⇒ spec[a]`. To obtain optimized versions, one can use the type-classes `Optimised_op` and `Optimised_f` that only take as argument the specification. The optimized versions do not need to be known beforehand: they can be discovered while proving the instances. In our example, the operation is mostly the addition of the first components of the argument pairs (replaced by 0 if the second component is 0), and the function is `fun a ⇒ (a, 1)`.

Finally, the extracted[1] OCaml code (with calls to BSML functions in a module `MapReduce` similar to the functions of Fig. 2) is given Fig. 3. Such a program can be compiled and run on (possibly massively) parallel machines. The SYDPACC framework provided a guide towards the development of such a parallel program, but also the proof that this program is correct with respect to the initial specification.

---

[1] The type annotations have been added manually and the argument renamed to increase readability.

```
let par_avg (numbers : (nat list) par) : nat =
  uncurry div
    (MapReduce.par_reduce
      (fun a b →
        (add (match snd a with | 0 → 0 | S _ → fst a)
             (match snd b with | 0 → 0 | S _ → fst b),
          add (snd a) (snd b)))
      (spec Nil)
      (MapReduce.par_map (fun a → (a, 1))) numbers)
```

Fig. 3. OCaml Code Extracted from CoQ

4 Verified Parallel Maximum Segment Sum

The goal of maximum segment sum problem is to obtain the maximum value among the sums of all segments (i.e. sub-structures) of a structure. We consider here lists, but algorithms are equivalent for 1D arrays.

Basically, the specification for this problem can be written as follows:

Definition **mss_spec** := maximum ∘ (map sum) ∘ segs.

There are several derivations of parallel algorithms for the maximum segment sum problem. The first, informal one, was proposed by Cole [7]. Takeichi et al. [20] gave a formal account of this construction using a theory of tupling and fusion. Their theory may be expressed in CoQ, but it is not simple as theorems are stated for an arbitrary number of mutually recursive functions which are tupled, hence it is necessary to deal with tuples of an arbitrary size. The algorithm they obtain (from a similar specification than the one above) is a list homomorphism and therefore SyDPaCC could automatically parallelized it. The GTA (generate-test-aggregate) approach [11] — which was implemented in CoQ [12], but this implementation is not compatible with the current version of SyDPaCC — is also applicable. Both solutions are not well suited as we want to consider in the future the variant problem of maximum segment sum with a bound on the segment lengths. Thus, we based our contribution on the calculation proposed by Morihata [36].

Morihata only considered non-empty lists. There is support in SyDPaCC to deal with non-empty lists [28], but it requires for example to use different function compositions that transport facts about the non-emptyness of lists across function composition. For example, segs is the function that generates all the segments of a list, and it returns a non-empty list even if its argument is an empty list. The map function preserves non-emptiness. Finally, if maximum returns a number then it is defined only on non-empty lists.

Here, we choose to deal with empty lists. Therefore, the function maximum used in the specification has type list N.t → option N.t where N.t is an abstract type of numbers that possess the required algebraic properties, and option is the CoQ type:

Inductive option (A: Type) : Type := | Some: A→ option A | None: option A.

which basically adds a value None to the type given as argument to option. In the case of maximum we interpret None as $-\infty$. The definition of sum and maximum follow:

```
Definition sum : list t → t := reduce add.
Definition optionize '(f:A→ A→ A) (a b: option A) : option A :=
  match (a,b) with
  | (None, None) ⇒ None
  | (None, _ ) ⇒ b
  | (_, None) ⇒ a
  | (Some a, Some b) ⇒ Some(f a b)
  end.
Definition max_option := optionize max.
Definition maximum := reduce max_option ∘ (map Some).
```

reduce is a higher-order function that "sums" all the elements of a list using the binary operation given as first argument. We proved that is f is associative then optionize f forms a monoid with the neutral element being None.

During the transformations of mss_spec, a version of add that deals with option N.t values instead of N.t values is needed. The add_option function is:

```
Definition optionize_none '(f:A→ A→ A)(a b: option A) : option A :=
  match (a,b) with
  | (Some a, Some b) ⇒ Some(f a b)
  | _ ⇒ None
  end.
Definition add_option :— optionize_none N.add.
```

If the original operation f forms a monoid with neutral element e, then the optionzed version forms a monoid with Some e. None is an absorbing element of optionize_none f.

The function generating all the segments is defined in terms of prefix and tails which are two functions already defined in SYDPACC that respectively return the prefixes of a list and its suffixes (List.app is part of COQ's standard library and is list concatenation):

```
Definition segs {A}:= reduce (@List.app (list A)) ∘ (map prefix) ∘ tails.
```

We then prove the following instance of Opt to give an equivalent but optimized version of mss_spec:

```
Instance opt_mss :
  Opt mss_spec
    ( (reduce max_option) ∘ (map fst) ∘
      (scanr (oslash add_option max_option) (None, Some 0)) ∘
      (map (fun x : t ⇒ (Some x, Some x))) ).
```

The proof of this instance follows roughly the calculation of Morihata but for the treatment of empty lists. This proof is simple in term of structure: just a sequence of applications of rewriting steps, each step being the application of a transformation lemma. Most of the lemmas were already in COQ or SYDPACC libraries but the definition of oslash and related lemma (and instances omitted here):

```
Definition oslash [A] otimes oplus
  '{Monoid A otimes e_t} '{Monoid A oplus e_p}: (A*A)→ (A*A)→ (A*A) :=
  fun a_b c_d ⇒
  ( oplus (fst a_b)(otimes (snd a_b)(fst c_d)),
    otimes (snd a_b) (snd c_d) ).
```

```
Lemma distributivity_reduce_scanl A
  '{Ht: Monoid (A:=A) otimes e_t} '{Hp: Monoid (A:=A) oplus e_p}
  {Ha: RightAbsorbing otimes e_p} {Hd: LeftDistributive otimes oplus}:
  ∀ l,
    (reduce oplus) (scanl otimes e_t l) =
    fst(reduce (oslash otimes oplus) (map dup l)).
```

Morihata used this operator and a lemma based on a method first proposed by Smith [41].

The optimized version also uses scanr which is linear on the length of its list argument. We implemented a tail recursive version of scanr (as we do for all the function on lists that are supposed to be part of the final optimized code) and satisfies the following expected property for a scanr:

```
Lemma scanr_spec_monoid:
  ∀ A op e {Hm: @Monoid A op e} l,
    scanr op e l = map (reduce op) (tails l).
```

The optimized version has a linear complexity in the length of its argument while the specification has a cubic one. The goal of the transformations was to remove the calls to prefix and tails. These transformations are not automatic, but the support provided by SYDPACC is a collection of already proved transformations.

```
Module Make (Import Bsml: Core.BSML)(N: Number).
  (* ... application of a few parametric modules omitted *)
  Definition par_mss : par(list N.t) → option N.t :=
    Eval sydpacc in
      parallel (Mss.mss_spec).
End Make.
```

Fig. 4. Automatic parallelization of MSS

The last step is fully automatic and very simple as shown in Fig. 4. With the call to parallel, SYDPACC uses the instance opt_mss as well as instances of types and functions correspondences that are part of the framework to generate a parallel version of mss_spec by replacing the list functions by their algorithmic skeletons counter-parts: par_reduce, par_map and par_scanr.

5   Experiments

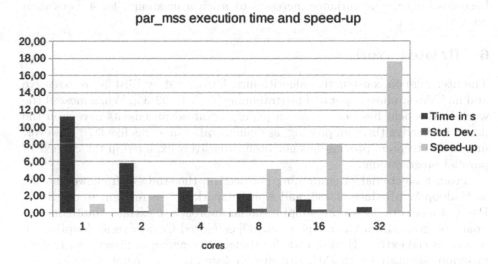

Fig. 5. Time and relative speed-up ($64 \cdot 10^6$ elements, median of 30 measures)

The Coq proof assistant offers an extraction mechanism [25] able to generate compilable code from Coq definitions and proofs. In particular, it can generate OCaml code. Extracting the parametric module of Fig. 4 generates an OCaml functor (which is basically a parametric module). To be able to execute the function par_mss, we first need to apply this functor. For the number part, we just wrote a module using OCaml native integers of type int for N.t. For the parameter, Bsml we simply apply the actual parallel implementation of BSML primitives as provided by the BSML library for OCaml. This library is implemented on top of an API for parallel processing library in C named MPI [42] (several implementations of this API exist). For the moment, the Bsml module of the BSML library cannot directly be given as argument to the Make functor. Indeed, processor identifiers are represented by mathematical natural numbers in Coq while they are encoded as OCaml bounded int values. SyDPaCC features a wrapper module BsmlWrapperN that performs number conversions when needed.

The application of the verified extracted function and aspects such as input/output operations and command line argument management are not verified and written in plain OCaml. The final program was run on a shared memory parallel machine, but it could run on large scale distributed memory machines.

We ran the program on a machine having an Intel Xeon Gold 5218 processor with 32 cores. The operating system was Ubuntu 22.04. To compile we used OCaml 4.14.1. The MPI implementation was OpenMPI 4.1.2. We ran par_mss on a list of length $64 \cdot 10^6$ and measured the time required for this computation

30 times. The results for the *relative* speed-up are presented in Fig. 5 for an increasing number of cores. The speedup is fine but of course as the number of cores increases the relative impact of communication and synchronization time becomes bigger. The variance increases to reach a maximum for 4 cores then decreases again.

6   Related Work

The literature on constructive algorithmics, introduced by Bird [3], is extensive and includes studies on parallel programming [7,10,18,22,35]. While most of the work in this field has been done on paper, recent advancements have seen the use of interactive theorem proving, as demonstrated in works like [37]. However, interactive theorem proving has not been extensively explored in the context of parallel programming.

From a functional programming perspective, the study of frameworks such as Hadoop MapReduce [23,33] and Apache Spark [1,5] is relevant to our SYD-PACC framework, as we can adopt a similar approach to extract MapReduce or Spark programs from COQ. Ono et al. [39] employed COQ to verify MapReduce programs and extract Haskell code for Hadoop Streaming or directly write Java programs annotated with JML, utilizing Krakatoa [14] to generate COQ lemmas. However, their work is less systematic and automated than SYDPACC.

There have been contributions that formalize certain aspects of parallel programming, but as far as we know, these approaches do not directly yield executable code like our SYDPACC framework. Swierstra [43] formalized mutable arrays with explicit distributions in Agda, while BSP-Why [15] allows for deductive verification of imperative BSP programs, although they represent models of C BSPlib [19] programs rather than executable code. Another example is the formalization of the Data Parallel C programming language using Isabelle/HOL [8], where Isabelle/HOL expressions representing parallel programs were generated.

7   Conclusion

We developed a verified parallel implementation of a functional scalable parallel program for solving the maximum segment sum problem and studied its parallel performances. Experiments on a larger number of processors are planned.

Often in applications, the domain is 2D rather than 1D, and it may be interesting to consider segments of a given bounded size, for example in genomics. We therefore plan to systematically develop parallel algorithms for these problems starting from the work of Morihata [36].

The development of SYDPACC started in 2015 while preparing a graduate course for a summer school, on the predecessor of SYDPACC named SDPP. There are SDPP theories, namely BSP homomorphisms [16,31] and generate, test, aggregate [11,12] that have not been ported to SYDPACC yet. We also plan to work on additional data-structures such as trees. For the moment, SYDPACC only targets BSML+OCaml, but there is ongoing work to extend it to generate Scala [38] code with Apache Spark for parallel processing [30].

Acknowledgments. We wish to thank the reviewers for their suggestions and highlighting some typos.

References

1. Armbrust, M., et al.: Scaling spark in the real world: performance and usability. PVLDB **8**(12), 1840–1851 (2015). http://www.vldb.org/pvldb/vol8/p1840-armbrust.pdf
2. Bertot, Y.: Coq in a hurry (2006). http://hal.inria.fr/inria-00001173
3. Bird, R.: An introduction to the theory of lists. In: Broy, M. (ed.) Logic of Programming and Calculi of Discrete Design. NATO ASI Series, vol. 36, pp. 5–42. Springer, Heidelberg (1987). https://doi.org/10.1007/978-3-642-87374-4_1
4. Cao, L.: Data science: a comprehensive overview. ACM Comput. Surv. **50**(3), 1–42 (2017). https://doi.org/10.1145/3076253
5. Chen, Y.-F., Hong, C.-D., Lengál, O., Mu, S.-C., Sinha, N., Wang, B.-Y.: An executable sequential specification for spark aggregation. In: El Abbadi, A., Garbinato, B. (eds.) NETYS 2017. LNCS, vol. 10299, pp. 421–438. Springer, Cham (2017). https://doi.org/10.1007/978-3-319-59647-1_31
6. Cole, M.: Algorithmic Skeletons: Structured Management of Parallel Computation. MIT Press, Cambridge (1989)
7. Cole, M.: Parallel programming, list homomorphisms and the maximum segment sum problem. In: Joubert, G.R., Trystram, D., Peters, F.J., Evans, D.J. (eds.) Parallel Computing: Trends and Applications, PARCO 1993, pp. 489–492. Elsevier (1994)
8. Daum, M.: Reasoning on Data-Parallel Programs in Isabelle/Hol. In: C/C++ Verification Workshop (2007). http://www.cse.unsw.edu.au/rhuuck/CV07/program.html
9. Dean, J., Ghemawat, S.: MapReduce: simplified data processing on large clusters. In: OSDI, pp. 137–150. USENIX Association (2004)
10. Dosch, W., Wiedemann, B.: List homomorphisms with accumulation and indexing. In: Michaelson, G., Trinder, P., Loidl, H.W. (eds.) Trends in Functional Programming, pp. 134–142. Intellect (2000)
11. Emoto, K., Fischer, S., Hu, Z.: Filter-embedding semiring fusion for programming with MapReduce. Formal Aspects Comput. **24**(4–6), 623–645 (2012). https://doi.org/10.1007/s00165-012-0241-8
12. Emoto, K., Loulergue, F., Tesson, J.: A verified generate-test-aggregate Coq library for parallel programs extraction. In: Klein, G., Gamboa, R. (eds.) ITP 2014. LNCS, vol. 8558, pp. 258–274. Springer, Cham (2014). https://doi.org/10.1007/978-3-319-08970-6_17
13. Fang, R., Pouyanfar, S., Yang, Y., Chen, S.C., Iyengar, S.S.: Computational health informatics in the big data age: a survey. ACM Comput. Surv. **49**(1), 1–36 (2016). https://doi.org/10.1145/2932707
14. Filliâtre, J.-C., Marché, C.: The why/Krakatoa/Caduceus platform for deductive program verification. In: Damm, W., Hermanns, H. (eds.) CAV 2007. LNCS, vol. 4590, pp. 173–177. Springer, Heidelberg (2007). https://doi.org/10.1007/978-3-540-73368-3_21
15. Gava, F., Fortin, J., Guedj, M.: Deductive verification of state-space algorithms. In: Johnsen, E.B., Petre, L. (eds.) IFM 2013. LNCS, vol. 7940, pp. 124–138. Springer, Heidelberg (2013). https://doi.org/10.1007/978-3-642-38613-8_9

16. Gesbert, L., Hu, Z., Loulergue, F., Matsuzaki, K., Tesson, J.: Systematic development of correct bulk synchronous parallel programs. In: Parallel and Distributed Computing, Applications and Technologies (PDCAT), pp. 334–340. IEEE (2010). https://doi.org/10.1109/PDCAT.2010.86

17. Gibbons, J.: The third homomorphism theorem. J. Funct. Program. **6**(4), 657–665 (1996). https://doi.org/10.1017/S0956796800001908

18. Gorlatch, S., Bischof, H.: Formal derivation of divide-and-conquer programs: a case study in the multidimensional FFT's. In: Mery, D. (ed.) Formal Methods for Parallel Programming: Theory and Applications, pp. 80–94 (1997)

19. Hill, J.M.D., et al.: BSPlib: the BSP programming library. Parallel Comput. **24**, 1947–1980 (1998)

20. Hu, Z., Iwasaki, H., Takeichi, M.: Construction of list homomorphisms by tupling and fusion. In: Penczek, W., Szałas, A. (eds.) MFCS 1996. LNCS, vol. 1113, pp. 407–418. Springer, Heidelberg (1996). https://doi.org/10.1007/3-540-61550-4_166

21. Hu, Z., Takeichi, M., Iwasaki, H.: Diffusion: calculating efficient parallel programs. In: ACM SIGPLAN Workshop on Partial Evaluation and Semantics-Based Program Manipulation (PEPM 1999), pp. 85–94. ACM (1999)

22. Hu, Z., Iwasaki, H., Takeichi, M.: Formal derivation of efficient parallel programs by construction of list homomorphisms. ACM Trans. Program. Lang. Syst. **19**(3), 444–461 (1997). https://doi.org/10.1145/256167.256201

23. Lämmel, R.: Google's MapReduce programming model - revisited. Sci. Comput. Program. **70**(1), 1–30 (2008). https://doi.org/10.1016/j.scico.2007.07.001

24. Leroy, X., Doligez, D., Frisch, A., Garrigue, J., Rémy, D., Vouillon, J.: The OCaml system release 5.00 (2022). https://v2.ocaml.org/manual/

25. Letouzey, P.: Extraction in Coq: an overview. In: Beckmann, A., Dimitracopoulos, C., Löwe, B. (eds.) CiE 2008. LNCS, vol. 5028, pp. 359–369. Springer, Heidelberg (2008). https://doi.org/10.1007/978-3-540-69407-6_39

26. Loulergue, F.: A BSPlib-style API for bulk synchronous parallel ML. Scalable Comput. Pract. Experience **18**, 261–274 (2017). https://doi.org/10.12694/scpe.v18i3.1306

27. Loulergue, F.: A verified accumulate algorithmic skeleton. In: Fifth International Symposium on Computing and Networking (CANDAR), pp. 420–426. IEEE, Aomori, Japan (2017). https://doi.org/10.1109/CANDAR.2017.108

28. Loulergue, F., Bousdira, W., Tesson, J.: Calculating parallel programs in Coq using list homomorphisms. Int. J. Parallel Prog. **45**(2), 300–319 (2016). https://doi.org/10.1007/s10766-016-0415-8

29. Loulergue, F., Gava, F., Billiet, D.: Bulk synchronous parallel ML: modular implementation and performance prediction. In: Sunderam, V.S., van Albada, G.D., Sloot, P.M.A., Dongarra, J.J. (eds.) ICCS 2005. LNCS, vol. 3515, pp. 1046–1054. Springer, Heidelberg (2005). https://doi.org/10.1007/11428848_132

30. Loulergue, F., Philippe, J.: Towards verified scalable parallel computing with Coq and Spark. In: Proceedings of the 25th ACM International Workshop on Formal Techniques for Java-like Programs (FTfJP), pp. 11–17. ACM, New York, NY, USA (2023). https://doi.org/10.1145/3605156.3606450

31. Loulergue, F., Robillard, S., Tesson, J., Légaux, J., Hu, Z.: Formal derivation and extraction of a parallel program for the all nearest smaller values problem. In: ACM Symposium on Applied Computing (SAC), pp. 1577–1584. ACM, Gyeongju, Korea (2014). https://doi.org/10.1145/2554850.2554912

32. Malewicz, G., et al.: Pregel: a system for large-scale graph processing. In: SIGMOD, pp. 135–146. ACM (2010). https://doi.org/10.1145/1807167.1807184

33. Matsuzaki, K.: Functional models of hadoop mapreduce with application to scan. Int. J. Parallel Prog. **45**(2), 362–381 (2016). https://doi.org/10.1007/s10766-016-0414-9

34. Minsky, Y.: OCaml for the masses. Commun. ACM **54**(11), 53–58 (2011). https://doi.org/10.1145/2018396.2018413

35. Morihata, A., Matsuzaki, K., Hu, Z., Takeichi, M.: The third homomorphism theorem on trees: downward & upward lead to divide-and-conquer. In: Shao, Z., Pierce, B.C. (eds.) POPL 2009, pp. 177–185. ACM (2009). https://doi.org/10.1145/1480881.1480905

36. Morihata, A.: Calculational developments of new parallel algorithms for size-constrained maximum-sum segment problems. In: Schrijvers, T., Thiemann, P. (eds.) FLOPS 2012. LNCS, vol. 7294, pp. 213–227. Springer, Heidelberg (2012). https://doi.org/10.1007/978-3-642-29822-6_18

37. Mu, S., Ko, H., Jansson, P.: Algebra of programming in Agda: dependent types for relational program derivation. J. Funct. Program. **19**(5), 545–579 (2009). https://doi.org/10.1017/S0956796809007345

38. Odersky, M., Spoon, L., Venners, B.: Programming in Scala, 2nd edn. Artima, Walnut Creek (2010)

39. Ono, K., Hirai, Y., Tanabe, Y., Noda, N., Hagiya, M.: Using Coq in specification and program extraction of hadoop mapreduce applications. In: Barthe, G., Pardo, A., Schneider, G. (eds.) SEFM 2011. LNCS, vol. 7041, pp. 350–365. Springer, Heidelberg (2011). https://doi.org/10.1007/978-3-642-24690-6_24

40. Skillicorn, D.B., Hill, J.M.D., McColl, W.F.: Questions and answers about BSP. Sci. Program. **6**(3), 249–274 (1997)

41. Smith, D.R.: Applications of a strategy for designing divide-and-conquer algorithms Sci. Comput. Program. **8**(3), 213–220 (1987). https://doi.org/10.1016/0167-6423(87)90034-7

42. Snir, M., Gropp, W.: MPI the Complete Reference. MIT Press, Cambridge (1998)

43. Swierstra, W.: More dependent types for distributed arrays. Higher-Order Symbolic Comput. **23**(4), 489–506 (2010). https://doi.org/10.1007/s10990-011-9075-y

44. Valiant, L.G.: A bridging model for parallel computation. Commun. ACM **33**(8), 103 (1990). https://doi.org/10.1145/79173.79181

A QoE Driven DRL Approach for Network Slicing Based on SFC Orchestration in SDN/NFV Enabled Networks

Wiem Taktak[1], Mohamed Escheikh[1], and Kamel Barkaoui[2(✉)]

[1] Syscom Laboratory, ENIT, University of Tunis El Manar, Tunis, Tunisia
{wiem.taktak,mohamed.escheikh}@enit.utm.tn
[2] CNAM-Laboratory Cédric, Paris, France
kamel.barkaoui@cnam.fr

Abstract. In this paper, we provide a comparative performance evaluation study of Deep-Q-Network (DQN) and Dueling DQN in the context where we address network slicing in 5G networks and beyond through solving SFC orchestration problem leveraging Software Defined Networking (SDN) and Network Function Virtualization (NFV) capabilities and using Deep Reinforcement Learning (DRL) approach aiming to maximize Quality of Experience (QoE) while meeting Quality of Service (QoS) requirements. We intend through such investigation to highlight how the DRL agent behaves along the training phase while orchestrating each network slice (or Service Function Chain (SFC)) on a Physical Substrate Network (PSN) in terms of reaching a suitable compromise between performance and convergence. The network slice orchestration is achieved by deploying the corresponding SFC request composed of a set of ordered Virtualized Network Functions (VNFs) linked through virtual links that packets need to traverse within a network slice to achieve specific service requirements. We show throughout numerical experiments how Dueling DQN outperforms DQN in this scenario and how we can compare its performances with those of reference algorithms referred to as violent and random. The investigated performance evaluation study is based on two performance metrics concerning the QoE score and the rejection ratio (RR). Furthermore we assess the quality of learning for the two metrics by testing the ability of the DRL agent to reach a near-optimal solution, along the last 100 runs of the learning phase, quantified by a pre-defined QoE threshold score.

Keywords: Orchestration · DRL · Dueling DQN · SDN/NFV · Network Slicing · SFC · 5G networks and beyond

1 Introduction

SDN and NFV are two key technologies that have revolutionized network architectures, and they play nowadays a significant role in the evolution of 5G and

© The Author(s), under exclusive license to Springer Nature Switzerland AG 2024
B. Ben Hedia et al. (Eds.): VECoS 2023, LNCS 14368, pp. 30–44, 2024.
https://doi.org/10.1007/978-3-031-49737-7_3

beyond networks [2]. These technologies are considerd as essential enablers in achieving the vision of highly flexible, efficient, and intelligent networks of the future. SDN/NFV enabled networks promise to shape the future of telecommunications through bringing several benefits including network programmability, service orchestration, network automation and enhanced scalability and flexibility. 5G introduces the concept of network slicing, which allows operators to partition a single PSN into multiple virtual networks. The combination of SDN and NFV is instrumental in realizing network slicing by dynamically allocating resources and deploying specific network functions for each slice [8]. Network slicing can indeed be considered as Network Slice as a Service (NSaaS), an emerging business model, that leverages network slicing capabilities to offer customized, differentiated, and flexible network services to various tenants or customers such as enhanced Mobile Broadband (eMBB), massive Machine-Type Communications (mMTC), or Ultra-Reliable Low-Latency Communications (URLLC) [15]. It enables operators rapid service deployment reducing time-to-market for new services and fostering innovation. Furthermore it allows to monetize their network infrastructure effectively and meet the diverse needs of different industries and applications. With NSaaS, each slice is tailored and optimized. However, network slicing introduces several technical challenges that need to be addressed to ensure better-performing and cost-efficient services. In order to raise these challenges an efficient resource management and particularly service network slicing Management and Orchestration (MANO) is needed to handle the complexities of network slicing [10]. This complexity concerns scalability issues, dynamic resource management, slice life-cycle management, and successful deployment and operation. Notice that network slicing may be achieved through SFC orchestration. By combining network slicing and SFC orchestration, operators can provide customized end-to-end network services, with specific service paths tailored to the needs of different tenants usually imposing stringent requirements on QoE perceived by users. This approach allows efficient resource utilization, isolation, and management of the network slices. [4]. Resource management for network slicing is a perpetual topic during the evolution of wireless communication where efficient matching of the allocated resource to each network slice while accounting for the users' activity requirements especially in terms of QoE is the most critical challenge. In this regard, DRL seems nowadays one of the most promising solutions to raise this challenge [1,5]. Comparing different implementations of DRL in this context is essential for performance evaluation, benchmarking, optimization and generalization. It facilitates the development of more efficient and effective DRL algorithms and helps better understanding the strengths and weaknesses of different approaches. It enables also to identify areas of improvement and optimization and promotes the selection of the most effective implementation for a specific wireless network scenario.

In this paper, we investigate a comparative study between DQN and Dueling DQN in the context where network slicing is addressed as SFC orchestration problem based on DRL approach and aiming to maximize QoE while meeting QoS requirements. We intend through such investigation to highlight how

DQN and Dueling DQN algorithms behave in ever changing environments while learning to successfully to determine both the optimal placement of VNFs and the mapping of virtual links involved in a chain of Service Functions (SF)s and efficient routing paths within each network slice.

The rest of this paper is organized as follows. Section 2 describes the role of SDN and NFV for network slicing in 5G and beyond. Section 3 highlights how SFC may be leveraged to achieve network slicing. Section 4 examines DRL Implementation via DQN and Dueling DQN. Section 5 addresses performance evaluation and numerical results before concluding this paper in Sect. 6.

2   SDN and NFV for Network Slicing in 5G and Beyond

The combined use of SDN, NFV, and SFC in 5G and beyond offers several benefits for network slicing. Among the key advantages of this combination:

- *Flexible and customized network slicing:* SDN provides centralized control and programmability, allowing dynamic creation, management, and orchestration of network slices. On the other hand, NFV allows the deployment of VNFs on commodity hardware, facilitating the customization of network slices based on specific requirements. Furthermore, SFC provides the ability to chain and sequence these VNFs to create end-to-end service paths.
- *Efficient resource utilization and scalability:* Thanks to SDN's centralized control, efficient allocation and sharing of network resources based on the requirements of individual slices is enabled. Also leveraging NFV capabilities allows dynamic scaling of VNFs, and resource allocation based on demand, reducing the need for dedicated hardware. In this context, SFC ensures that traffic flows through the necessary sequence of VNFs, enabling efficient use of resources and optimizing performance within the slice.
- *Faster service deployment and innovation:* SDN's programmability and automation capabilities enable rapid provisioning, configuration, and reconfiguration of network slices. NFV's software-based approach allows for quicker deployment and scaling of VNFs without relying on PSN changes. SFC ensures efficient service chaining and sequencing, enabling the deployment of new services with reduced time-to-market. This agility empowers service providers to respond quickly to evolving customer demands, deploy innovative services, and support emerging use cases in 5G and beyond.
- *Isolation and security:* Each network slice operates as a separate virtual network with its dedicated resources, control plane, and service paths. SDN's centralized control enables the enforcement of slice-specific policies and security mechanisms. On the other hand NFV allows for the isolation of VNFs within their respective slices. Furthermore, SFC ensures that traffic flows through the defined sequence of VNFs, enhancing security and ensuring that each slice's traffic remains isolated.
- *Network efficiency and optimization:* SDN's centralized control and visibility allow for efficient allocation and optimization of network resources. Also,

NFV's dynamic scaling and load balancing capabilities optimize resource utilization for VNFs. In addition, SFC ensures that traffic flows through the required SFs, minimizing latency and maximizing performance within the slice.

- *End-to-end service orchestration:* SDN controllers can manage network slices across access networks, transport networks, and core networks, ensuring seamless service delivery. NFV enables the virtualization and chaining of network functions across these domains, allowing SFs to be dynamically instantiated and chained based on service requirements. Moreover, SFC ensures that traffic flows through the specified sequence of VNFs across domains.
- *Enhanced service functionality:* NFV enables the deployment of a wide range of VNFs, including firewalls, load balancers, intrusion detection systems, and more, providing advanced services and capabilities within slices. SFC ensures correct SFCs ordering and chaining to create service paths.
- *Flexible network slicing:* SDN and NFV enable the dynamic creation, management, and orchestration of network slices. Network slicing allows the partitioning of a PSN into multiple virtual networks, each tailored to specific requirements. Furthermore, SDN provides centralized control and programmability, while NFV allows the deployment of VNFs on commodity hardware.

3 SFC for Network Slicing in 5G and Beyond

In 5G and beyond, SFC promise to play a pivotal role in addressing varied vertical applications and enabling network slicing through delivering a wide range of services with specific requirements [3]. When it comes to network slicing in 5G and beyond, SFC can be incorporated by network operators within individual slices to define the sequence of SFs (such as traffic classification, security functions (firewall, intrusion detection), Network Address Translation (NAT), traffic optimization, or content filtering) that network packets or flows need to traverse. This allows for the creation, within the limits imposed by the underlying PSN, of customized slices with their own logical topology, security rules and performance characteristics (in terms of latency requirements, bandwidth allocation, QoS and QoE guarantees) (see Fig. 1). It empowers providing fine-grained control over the traffic flow and the application of specific services through customizing the order and composition of SFs for each network slice, based on the specific requirements of the services or applications hosted in that slice.

3.1 SFC Orchestration Based on QoE

Ensuring efficient SFC orchestration and satisfactory QoE for different network slices can significantly strengthen the overall performance and user satisfaction. Network slice orchestration involves the management and coordination of resources, functions, and policies across the network to instantiate, configure, and manage network slices according to dynamic consumer needs. SFC orchestration, on the other hand, focuses on SFC instantiation and management within

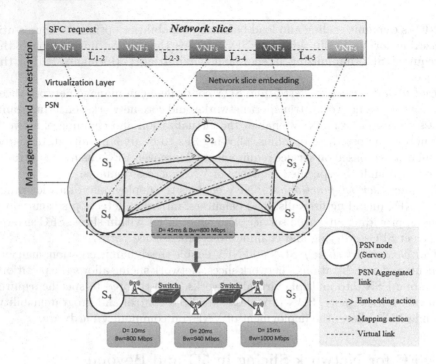

Fig. 1. Network Slice Management and Orchestration

each network slice. The orchestration process uses automation platform to ensure several services such as efficient resources allocation, appropriate placement of SFs, and dynamic scaling based on demand. As different services and applications have varying requirements and performance expectations, a crucial aspect of network slicing is QoE. QoE may involve several metrics such such as latency, throughput, reliability, availability, and overall user satisfaction.

3.2   Formulating QoE with Respect to QoS

The goal of formulating QoE with respect to QoS is to quantify the user's quality perception based on objective measurements of QoS and contextual factors. However, there is no universally applicable formula, and it often requires continuous monitoring, user feedback, and iterative refinement to accurately capture the relationship between QoE and QoS. Indeed, the relationship between QoE and QoS is complex and subjective, as QoE represents the end-user's perception of the service quality, while QoS refers to the measurable performance parameters of the underlying network. However, it is possible to establish a general formula and fundamental laws to express and governs the relationship between QoE and QoS. One widely used approach to establish this relationship is the Mean Opinion Score (MOS) model, which quantifies QoE based on subjective ratings provided by users. The actual form of this relationship should represent the mapping or transformation of QoS and contextual factors into the QoE score and may vary depending on the application, service, or industry domain. Different QoE models may be considered according to the application nature (video streaming services, voice communications, online gaming). Additionally, in order to capture the complex relationships between QoE and QoS, Machine Learning (ML) and Artificial Intelligence (AI) techniques may be leveraged for developing more sophisticated models. In literature the investigation of multi-dimensional QoE models establishing fundamental laws and principles that govern the relationship between user experience and various QoS dimensions is usually embodied through Web Quality and Functionality (WFL) (Eq. (1)) and Interaction Quality eXperience (IQX) (Eq. (2)) models [12]. Such models attempt to provide a deeper understanding of QoE and establish frameworks for measuring and improving user satisfaction. The WFL model specifically focuses on web-based applications and services. It considers the dimensions of web quality and functionality that impact user experience. These dimensions can include factors such as content quality, ease of navigation, page loading speed, visual appeal, accessibility, and privacy. The investigation of WFL involves studying the relationships between these web quality and functionality dimensions and user satisfaction [7]. On the other hand, the IQX model aims to capture the overall user perception of the quality of interactions, taking into account both subjective and objective measures. It focuses on the quality of interactive systems, such as web applications, mobile apps, or multimedia platforms and considers various factors that impact the user experience during interactions, including usability, responsiveness, aesthetics, efficiency, and reliability.

$$QoE^t = \gamma_p \times log(\alpha_p \times qos^t + \beta_p) + \theta_p, t \in \{1, 2, .., k\} \tag{1}$$

$$QoE^t = \gamma_n \times e^{(\alpha_n \times qos^t + \beta_n)} + \theta_n, t \in \{k+1, k+2, .., L\} \tag{2}$$

Both in Eq. (1) and Eq. (2), QoE^t denotes the QoE gain related to the tth QoS metric of the SFC instance. The SFC instance is defined as the set of distributed resources to be allocated in the PSN to successfully handle (embed/map) the set of ordered VNFs and the corresponding virtual links belonging to the same SFC request. These resources are dynamically chosen along the SFC request deployment process among available resources in the PSN nodes and PSN links. Notice also that, the constant parameters α_p, β_p, γ_p, θ_p, α_n, β_n, γ_n and θ_n in Eq. (1) and Eq. (2) may be leveraged to achieve fine tuning of the quantitative inter-dependency between QoE and QoS.

In this paper, we formulate a reward function similar to that provided in [6] and assigning a reward quantified by a QoE gain (Eq. (3)) combining WFL and IQX models when a SFC request is successfully deployed and a penalty $P = 10$ otherwise. Along the training phase, the DRL agent attempts to maximize the expected accumulated reward while meeting QoS requirements and considering PSN's resources limitations.

$$QoE = \sum_{t=1}^{K} w^t \times QoE^t - \sum_{t=K+1}^{L} w^t \times QoE^t \tag{3}$$

4   DRL Implementation via DQN and Dueling DQN

In this paper, we implement DRL by considering two algorithms DQN (Algorithm 1) and Dueling DQN (Algorithm 2), a variant of DQN. This implementation aims to maximize QoE while meeting QoS constraints. Among these constraints we consider several assumptions related to VNF license as well as limitations in terms PSN link capacity (in terms of bandwidth) and PSN link delay. In the rest of this section, we describe first DQN principle and we detail next Dueling DQN concept and related improvements.

4.1   DQN

Q-learning is a model free Reinforcement Learning (RL) algorithm based on a tabular method that requires explicitly maintaining a table (Q-table) to store the action-value function for each state-action pair. It works well for problems with discrete small state and action spaces. On the other hand, DQN [11] as a DRL algorithm generalizes Q-learning and leverages deep neural networks DNN [13] to approximate the action-value function, enabling it to handle large and and high-dimensional continuous state space, making it scalable and more suitable for complex real-world problems. DQN uses a parameterized Q-function $Q(s, a; \theta) \approx Q(s, a)$ where, θ represents the DNN parameters. By training DNN with gradient descent instead of the Q-Learning iterative update process, DQN aims to minimize a loss function at iteration i:

$$L_i(\theta_i) = \mathbb{E}_{s,a,r,s'}[(y_i^{DQN} - Q(s, a; \theta_i))^2] \tag{4}$$

In order to address instability caused by using function approximation, DQN uses two innovative techniques referred to as experience replay and target Q-networks. Experience replay stores and reuses past experiences (history) with a replay buffer for the update of current policy. and randomly samples from the buffer during training [9], in order to break the correlation between consecutive experience tuples and to stabilize the training process. On the other hand, target Q-network is used to make training more stable. It is a copy of the action-value function (or Q-function, main network) that is held constant to serve as a stable and frozen target. DQN leverages this frozen target network to generate the target Q-values, used for updating the main network. By freezing the target network, DQN tries enhancing the training targets stability by decoupling them from the parameters being updated and avoid over-fitting [11]. Freezing covers the target network parameters $Q(s', a'; \theta^-)$ for some fixed number of iterations while updating the online network $Q(s, a; \theta_i)$ by gradient descent in order to minimize the loss function. The specific gradient update is given as follows:

$$\nabla_{\theta_i} L_i(\theta_i) = \mathbb{E}_{s,a,r,s'}[(y_i^{DQN} - Q(s, a; \theta_i))\nabla_{\theta_i} Q(s, a; \theta_i)] \tag{5}$$

Given the state s', reward r, discount factor γ, DQN computes the target Q-value y_i^{DQN} as follows:

$$y_i^{DQN} = r + \gamma max_{a'} Q(s', a'; \theta^-) \tag{6}$$

where θ^- corresponds to the parameters (weights) of a fixed and separate target network. While DQN has achieved remarkable success in various domains, it presents some common limitations and challenges. Indeed training DQN may be unstable. and can lead to oscillations or divergence. Also DQN suffers from sample inefficiency since it can require a substantial amount of data to converge to an optimal policy. Also, insufficient exploration of DQN can result in sub-optimal policies or the agent getting stuck in local optima. Furthermore, although DQN can handle continuous state spaces, its generalization capabilities through neural network approximation are still limited compared to more advanced algorithms. Finally, the DQN training process may require substantial computational resources to handle the network training, experience replay, and exploration-exploitation balance efficiently. In this regard, the major challenge is to find suitable performance-convergence compromise while computing NNs.

4.2   Dueling DQN

Dueling DQN [14] proposes a new variant of the DQN algorithm, using a model-based RL method to learn a control policy for the decision maker (an agent interacting with an environment in discrete time steps). In standard DQN algorithm, the estimation of the Q-function is achieved by a NN taking as input the current state of the environment and action and as outputs the expected return for each possible action. In order to enhance the DQN algorithm learning efficiency, Dueling DQN architecture separates the estimator (Q-function) into two estimators using two new streams, the value function $V(s)$ and the advantage function $A(s, a)$. This is achieved through splitting the last layer of the same NN in two parts. Whereas $V(s)$ gives information about how much reward will be collected from state s, $A(s, a)$ provides information about how much better one action when compared to the other actions. Accordingly, the Q-values is obtained as the sum of $V(s)$ and $A(s, a)$ for each action. The aggregation of the two streams (Eq. (7)) into a single Q-function (the Q-value stream) is only achieved via a special aggregating layer. This will be useful to quantify the Q-values and to estimate how good it is to take a certain action given a certain state.

$$Q(s, a; \theta, \alpha, \beta) = V(s; \theta, \beta) + A(s, a; \theta, \alpha) \tag{7}$$

Here, θ denotes the parameters of the convolutional layers, while α and β are the parameters of the two streams of fully-connected layers. This change is helpful, because sometimes it is unnecessary to know the exact value of each action, so just learning $V(s)$ can be enough is some cases. Unfortunately, knowing the Q-value (Eq. (7)) (that simply sums $V(s)$ and $A(s, a)$) through training the NN cannot provide explicitly $V(s)$ and $A(s, a)$. In other terms knowing the sum of two terms $(Q = A + V)$ does not allow to know $V(s)$ and $A(s, a)$ separately (since there is an infinite possible solutions). In order to solve this problem

---

Algorithm 1. DQN_QoS/QoE_SFC

---

initialize replay memory D to capacity RS and initialize $QoE_{Sc-Th} = 2500, Sum = 0$
initialize action value function Q_θ, with random weights θ
initialize target action value function $Q_{\theta-}$ with weights θ^-
for *episode* = 1..E **do** //E = 5000
    `reset environment,` $Sum_r = 0$
    for *sfc_req* = 1..*Req* **do** //*Req* = 100
        `initialize chain c and observe initial observation state` s
        for i = 1..N **do**
            `select action a and observe reward r and` s `by QoS`
            `store transition (s,a,r,s`$'$`) in D and s=s`$'$
        end for
        $Sum_r+ = r$
        if enough experiences in D **then**
            `sample mini-batch of` BS `transitions from` D
            `compute target` Q `value by Eq. (6)`
            `perform a gradient descent step on by Eq. (4)`
            `every` C `iterations, reset` $Q_{\theta-} = Q_\theta$
        end if
    end for
    `calculate` Sum `the sum of last 100 mean rewards ((`Sum_r/Req`))`
    if $(Sum/100) \geq QoE_{Sc-Th}$ **then** break
    end if
end for

Dueling DQN suggests to force the highest Q-value to be equal to $V(s)$, making the highest value in the advantage function be at most zero (Eq. (8)). In this way $V(s)$ is exactly known, and we can deduce all the advantages from there, solving the problem. Hence the training is described by the following equation:

$$Q(s, a; \theta, \alpha, \beta) = V(s; \theta, \beta) + (A(s, a; \theta, \alpha) - max_{a' \in |A|} A(s, a'; \theta, \alpha)) \quad (8)$$

In order to increase optimization stability, in [14], authors suggest to replace the max of A (Eq. (8)) by the mean of A (Eq. (9)) to train the network.

$$Q(s, a; \theta, \alpha, \beta) = V(s; \theta, \beta) + (A(s, a; \theta, \alpha) - \frac{1}{|A|} \sum_{a'} A(s, a'; \theta, \alpha)) \quad (9)$$

This enables a quicker identification of the correct action during the policy evaluation as the network can learn the effectiveness of the states without having to learn the value of each action for each state. With this separation, defined in Eq. (10) (in a similar way as in Eq. (6)), the target Q-value given in (Eq. (10)) is now expressed as follows (Eq. (11)):

$$y_i^{DuelDQN} = r + \gamma max_{a'} Q(s', a'; \theta^-, \alpha^-, \beta^-) \quad (10)$$

where the β^- and α^- denote the weights of the fully connected layers for value function stream and advantage function stream respectively.

$$y_i^{DuelDQN} = r + \gamma max_{a'}[V(s';\theta^-,\beta^-) + (A(s',a';\theta^-,\alpha^-) - \frac{1}{|A|}\sum_a A(s',a;\theta^-,\alpha^-))]$$

(11)

Dueling DQN offers a more structured and refined approach to estimating Q-values, allowing for better learning efficiency, improved action selection, enhanced generalization, and increased stability during training. These advantages make it a suitable choice in various RL tasks where value estimation and action selection are crucial.

Algorithm 2. Dueling DQN_QoS/QoE_SFC

---

initialize replay memory D to capacity RS and initialize $QoE_{Sc-Th} = 2500, Sum = 0$
initialize action value function Q_θ, with random weights θ, α and β
initialize target action value function Q_{θ^-} with weights θ^-, β^- and α^-
for $episode = 1..E$ **do** $//E = 5000$
   reset environment, $Sum_r = 0$
   for $sfc\_req = 1..Req$ **do** $//Req = 100$
      initialize chain c and observe initial observation state s
      for $i = 1..N$ **do**
         select action a and observe reward r and s by QoS
         store transition (s,a,r,s') in D and $s=s'$
      end for
      $Sum_r+=r$
      if enough experiences in D **then**
         sample mini-batch of BS transitions from D
         compute target Q value by Eq. (11)
         perform a gradient descent step on by Eq. (4)
         every C iterations, reset $Q_{\theta^-} = Q_\theta$
      end if
   end for
   calculate Sum the sum of last 100 mean rewards $((Sum_r/Req))$
   if $(Sum/100) \geq QoE_{Sc-Th}$ **then** break
   end if
end for

---

5 Performance Evaluation and Simulation Results

Performance evaluation of DRL algorithms requires defining the simulation environment and related parameters as well as the considered assumptions related to the used PSN topology (Fig. 1), the workload (SFC requests (SR)), and the investigated performance metrics.

5.1   Key Assumptions

- PSN nodes: Each PSN node is assumed hosting one or more VNF(s).
- PSN links: Each PSN link is assumed with limited bandwidth capacity (Bw_{link}) and non zero transmission delay (D_{link}). It may handle one or more Vlink(s). Bw_{link} is randomly chosen in the range of [768–1280]Mbps, and D_{link} is randomly selected in [10–20]ms.
- PSN attributes:
  - M: is the number of nodes in PSN ($M = 5$).
  - M_{link}: The number of PSN links ($M_{link} = M * (M - 1)/2 = 10$), (PSN is assumed fully interconnected).
- SR attributes:
  - N_{VNF}: The number of VNF instances ($N_{VNF} = 5$) involved in deploying the SR. The embedding of each VNF instance on each PSN node is assumed requiring no CPU capacity and no processing delay. Such assumption may be easily relaxed by affecting a non null processing capacity and non null time delay in the PSN node. This is out of the scope of this paper.
  - N_{Vlink}: The number of Vlinks ($N_{Vlink} = 4$) involved in deploying the SR.
  - Bw_r: The SR End-to-End Bandwidth is assumed varying according to a random law in the range of [16–256]Mbps.
  - D_r: The SR End-to-End Delay is assumed varying randomly in the range of [50–90]ms.
- Performance evaluation metrics;
  - The average QoE score (QoE) quantifying the expected cumulative reward.
  - The standard deviation (Std) quantifying the amount of variability or dispersion of the expected cumulative reward.
  - The Rejection Ratio (RR) quantifying the rejection rate of SR.

In the conducted experiments every cycle of state-action-reward corresponds to one step. Each SFC request involves 5 steps or actions and each action corresponds to embedding one VNF on a PSN node. Notice also that during one run we assume processing 100 SFC requests and the expected accumulated reward along this time period is used to plot one point in the training curve. The learning phase is observed along a set of runs referred to as one episode. The episode is considered ended whenever a maximum number of runs expired (20000 runs). The training phase is considered finished whenever a training goal (or a final state corresponding to QoE_{Th_Sc} reached on average during the last 100 runs of the training phase) is fulfilled by the DRL agent. The training goal is achieved whenever the quality of the agent's learning performance is considered enough satisfactory (whenever reaching a near-optimal solution as close as possible to optimal solution). The target quality of learning is assessed through a QoE_{Th_Sc}. Along the simulation process and whenever an episode ends the environment is reset to its initial state and the agent begins a new episode. Such configuration allows the agent to learn from its experience in every episode and leverages such information (knowledge) to improve its performance in the following episodes.

5.2   Simulation Results

In order to establish performance comparison along training phase of DQN and Dueling DQN algorithms with two other standard algorithms referred to as violent and random a set of simulation experiments (Fig. 2) are conducted. Notice that all these algorithms (violent, random, DQN and Dueling DQN) use the same reward function. Along each experience each algorithm seeks to solve network slicing orchestration problem through dynamically deploying an incoming SFC request (with both variable end-to-end delay and end-to-end bandwidth) on PSN with limited resources. This task is fulfilled by each algorithm in a different way taking into account specific hypotheses.

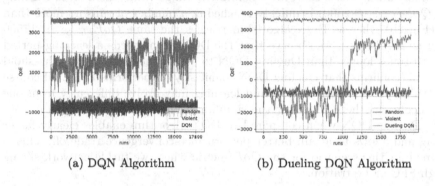

(a) DQN Algorithm   (b) Dueling DQN Algorithm

Fig. 2. QoE vs runs ($QoE_{Sc-Th} = 2500$)

Before investigating simulation results, we provide in what follows detailed description of two reference algorithms (violent and random) as well as DQN and Dueling DQN from knowledge and observability perspective.

Violent Algorithm: This algorithm possesses full network observability. This knowledge is fully leveraged to find a optimal solution to the network slicing orchestration problem. This is fulfilled by decision making based on selecting, among all the SFC instances enabling to successfully deploy the SFC request, the one that produces the highest expected accumulated reward. Obviously the adopted approach of violent algorithm is expected to bring the best QoE with the sacrifice of costly simulation time.

Random Algorithm: This algorithm has no network observability that may be leveraged to help achieving optimal decisions or actions, instead, it randomly selects a SFC instance enabling successfully deployment of the SFC request (without worrying about selecting the optimal SFC instance yielding the highest reward (QoE score)). Random algorithm is obviously expected to be the fastest one, however since it does not use any learning to arrive at the final solution of the problem to be solved and does not seek to maximize any reward along the training episode, It is also expected to produce the worst QoE.

DQN and Dueling DQN: These algorithms are classified as DRL algorithms and as a consequence there is no need for them to any prior knowledge on the environment and its dynamic to initiate the training phase. Instead, they attempt through RL via trials and errors, exploration and exploitation to train DRL agent to perform near-optimal solution in terms of QoE score. The objective is to get as close as possible to the optimal policy provided by the violent algorithm by maximizing the expected cumulative reward formulated by considering both QoE requirements and QoS constraints.

Simulation experiments conducted in this paper are provided through the evaluation of a set of performance metrics defined above in this same section. Along the training phase, Fig. 2a (resp. Figure 2b) shows the evolution of the *QoE* score with respect to the number of runs for respectively DQN and Dueling DQN algorithms. Notice that, for Dueling DQN algorithm, the desired learning level ($QoE_{Th-Sc} = 2500$) is quickly reached in a number of runs no more than 1861 (Fig. 2b) whereas DQN algorithm reaches the same QoE_{Th-Sc} in 17500 runs (Fig. 2a). Indeed, we observe that the DQN agent needs a learning period about 10 times longer than Dueling DQN to attain the desired QoE threshold score. This confirms that Dueling DQN manifestly outperforms DQN. Of course the learning process is stochastic and learning may evolve differently from one experience to anotherğ. However the significant enhancements provided in conceiving Dueling DQN when compared to DQN algorithm enables clearly faster learning and allows to attain better performance-convergence trade-off. This is confirmed for this scenario for the *QoE* metric where we tackle network slicing through SFC orchestration.

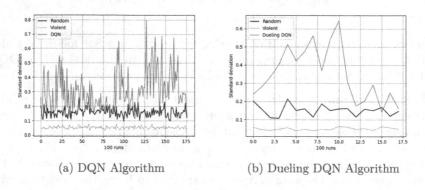

(a) DQN Algorithm   (b) Dueling DQN Algorithm

Fig. 3. Standard Deviation ($QoE_{Sc-Th} = 2500$)

One of the major improvements considered by Dueling to remedy the shortcomings of DQN is stability. To highlight this advantage we have considered experiments where we propose to compare the performance of Dueling DQN with DQN in terms of standard deviation in Fig. 3. The curves plot every 100 runs the standard deviation of each algorithm. We notice that fluctuations and oscillations of DQN (Fig. 3a) are more pronounced than those generated by Dueling

DQN (Fig. 3b). Also DRL algorithms (DQN and Dueling DQN) give rise to more severe oscillations than violent and random. This may be explained by the following arguments. During exploitation DRL algorithms select the action yielding the best reward (QoE) whereas during exploration the agent may obtain better reward but also risks to obtain severe penalties. Also, since along the training phase the agent alternates between exploration and exploitation it is very likely to show large oscillations when compared to random and violent algorithms until converging at the end of the training phase.

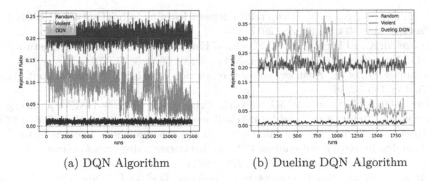

(a) DQN Algorithm   (b) Dueling DQN Algorithm

Fig. 4. RR vs runs ($QoE_{Sc-Th} = 2500$)

It is also confirmed again for another performance metric (RR) where we investigate in Fig. 4 along the training phase of the agent the rejection ratio evolution with respect to the number of runs for DQN (Fig. 4a) and Dueling DQN (Fig. 4b). Obviously the random and violent algorithms are used in the same plot as reference algorithms as detailed above in this same section.

Evidently, further numerical explorations may be investigated in future works to better understand the enhancements provided by Dueling DQN and also other variants of DQN through the performance metrics provided in this paper or other metrics to be defined.

6 Conclusion

Comparing DRL algorithms is essential for evaluating performance, driving algorithmic advancements, understanding their behaviors, aiding in algorithm selection, and establishing benchmarks for future research. It contributes to the growth and development of the field of DRL, enabling to make informed decisions and advancements in the application of RL. In this paper, we investigated a comparative study between DQN and Dueling DQN in a scenario where we tackle network slicing orchestration problem aiming to maximize QoE while meeting QoS requirements. The network slicing orchestration is considered based on deploying each incoming SFC request on 5G networks and beyond leveraging flexibility and agility of SDN and NFV and their capacities to abstract networks through virtualization. Numerical investigation confirms that Dueling DQN manifestly outperforms DQN and highlights related enhancements leading to better convergence-performance trade-off in terms of reaching a predefined QoE_{Th_Sc} and in minimizing RR. In future researches, we intend to investigate further performance metrics and to establish performance comparison between DQN and other DQN variants for the same scenario addressed in this paper.

References

1. Arulkumaran, K., et al.: Deep reinforcement learning: a brief survey. IEEE Signal Process. Mag. **34**(6), 26–38 (2017)
2. Benzekki, K., El Fergougui, A., Elbelrhiti Elalaoui, A.: Software-defined networking (SDN): a survey. Secur. Commun. Netw. 9(18), 5803–5833 (2016)
3. Bhamare, D., et al.: A survey on service function chaining. J. Netw. Comput. Appl. **75**, 138–155 (2016)
4. Barakabitze, A.A., et al.: 5G network slicing using SDN and NFV: a survey of taxonomy, architectures and future challenges. Comput. Netw. **167**, 106984 (2020)
5. Moreno, C., Fernando, J., et al.: Online service function chain deployment for live-streaming in virtualized content delivery networks: a deep reinforcement learning approach. Future Internet **13**(11), 278 (2021)
6. Chen, X., et al.: Reinforcement learning-based QoS/QoE-aware service function chaining in software-driven 5G slices. Trans. Emerg. Telecommun. Technol. **29**(11), e3477 (2018)
7. Fiedler, M., Hossfeld, T., Tran-Gia, P.: A generic quantitative relationship between quality of experience and quality of service. IEEE Netw. **24**(2), 36–41 (2010)
8. Sánchez, H., Andrea, J., Casilimas, K., Rendon, O.M.C.: Deep reinforcement learning for resource management on network slicing: a survey. Sensors **22**(8), 3031 (2022)
9. Lin, L.J.: RL for Robots Using Neural Networks. Carnegie Mellon University, Pittsburgh (1992)
10. Li, R., et al.: Deep reinforcement learning for resource management in network slicing. IEEE Access **6**, 74429–74441 (2018)
11. Mnih, V., et al.: Human-level control through deep reinforcement learning. Nature **518**(7540), 529–533 (2015)
12. Reichl, P., et al.: The logarithmic nature of QoE and the role of the Weber-Fechner law in QoE assessment. In: 2010 IEEE International Conference on Communications. IEEE (2010)
13. Sarker, I.H.: Deep learning: a comprehensive overview on techniques, taxonomy, applications and research directions. SN Comput. Sci. **2**(6), 420 (2021)
14. Wang, Z., et al.: Dueling network architectures for deep reinforcement learning. In: International Conference on Machine Learning. PMLR (2016)
15. Yang, W., et al.: Dynamic URLLC and eMBB multiplexing design in 5G new radio. In: 2020 IEEE 17th Annual Consumer Communications & Networking Conference (CCNC). IEEE (2020)

On Language-Based Opacity Verification Problem in Discrete Event Systems Under Orwellian Observation

Salwa Habbachi[1]([✉]), Imene Ben Hafaiedh[2], Zhiwu Li[1,3], and Moez Krichen[4]

[1] Institute of Systems Engineering (MISE), Macau University of Science and Technology (MUST), Taipa, Macau
Salwahabbachi29@gmail.com

[2] Institut Supérieur d'informatique (ISI), Université Tunis El Manar (UTM), LIPSIC Laboratory Tunis, Tunis, Tunisia

[3] School of Electro-Mechanical Engineering, Xidian University, Xi'an 710071, China

[4] AlBaha University, AlMandaq, AlBaha, Kingdom of Saudi Arabia

Abstract. Opacity is an important information flow property that is concerned with the secret leakage of a system to a malicious observer called an "intruder". Usually, opacity analyses are made under static or dynamic observation, i.e., the observability of events in a system is fixed or changeable over time by a mask. In this paper, we address the verification of language-based opacity in the context of discrete-event systems under Orwellian observation. We consider an Orwellian partial observability model, where some unobservable events, not visible when occurring, may become noticeable in the future. Specifically, we propose a set of unobservable events that are no longer unobservable once an event in another particular disjoint event subset is triggered. First, we define and solve an integer linear programming problem to verify language-based opacity in discrete event systems using labeled Petri nets. We then propose a new Orwellian projection function that is event-based, i.e., the system is allowed to re-interpret the observation of the already triggered events when a particular observable event occurs. Finally, the verification of language-based opacity in discrete event systems under Orwellian projection is addressed.

Keywords: Language-based opacity · labeled Petri net · Discrete-event system · Orwellian projection · Integer linear programming

1 Introduction

With more and more information exchanges in cyber-systems, serious security issues have been raised. Ensuring the safety and reliability of such systems becomes challenging. Security analysis and control in cyber-systems has received a great deal of attention in the past decade. Some security notions are related to information flows. Information flows should be governed in a safe manner to prevent secret information from being leaked to an outside observer with malicious intention called an "intruder". Opacity is one of the most important information flow properties studied in the literature. Opacity reflects the ability of a system to hide a given secret from an intruder during the system's evolution. For the opacity issue in a DES, it usually assumes that the intruder has full knowledge of the system's structure but has only a partial observation ability of its evolution.

In recent years, opacity-related problems have been extensively studied in the context of discrete event systems. In a DES, opacity is first addressed in [1] for transition systems, further developed in [2], and extended in [3] using Petri nets (PNs) as a modeling formalism. The opacity notion is then framed in the context of finite state automata in [4]. A system is said to be opaque if, during its evolution, an intruder is unable to determine the system's secret based on its observations. Different opacity notions have been proposed such as language-based opacity, current-state opacity, initial-state opacity, K-step opacity, and infinite-step opacity [5]. The opacity verification problem in discrete event systems has received a great deal of attention from researchers over the last few years. Verification methods have been proposed in various ways to deal with different categories of opacity [6].

The observation model of a system is the key to its opacity analysis. In the DES literature, the observation mechanisms can be classified mainly into three types: static, dynamic, and Orwellian, depending on the computational power of an observer that it reflects. Broadly speaking, in the setup of the static observation, the set of observable events and the observer interpretation are fixed off-line. For dynamic observability, the set of observable events changes over time depending on the history of the trace. However, in the setting of Orwellian observation, a system is allowed to re-interpret the observation of an internal string, in which the observability of an event depends on the prefix up to the current instant and on the future suffix.

For instance, the work in [7] introduces dynamic partial observability, in which the observation of a set of events is controlled by a dynamic mask and changes over time. Opacity verification under a dynamic projection is then addressed. Moreover, the authors in [8] introduce the synthesis of infinite-step opacity under a dynamic projection. Opacity under an Orwellian observation is first investigated in [9], in which the authors prove that opacity and intransitive non-interference are equivalent. Therein, the Orwellian projection reveals the entire trajectory when a particular event, named a downgrading event, occurs, i.e., the outsider knows the current state precisely. However, in this paper, it is assumed that only some of the unobserved events (not all of the entire path) are revealed (become noticeable) when a particular event occurs in order to preserve the uncertainty of the intruder. The work in [10] extends the approach in [9] to address opacity verification and enforcement under the proposed Orwellian observation model. The authors in [10] show that opacity verification is decidable under their suggested Orwellian observation function with PSPACE-complete complexity, while it is undecidable under a general Orwellian observation function. Later, the authors in [11] propose a new Orwellian-type observation model called a dynamic information release mechanism (DIRM) which is state-dependent, where they assume that only partial information of the trajectory can be released when a particular state is reached. The verification of current-state opacity under the proposed Orwellian-type observation is then discussed. In this paper, we address language-based opacity (LBO) verification in discrete event systems under an Orwellian observation model using Petri nets (PNs).

In the context of an automaton framework, the work in [12] proposes algorithms to verify both strong and weak LBO, in which the construction of nine types of graphs is required and the complexity of the proposed approach is PSPACE-complete. Later, weak opacity has been checked by an algorithm with polynomial time complexity, which is proposed in [13]. On the other side, the authors in [20] introduce an algebraic representation of labeled PNs to verify initial state opacity. However, only the works in [14] and [15] study language-based opacity verification using labeled PNs. The study in [14] verifies language-based opacity using a special structure called a verifier under the assumption that an intruder is interested in the set of observable transitions only. This work constructs the basis reachability graph (BRG) of a given PN and applies the related approach proposed in [12]. In [15], an approach based on integer linear programming is proposed, where an algebraic representation of labeled Petri net (LPN) is exploited and two conditions are derived to check LBO with respect to a given finite secret language.

As stated, this paper addresses the verification of language-based opacity in the context of discrete-event systems under Orwellian observations. We consider Orwellian partial observability, where some unobservable events, not visible when occurring, can be noticeable due to the further system evolution. In other words, besides the standard sets of observable and unobservable events, we propose a set of unobservable events that are no longer unobservable once an event in another particular disjoint event subset is triggered. This concept is invented in order to release information as much as possible to maintain accountability while keeping the system's security. First, the verification of language-based opacity in discrete event systems is addressed using integer linear programming, which helps us further consider unbounded Petri nets. A new Orwellian projection is then proposed that is event-based, i.e., the system is allowed to re-interpret the observation of the already triggered events when a particular observable event occurs. Finally, language-based opacity in modular systems under Orwellian observation is defined.

2 Preliminaries

2.1 Petri Net

A Petri net is a four-tuple $N = (P, T, Pre, Post)$, where P is a finite set of m places, graphically represented by circles; T is a finite set of n transitions, graphically represented by bars, with $P \cap T = \emptyset$ and $P \cup T \neq \emptyset$; $Pre: P \times T \to \mathbb{N}$

and $Post : P \times T \to \mathbb{N}$ are the pre- and post-incidence functions that respectively specify the arcs directed from places to transitions and vice versa, where $\mathbb{N} = \{0, 1, 2, \ldots\}$ is a set of non-negative integers. In a Petri net, the pre- (post-) incidence function Pre ($Post$) can be represented by a matrix indexed by P and T, i.e., $Pre, Post \in \mathbb{N}^{m \times n}$. We use $C = Post - Pre$ to represent the incidence matrix of a net.

A marking is a mapping $M : P \to \mathbb{N}$ that assigns tokens to places; graphically a token is drawn by a black dot. The marking of a place p at a marking M is denoted by $M(p)$. For economy of space, the multi-set notation is used, i.e., write $M = \Sigma_{p \in P} M(p).p$ to denote a marking M. For mathematical convenience, a marking M can be represented as a vector with its i-th entry being $M(p_i)$.

A Petri net system $\langle N, M_0 \rangle$ is a net N equipped with an initial marking M_0. A transition t is enabled at a marking M if $M \geq Pre(\cdot, t)$. The firing of t at M yields a marking M', satisfying $M' = M + C(\cdot, t)$. We write $M[t\rangle$ to denote that t is enabled at M and $M[t\rangle M'$ to denote that the firing of t drives a system from M to M'.

Write $M[\sigma\rangle$ if a sequence of transitions $\sigma = t_1 \ldots t_i \in T^*$ is sequentially enabled at the marking M such that $M[t_1\rangle M_1[t_2\rangle M_2 \ldots [t_i\rangle M_i$ holds, denoted as $M[\sigma\rangle M_i$. The set of all firable (feasible) transition sequences in $\langle N, M_0 \rangle$ is denoted as $L(N, M_0) = \{\sigma \in T^* | M_0[\sigma\rangle\}$. Given a transition sequence $\sigma \in T^*$, function $\tau : T^* \to \mathbb{N}^n$ defines the firing count vector of the transition sequence σ, i.e., $\tau(\sigma) \in \mathbb{N}^n$, where $\tau(\sigma) = y$ with $y(t) = k$ representing that the number of occurrences of t in σ is k. By a slight abuse of notation, we write $t \in \sigma$ if t is contained in σ.

A marking M is said to be reachable in $\langle N, M_0 \rangle$ if there exists a transition sequence $\sigma \in T^*$ such that $M_0[\sigma\rangle M$. The reachability set of $\langle N, M_0 \rangle$, denoted by $R(N, M_0)$, contains all markings of the net system reachable from M_0, i.e., $R(N, M_0) = \{M \in \mathbb{N}^m \mid \exists \sigma \in T^* : M_0[\sigma\rangle M\}$. If $M_0[\sigma\rangle M$, then the state equation of the net is $M = M_0 + C \cdot y$, where $y = \tau(\sigma)$.

2.2   Labeled Petri Net

A *labeled Petri net* (LPN) is a four-tuple $\mathcal{G} = (N, M_0, E, \lambda)$, where $\langle N, M_0 \rangle$ is a net system, E is an alphabet, and $\lambda : T \to E$ is a labeling function that assigns a label in E to a transition $t \in T$. The labeling function can be extended in a usual way, written again as λ in the case of no confusion. The extended labeling function $\lambda : T^* \to E^*$ is defined as follows: $\lambda(\varepsilon) = \varepsilon$ and $\lambda(\sigma t) = \lambda(\sigma)\lambda(t)$, in which $\sigma \in T^*$ and $t \in T$, where ε is the empty string.

Due to the partially observable characteristics of a system, the set E is partitioned into two disjoint parts: namely E_o and E_u, representing the sets of observable and unobservable events, respectively. Accordingly, transition set T in an LPN can be divided into two disjoint sets $T = T_o \cup T_u$, where $T_o = \{t \in T \mid \lambda(t) \in E_o\}$ is the set of observable transitions, while $T_u = T \setminus T_o = \{t \in T \mid \lambda(t) \in E_u\}$ is the set of unobservable transitions, also called *silent* transitions. Herein, we assume that a label $e \in E$ can be associated with more than one transition. We then define the set of transitions associated with the same label e as $T(e) = \{t \in T_o | \lambda(t) = e\}$.

Given a word $\omega \in E^*$, its observation is the output of a natural projection function $Pr : E^* \to E_o^*$, which is recursively defined as $Pr(\varepsilon) = \varepsilon$; $Pr(e) = e$ if $e \in E_o$ and $Pr(e) = \varepsilon$ if $e \in E_u$; $Pr(\omega e) = Pr(\omega)Pr(e)$, where $\omega \in E^*$ and $e \in E$. The natural projection Pr can be extended to $Pr : 2^{E^*} \to 2^{E_o^*}$, i.e., given a language $L \subseteq E^*$, $Pr(L) = \{Pr(\omega) \in E_o^* \mid \omega \in L\}$. The inverse project of Pr, denoted by Pr^{-1}, can be accordingly defined by $Pr^{-1} : 2^{E_o^*} \to 2^{E^*}$. Let $s \in E^*$ be a string. Write, as before, $e \in s$ if s contains e. Set $||s|| = \{e \in E \mid e \in s\}$ is called the support of s. The length of s is the number of symbols contained in it.

The language generated by an LPN system $\mathcal{G} = (N, M_0, E, \lambda)$ from M_0 that defines its behavior is given by

$$\mathcal{L}(\mathcal{G}, M_0) = \{\omega \in E^* | \exists \sigma \in T^* : M_0[\sigma\rangle, \lambda(\sigma) = \omega\} \tag{1}$$

Given a subset of transitions $T' \subseteq T$, we define the T'-derived subnet of N as $N' = (P, T', Pre', Post')$ that is the net resulting by removing all transitions in $T\backslash T'$ from N, where Pre' and $Post'$ are the restrictions of Pre and $Post$ to T', respectively. The incidence matrix of the T'-derived subnet is defined by $C' = Post' - Pre'$.

2.3 Some Results on Reachability in Petri Nets

Definition 1 (Basis Partition [16]). *Given a Petri net $N = (P, T, Pre, Post)$, a pair $\pi = (T_E, T_I)$ is called a basis partition of transition set T if $T_I \subseteq T$, $T_E = T \setminus T_I$, and the T_I-induced subnet is acyclic.*

Sets T_E and T_I collect the explicit and implicit transitions, respectively. In simple words, π divides T into two disjoint sets T_E and T_I such that the T_I-induced subnet is acyclic. Note that terms "implicit" and "explicit" are not related to the physical meanings of transitions. Let $|T_E| = n_E$ and $|T_I| = n_I$, where n_E and n_I represent the cardinalities of T_E and T_I, respectively.

Definition 2 (Explanations [16]). *Given a marked net (N, M_0) with $N = (P, T, Pre, Post)$, a basis partition $\pi = (T_E, T_I)$, a marking $M \in R(N, M_0)$, and a transition $t \in T_E$, the set of explanations of t at M is defined as*

$$\Sigma(M, t) = \{\sigma \in T_I^* | M[\sigma\rangle M', M' \geq Pre(\cdot, t)\} \tag{2}$$

The set of e-vectors (explanation vectors), denoting the firing vectors associated with the sequences in $\Sigma(M, t)$, is defined as $Y(M, t) = \{y_\sigma \in \mathbb{N}^{n_I} \mid \sigma \in \Sigma(M, t) : y_\sigma = \tau(\sigma)\}$.

Definition 3 (Minimal Explanations [16]). *Let (N, M_0) be a marked net with $N = (P, T, Pre, Post)$. Given a basis partition $\pi = (T_E, T_I)$, a marking M*

$\in R(N, M_0)$, and an explicit transition $t \in T_E$, the set of minimal explanations of t at M is defined as

$$\Sigma_{min}(M,t) = \{\sigma \in \Sigma(M,t) | \nexists \sigma' \in \Sigma(M,t) : y_{\sigma'} \lneq y_\sigma\} \tag{3}$$

and the corresponding set of minimal e-vectors is defined by $Y_{min}(M,t) = \{y_\sigma \in \mathbb{N}^{n_I} | \sigma \in \Sigma_{min}(M,t) : y_\sigma = \tau(\sigma)\}$.

Definition 4 (Basis Marking [16]). *Given a net $N = (P, T, Pre, Post)$ with initial marking M_0 and a basis partition $\pi = (T_E, T_I)$, the set of its basis markings $\mathcal{M}$ is a subset of $R(N, M_0)$ such that:*

a) $M_0 \in \mathcal{M}$;
b) *If $M \in \mathcal{M}$, then for all $t \in T_E$, for all $y_I \in Y_{min}(M,t)$, it holds $M' \in \mathcal{M}$, where $M' = M + C_I \cdot y_I + C(\cdot, t)$.*

Note that C_I is the incidence matrix of the subnet derived from T_I. A marking $M \in \mathcal{M}$ is called a basis marking with respect to $\pi = (T_E, T_I)$.

3   Verification of Language-Based Opacity

Opacity is a safety property for analyzing secret leakages of DESs. A secret is usually represented by a set of states or a set of event sequences. When the second type of secret is considered, opacity is referred to as language-based opacity (LBO). The definition of LBO of DESs is initially formulated based on automata and then consistently extended to the Petri net framework [14], where a secret is represented as a set of transition sequences. Given a transition sequence $\sigma \in T^*$, $\lambda(\sigma) \in E^*$ is by definition the string generated by σ and $Pr(\lambda(\sigma)) \in E_o^*$ is called the observation of σ. Accordingly, $Pr(\mathcal{L}(\mathcal{G}, M_0)) \subseteq E_o^*$ is called the observation language of $\mathcal{G}$.

3.1   Language-Based Opacity Description

Definition 5 ([14]). *Let $\mathcal{G} = (N, M_0, E, \lambda)$ be an LPN and $S \subseteq L(N, M_0)$ be a secret. A transition sequence $\sigma \in S$ is said to be opaque w.r.t S if there exists $\sigma' \in L(N, M_0) \backslash S$ such that $Pr(\lambda(\sigma)) = Pr(\lambda(\sigma'))$.*

Definition 6 ([14]). *Let $\mathcal{G} = (N, M_0, E, \lambda)$ be an LPN and $S \subseteq L(N, M_0)$ be a secret. The system $\mathcal{G}$ is said to be language-based opaque w.r.t. S if all the transition sequences in S are opaque.*

In other words, $\mathcal{G}$ is language-based opaque if, for all the strings generated by a secret transition sequence in S, there exists at least one string generated by a non-secret sequence in $L(N, M_0) \backslash S$ with the same observation under the natural projection Pr.

Definition 7. *Given an LPN $\mathcal{G} = (N, M_0, E, \lambda)$ and an observation $\omega \in Pr(\mathcal{L}(\mathcal{G}, M_0))$, the set of transition firing sequences consistent with ω is defined as*

$$S(\omega) = \{\sigma \in L(N, M_0) | Pr(\lambda(\sigma)) = \omega\} \tag{4}$$

Definition 8. *Given an LPN $\mathcal{G} = (N, M_0, E, \lambda)$ and a secret $S \subseteq L(N, M_0)$, the set of secret observations is defined as*

$$L_S = \{\omega \in E_o^* | \exists \sigma \in S : Pr(\lambda(\sigma)) = \omega\} \tag{5}$$

Lemma 1. *Let $\mathcal{G} = (N, M_0, E, \lambda)$ be an LPN and $S \subseteq L(N, M_0)$ be a secret. $\mathcal{G}$ is language-based opaque w.r.t. S if for all $\omega \in L_S$, $S(\omega) \nsubseteq S$.*

Proof. Consider the contrapositive case when there exists $\omega \in L_S$ such that $S(\omega) \subseteq S$. Following that, all the transition sequences that are consistent with ω are secret sequences. Accordingly, there does not exist any non-secret transition sequence $\sigma \in L(N, M_0) \backslash S$ consistent with the secret observation $\omega \in L_S$. Given that any sequence generating ω is a secret transition sequence, Definition 6 establishes that $\mathcal{G}$ is non-language opaque which contradicts the assumption and concludes the proof.

3.2 An Integer Linear Programming Solution

A specific basis partition $\pi = (T_E, T_I)$ is proposed to address language-based opacity verification. Consider an LPN $\mathcal{G} = (N, M_0, E, \lambda)$, we assume that the explicit transition set T_E is a combination of two sets T_o and $\hat{T}_u$ in which $T_E = T_o \cup \hat{T}_u$, where the set $\hat{T}_u$ denotes the set of unobservable transitions contained in the secret transition sequences, i.e., $\hat{T}_u = \{t \in T_u \mid \exists \sigma \in S : t \in \sigma\}$. To ensure a precise representation of a system's observable behavior, we additionally assume that the set T_o is included in T_E. In order to handle a specific scenario in which unobservable transitions can render a system opaque, the set $\hat{T}_u$ is also intended to be included in the set T_E. Thus, a non-null e-vector is required for a transition t from the transition sequences representing secret words in order for a system to be opaque (details will be provided later). Indeed, $T_E = T_o \cup \hat{T}_u$ represents the proposed explicit transition set, and $T_I = T \backslash T_E$ represents the implicit transition set. The basis partition formed from secret S in this instance is denoted by (T_E, T_I). In order to designate $|T_E|$ and $|T_I|$, respectively, we use n_E and n_I once more.

Theorem 1. *Given an LPN $\mathcal{G} = (N, M_0, E, \lambda)$ with $E = E_o \dot{\cup} E_u$, a secret $S \subseteq L(N, M_0)$, a secret sequence $\sigma \in S$ with $Pr(\lambda(\sigma)) = \omega = e_1 e_2 \cdots e_n$ and $y = \tau(\sigma)$, such that for all $j \in \{1, 2, \cdots, n\}$, $e_j \in E_o$, and the basis partition $\pi = (T_E, T_I)$ derived from S, the sequence σ is opaque if and only if there exists a non-negative integer $k \geq n$ such that the set of constraints (6) admits a feasible solution:*

$$\begin{cases} y_{E_i} \in \mathbb{N}^{n_E}, \forall i \in \{1, 2, \cdots, k\} \\ y_{I_i} \in \mathbb{N}^{n_I}, \forall i \in \{1, 2, \cdots, k+1\} \\ M_0 - Pre_I \cdot y_{I_1} \geq \vec{0} \qquad (6a) \\ M_0 + C_I \cdot y_{I_1} - Pre_E \cdot y_{E_1} \geq \vec{0} \qquad (6b) \\ \exists t_m \in T_{e_1} \cup \hat{T}_u, y_{E_1}(t_m) + y_{I_1}(t_m) \leq 1 \quad \forall m \in \mathbb{N} \\ M_0 + C_E \cdot y_{E_1} + C_I \cdot y_{I_1} - Pre_I \cdot y_{I_2} \geq \vec{0} \qquad (6c) \\ \exists t_m \in T_{e_1} \cup \hat{T}_u, y_{E_1}(t_m) + y_{I_2}(t_m) \leq 1 \quad \forall m \in \mathbb{N} \\ M_0 + C_E \cdot y_{E_1} + C_I \cdot \sum_{i=1}^{2} y_{I_i} - Pre_E \cdot y_{E_2} \geq \vec{0} \qquad (6d) \\ \exists t_m \in T_{e_2} \cup \hat{T}_u, y_{E_2}(t_m) + y_{I_2}(t_m) \leq 1 \quad \forall m \in \mathbb{N} \\ \cdots \\ M_0 + C_E \cdot \sum_{i=1}^{k-1} y_{E_i} + C_I \cdot \sum_{i=1}^{k} y_{I_i} - Pre_E \cdot y_{E_k} \geq \vec{0} \quad (6e) \\ M_0 + C_E \cdot \sum_{i=1}^{k} y_{E_i} + C_I \cdot \sum_{i=1}^{k} y_{I_i} - Pre_I \cdot y_{I_{k+1}} \geq \vec{0} \quad (6f) \\ M_0 + C_E \cdot \sum_{i=1}^{k} y_{E_i} + C_I \cdot \sum_{i=1}^{k+1} y_{I_i} \geq \vec{0} \qquad (6g) \\ \sum_{i=1}^{k} y_{E_i} = y_E \in \mathbb{N}^{n_E} \\ \sum_{i=1}^{k+1} y_{I_i} = y_I \in \mathbb{N}^{n_I} \\ \sum_{t_m \in T_{e_j} \cup \hat{T}_u} y_{E_i}(t_m) + y_{I_i}(t_m) \leq 1 \qquad (6h) \\ \qquad \forall i \in \{1, 2, \cdots, k+1\}, \forall m \in \mathbb{N} \\ y_E + y_I \neq \tau(\sigma) \qquad (6i) \end{cases}$$

where Pre_I and Pre_E, are the pre-incidence functions of subnets derived from T_I and T_E, respectively. C_I and C_E are the incidence matrices of subnets derived from T_I and T_E, respectively. y_{E_i} and y_{I_i} represent the firing vectors of an explicit transition and an implicit transition, respectively.

Before presenting the proof, let us explain the constraints of this theorem. Let $\omega = e_1 e_2 \cdots e_n$ be the observation of a secret transition $\sigma \in S$. Starting from the initial marking M_0 and by the event $e_1 \in \omega$, at each instant i, Constraints (6a)–(6g) indicate the firing of a transition that generates an event e_i that must be either observable with the same observability of the event $e_j \in \omega$, with $j \in \{1, 2, \cdots, n\}$, or unobservable, i.e., $e_i \in E_u$. The satisfaction of Constraints (6a)–(6g) implies the existence of two vectors $y_E = \sum_{i=1}^{k} y_{E_i}$ and $y_I = \sum_{i=1}^{(k+1)} y_{I_i}$. The y_E represents the firing vector of the transition sequence that generates the observation ω, which is guaranteed by Constraint (6h). This means that Constraint (6h) forced that the firable transitions must either have the same observation as the events in ω or be unobservable. In order to guarantee that y_E does not represent the secret transition sequence σ that generates ω, Constraint (6i) is presented to ensure the firing of a vector y_I that enables the firing of unobservable transitions, which makes $y_E + y_I \neq y$.

Proof. (If) Let us suppose that the set of Constraints (6a)–(6i) is satisfied. Starting from M_0, if there exist firing vectors y_I and y_E that satisfy Constraints (6a)–(6g), then there exists a sequence $\sigma' = t_{u_1} t_{o_1} t_{u_2} t_{o_2} \cdots t_{u_k} t_{o_k} t_{u_{k+1}}$ such that $M_0[\sigma'\rangle$ holds, where $\lambda(t_{ui}) \in E_u$ and $\lambda(t_{oi}) \in E_o$, $i \in \{1, 2, \ldots, k+1\}$. Note that in Constraints (6a)–(6g) the firing vector could be equal to an empty vector which means that any t_{ui} or t_{oi} could not exist. This means that σ' could be in any form while ignoring any t_{ui} or t_{oi} since its firing vector could be the $\vec{0}$.

Based on the proposed basis partition, we have $T_E = T_o \cup \hat{T}_u$, which implies that the elements in the firing vector y_E contain the observable transitions and the unobservable ones in the secret sequences. Thus, $y_E = \sum_{i=1}^{k} y_{E_i}$ and $y_I = \sum_{i=1}^{(k+1)} y_{I_i}$ hold, where $k \geq n$. At a time, each integer vector y_{E_i} enables only the firing of one transition which either has the same observation as the j-th observable event in the secret observation, i.e., $e_j \in \omega$, or has no observation due to the fact that it is included in $\hat{T}_u$ (unobservable transition contained in a secret sequence), which is forced by Constraint (6h).

The vector y_E represents the firing vector of the transition sequence that generates ω, where $\omega = Pr(\lambda(\sigma))$. Moreover, the firing vector y_E could represent the sequence σ, i.e., $y_E = y = \tau(\sigma)$. For this reason, the firing of a vector y_I that enables the firing of unobservable transitions is required in order to guarantee that $y_E + y_I \neq y$, i.e., $y_E + y_I \neq \tau(\sigma)$, $y_E + y_I = \tau(\sigma')$, and $\sigma \neq \sigma'$, which is assured by Constraint (6i). The satisfaction of the set of constraints (6) implies that there exists a sequence σ' that is different from σ but has the same observation ω under the natural projection Pr. Thus, the sequence σ is opaque.

(Only If) Let us now suppose that σ is opaque. Thus, there exists a sequence $\sigma' \in S(\omega)$ such that $\sigma \neq \sigma'$, $M_0[\sigma\rangle$, and $\sigma' = t_{u_1} t_{o_1} t_{u_2} t_{o_2} \cdots t_{u_n} t_{o_n} t_{u_{n+1}}$. This implies that there exists a firing vector $y' = y_E + y_I$ such that $y' = \tau(\sigma')$ and $y' \neq y$, i.e., $y_E + y_I \neq y$. Based on the proposed basis partition, we have $T_E = T_o \cup \hat{T}_u$. The vector y_E could represent the observable transitions and the unobservable ones that are contained in the secret sequences. For this reason, we have

$$y_E = \sum_{i=1}^{k} y_{E_i}, \ y_I = \sum_{i=1}^{k+1} y_{I_i},$$

where $k \geq n$.

By the state equation, the firing vectors y_E and y_I satisfy the following constraint

$$M_0 + C_E \cdot \sum_{i=1}^{k} y_{E_i} + C_I \cdot \sum_{i=1}^{k+1} y_{I_i} \geq \vec{0}.$$

Thus, Constraints (6a)–(6g) hold. Since $\sigma' \in S(\omega)$, for each firing vector y_{E_i} only one transition having the same observation as the j-th observable event, i.e., $e_j \in \omega$, or an unobservable transition from $\hat{T}_u$ can be fired, which requires the satisfaction of Constraint (6h). However, the firing vector y_E can be associated with the sequence σ, i.e., $y_E = \tau(\sigma)$. To deal with that, $y_E + y_I \neq y$ must hold, which can be imposed by Constraint (6i). Thus, the fact that the sequence σ is opaque implies that the set of Constraints (6) admits a feasible solution.

Corollary 1. *Given an LPN* $\mathcal{G} = (N, M_0, E, \lambda)$, *a particular basis partition* $\pi = (T_E, T_I)$, *and a secret* $S \in L(N, M_0)$, $\mathcal{G}$ *is said to be language opaque if and only if for all* $\sigma \in S$, *with* $Pr(\lambda(\sigma)) = \omega$, *the set of Constraints (6) admits a feasible solution.*

Example 1. *Let us consider the LPN* $\mathcal{G}$ *portrayed in Fig. 1, where* $T_o = \{t_1, t_3, t_5, t_6\}$ *and* $T_u = \{t_2, t_4, t_7\}$, *leading to* $E_o = \{a, b\}$ *and* $E_u = \{c\}$. *Let* $S = \{t_1 t_2 t_3\}$ *be a secret and accordingly the set* $L_S = Pr(\lambda(S)) = \{Pr(\lambda(t_1 t_2 t_3))\} = \{ab\}$ *represents the secret observations. Based on the proposed basis partition,* $T_E = \{t_1, t_2, t_3, t_5, t_6\}$ *and* $T_I = \{t_4, t_7\}$ *hold. According to Theorem 1, the sequence* $\sigma = t_1 t_2 t_3$ *is opaque if and only if the set of Constraints (6) admits a feasible solution. Let* $y = [1110000]^T$ *be the associated firing vector of* σ. *Executing the set of Constraints (6), there exists a sequence* $\sigma' = t_{I_1} t_{E_1} t_{I_2} t_{E_2} t_{I_3} t_{E_3} t_{I_4} = \varepsilon t_1 \varepsilon t_2 \varepsilon t_3 t_7$ *that is enabled at* M_0 *and has the same observation as* σ, *i.e.,* $Pr(\lambda(\sigma')) = Pr(\lambda(\sigma)) = ab$. *Thus, we have found seven firing vectors* $y_{I_1} = [00]_I^T$, $y_{E_1} = [10000]_E^T$, $y_{I_2} = [00]_I^T$, $y_{E_2} = [01000]_E^T$, $y_{I_3} = [00]_I^T$, $y_{E_3} = [00100]_E^T$, *and* $y_{I_4} = [01]_I^T$ *which satisfy Constraints (6a)–(6h). We also have* $y_E + y_I = [1110001]^T \neq y$, *which is assured by Constraint (6i). According to Corollary 1,* $\mathcal{G}$ *is language opaque.*

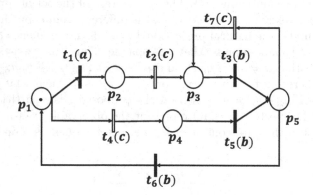

Fig. 1. A labeled Petri net example.

4   Orwellian Observation

In the DES community, opacity analysis, verification, and enforcement are usually addressed under the notion of natural projection due to the nature of partial observation of such systems. However, in real applications and for transparency reasons, it is desirable to release information as much as possible to maintain accountability. In this context, the notion of "information release to maintain opacity" is explored in order to compromise between security and transparency [17,19].

In order to keep a system's opacity, it is preferable to declassify (release) only partial history information to users. For this reason, the notion of Orwellian projection is defined [2,9]. Herein, we assume that some particular events are revealed only when a particular event in a system occurs. To this end, we identify two subsets, denoted by E_{or} and E_{ur}, from E_o and E_u, respectively. As before, E_o represents the set of standard observable events whose occurrences can be immediately observed and E_u represents a set of standard unobservable events whose occurrence can never be observed, where $E = E_o \cup E_u$ and $E_o \cap E_u = \emptyset$.

In this work, we assume that the set $E_{ur} \subseteq E_u$ groups the quasi-unobservable events whose occurrences may not be immediately observed but may be observed in the future when a particular observable event $e \in E_{or}$ occurs. Note that $E_{or} \subseteq E_o$ represents the set of particular observable events, called observability-triggering events, whose occurrences reveal the observability of the events in E_{ur} that have already occurred in the trajectories generated by a system. Thus, a transition with a label $e \in E_{ur}$ become observable only when an upcoming transition in E_{or} occurs, while the other transitions in E_{ur} with the same label e remain unobservable. For example, suppose that only a trajectory $s = \alpha\beta\gamma$ is generated by a system (from the initial marking) with $E_o = E_{or} = \{\gamma\}$, $E_u = \{\alpha, \beta\}$, and $E_{ur} = \{\beta\}$. Then, after the occurrence of γ, only the transition with the label β in this particular string s becomes observable, while the other transitions with label β (those not appearing in s) keep unobservable (a formal description will be given later).

Write $T_{ur} = \{t \in T \mid \lambda(t) \in E_{ur}\}$ and $T_{or} = \{t \in T \mid \lambda(t) \in E_{or}\}$. It is obvious that $T_{ur} \subseteq T_u$ and $T_{or} \subseteq T_o$. In the framework of static observation, the set of events is divided into observable and unobservable events, in which the observability of an event is fixed, i.e., either it is always observable or not observable. The event release mechanism used here is event-based. A system is allowed to re-interpret the observation of previously triggered events. Therefore, it is assumed that a system can hold on to the occurrence of events from E_{ur} and release their observation when an observability-triggering event occurs.

Let $\sigma \in L(N, M_0)$ be a transition sequence and $\lambda(\sigma) = \omega$ be its corresponding generated word. We define by $\omega[1, \mathbf{i}]$ the longest prefix of ω ending with an event $e \in E_{or}$. In this sense, notation $\mathbf{i}$ with $1 \leq \mathbf{i} \leq |\omega|$ represents the latest instant when an event in E_{or} is triggered. Then, we naturally use $\omega[\mathbf{i}+1, |\omega|]$ to represent the suffix of ω such that $\omega = \omega[1, \mathbf{i}]\omega[\mathbf{i} + 1, |\omega|]$. Formally, given an LPN $\mathcal{G}$ with $E = E_o \cup E_u \cup E_{or} \cup E_{ur}$, the Orwellian projection $Pr_o : E^* \rightarrow (E \backslash \{E_u \backslash E_{ur}\})^*$ of a given observation ω, denoted by $Pr_o(\omega)$, is defined as

$$Pr_o(\omega) = Pr_{E_o \cup E_{or} \cup E_{ur}}(\omega[1, \mathbf{i}])Pr(\omega[\mathbf{i} + 1, |\omega|]).$$

For the sake of succinctness, write $Pr_{E_o \cup E_{or} \cup E_{ur}}$ as $Pr_\triangle$. To formally define $Pr_\triangle$, suppose that $\omega = sts'$ and $\omega[1, \mathbf{i}] = st$, i.e., st is the longest prefix of ω

ending with an event $t \in E_{or}$. In this case we know that $s' = \omega[i+1, |\omega|]$ is the suffix of ω such that for all $e \in E_{or}$, $e \notin s'$ holds, where $s, s' \in E^*$ and $t \in E_{or}$. Thus, we define

$$Pr_\triangle(st) = \begin{cases} Pr_\triangle(s) & \text{if } t \in (E_u \backslash E_{ur}); \\ \varepsilon & \text{if } st = \varepsilon; \\ Pr_\triangle(s)t & \text{otherwise.} \end{cases}$$

Note that $Pr(s') = Pr(\omega[i+1, |\omega|])$ is the observation of the prefix s' under the standard natural projection Pr. In the setting of natural projection Pr, the users can observe the occurrence of observable events immediately, which are events in E_o (including of course E_{or}). Recall that "i" represents the latest instant to release the occurrence of already triggered events in E_{ur}. Thus, $Pr_\triangle(\omega[1, i])$ release (declassify) all the transitions in $\omega[1, i]$ except those in the set $(E_u \backslash (||st|| \cap E_{ur}))$. It is obvious that all the transitions with labels being in E_{ur} that occur before the instant "i" become observable. Meanwhile, the transitions with their labels being in E_{ur} that occur after the instant "i" remain unobservable, which is figured by $Pr(\omega[i+1, |\omega|])$.

Given an LPN $\mathcal{G}$, with $E = E_o \cup E_u \cup E_{or} \cup E_{ur}$, and a string $\omega \in \mathcal{L}(\mathcal{G}, M_0)$, a pre-language with respect to a string $\omega \in \mathcal{L}(\mathcal{G}, M_0)$ is defined as

$$L(\mathcal{G}, \omega) = \{\sigma \in T^* | \exists s_1 \in E_{or}, \exists \omega' \in E^* \cup \{\varepsilon\} :$$

$$\lambda(\sigma) = \omega[1, i], \omega[1, i]s_1 = \omega, \omega\omega' \in \mathcal{L}(\mathcal{G}, M_0)\}.$$

In summary, provided that an observation ω is observed, the current observable set will be $E_o \cup [\cup_{\sigma \in L(\mathcal{G}, \omega)}(||\lambda(\sigma)|| \cap E_{ur})]$. The following example illustrates the proposed Orwellian projection mechanism.

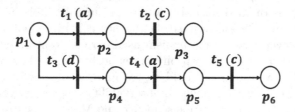

Fig. 2. An example of LPN.

Example 2. *Let us consider the LPN in Fig. 2, where $T_o = \{t_1, t_2, t_4, t_5\}$, $T_u = T_{ur} = \{t_3\}$, and $T_{or} \subseteq T_o = \{t_1, t_4\}$. We then have $E_o = \{a, c\}$, $E_{ur} = \{d\}$, and $E_{or} = \{a\}$. Let $S = \{t_1 t_2\}$ be a secret and $L_S = \{ac\}$ be its corresponding secret language. Under the standard natural projection, the system is language opaque since there exists another sequence $t_3 t_4 t_5$, in which $Pr(\lambda(t_3 t_4 t_5)) = Pr(\lambda(t_1 t_2)) = ac$. However, under the Orwellian projection,*

$Pr_o(\lambda(t_3t_4t_5)) = dac$ holds, where $d \in E_{ur}$, $a \in E_{or}$, and da is the longest prefix of dac that ends with an observability-triggering event, i.e., an event from the set E_{or} in which $\mathbf{i} = 2$. The observability of event d is released after the following event a is triggered. The Orwellian observation of the sequence $t_3t_4t_5$ is different from the Orwellian projection of the secret sequence, i.e., $Pr_o(\lambda(t_3t_4t_5)) = dac \neq Pr_o(\lambda(t_1t_2)) = ac$. Hence, the system is non-opaque under the Orwellian projection.

Remark 1. Note that the unobservable events in E_{ur} become observable after the occurrence of an event from E_{or} while the upcoming firable events from E_{ur} remain unobservable until the next occurrence of an observability-triggering event. For example, considering Example 2 again, where this time we suppose that $T_o = \{t_1, t_4\}$, $T_u = T_{ur} = \{t_2, t_3, t_5\}$, and $T_{or} \subseteq T_o = \{t_4\}$. Then, $E_{ur} = \{d, c\}$ holds. Suppose that the transition sequence $t_3t_4t_5$ occurs. We have $\lambda(t_3t_4t_5) = dac$ and $Pr_o(dac) = da$. The event d is released while the event c is still unobservable since there does not exist any observability-triggering event in E_{or} that has been occurred after the event c. $\triangle$

The Orwellian projection in this paper is closely related to the ones proposed in [9] and [11]. The main distinctions could be summarized as follows:

- As the same as the dynamic information release mechanism proposed in [11], the Orwellian projection in this paper is the partial information release, while the one in [9] is the full information release.
- The information release mechanism in [11] is state-based in which the occurrence of some unobservable events is released when the system reaches a particular state; however, herein, the information release is event-based.
- In [9], once a downgrading event (particular event) is triggered, the unobservable events that have been fired in the past become observable. Thus, an intruder infers immediately the exact reached state of the system, which is not the case in our research since only some events become observable once an observability-triggering event in E_{or} occurs.

5   Opacity Verification Under Orwellian Observation

In this section, the verification of language-based opacity in discrete event systems under an Orwellian mapping is presented. The Orwellian observation represents a conditional anonymity, in which some events may be initially anonymous but later in the future their occurrences can be revealed when certain conditions are satisfied. The Orwellian projection captures the trade-off between security and transparency by maintaining opacity during the release of information. Presently, sites, businesses, hospitals, and governments aim to be transparent while ensuring the requirement of critical information concealment or privacy. Thus, the notion of Orwellian projection becomes more applicable in practice than the standard natural projection [17]. Extending language-based opacity from natural projection to Orwellian projection in discrete event systems can be effected by simply replacing Pr by Pr_o. Thus, the following definition is introduced.

Definition 9 (Orwellian Opacity). *Given an LPN $\mathcal{G} = (N, M_0, E, \lambda)$, a basis partition $\pi = (T_E, T_I)$, a secret $S \subseteq L(N \cdot M_0)$, and an Orwellian projection Pr_o, $\mathcal{G}$ is said to be Orwellian opaque w.r.t. S if $Pr_o(\lambda(S)) \subseteq Pr_o(\lambda(L(N, M_0) \backslash S))$.*

Proposition 1 ([18]). *Deciding the opacity of regular languages under Orwellian projection is PSPACE-complete.*

A static or dynamic projection represents a particular case of Orwellian projection. It has been shown that the problems using such projections are already PSPACE-complete. Thus, deciding opacity under Orwellian projection is PSPACE-complete.

Proposition 2. *Given an LPN $\mathcal{G} = (N, M_0, E, \lambda)$, a basis partition $\pi = (T_E, T_I)$, a secret $S \subseteq L(N, M_0)$, and an Orwellian projection Pr_o, $\mathcal{G}$ is said to be Orwellian opaque w.r.t. S if it is opaque under the natural projection Pr and for all $\sigma \in S$, there does not exist any $t \in \sigma$ such that $t \in T_{ur}$.*

Proof. Assume that $\mathcal{G}$ is opaque under the natural projection Pr. For all $\sigma \in S$, there exists $\sigma' \in L(N, M_0 \backslash S$ such that $Pr(\lambda(\sigma)) = Pr(\lambda(\sigma'))$. Assume now that there does not exist $t \in \sigma$ such that $t \in T_{ur}$. As a result, there will be no unobservable transitions that will be noticed in the future, which may reveal the opacity of σ. This indicates that if σ is opaque under Pr, it will be opaque under Pr_o as well.

Proposition 3. *Given an LPN $\mathcal{G} = (N, M_0, E, \lambda)$, a basis partition $\pi = (T_E, T_I)$, a secret $S \subseteq L(N, M_0)$, and an Orwellian projection Pr_o, $\mathcal{G}$ is said to be Orwellian opaque w.r.t. S if it is opaque under the natural projection Pr and for all $\sigma \in S$, there does not exist any $t \in T_{or}$ that belongs to the secret σ's trajectory.*

Proof. Assume that $\mathcal{G}$ is opaque under the natural projection Pr. For all $\sigma \in S$, there exists $\sigma' \in L(N, M_0 \backslash S$ such that $Pr(\lambda(\sigma)) = Pr(\lambda(\sigma'))$. Assume now that there does not exist $t \in T_{or}$ that belongs to the secret σ's trajectory. As a result, there will be no unobservable transitions that will be noticed in the future since there does not exist any $t \in T_{or}$ that may reveal the observation of the quasi-unobservable transitions. This indicates that if σ is opaque under Pr, it will be opaque under Pr_o as well.

6   Conclusion

In this paper, we address the problem of language-based opacity verification in discrete event systems under a newly proposed Orwellian projection function. First, language-based opacity verification is presented by solving an integer linear programming problem to deal with unbounded Petri nets. Then, we propose a new observation model based on an Orwellian-type projection. Finally, a framework for language opacity verification under Orwellian projection is established.

References

1. Mazaré, L.: Using unification for opacity properties. In: Proceedings of the 4th IFIP WG1.7 Workshop Issues Theory Security (WITS 2004), Spain, vol. 7, pp. 165–176. (2004)
2. Bryans, J.W., Koutny, M., Mazaré, L., Ryan, P.Y.: Opacity generalised to transition systems. Int. J. Inform. Secur. **7**(6), 421–435 (2008)
3. Bryans, J.W., Koutny, M., Ryan, P.Y.: Modelling opacity using Petri nets. Electron. Notes Theor. Comput. Sci. **121**, 101–115 (2005)
4. Saboori, A., Hadjicostis, C.N.: Notions of security and opacity in discrete event systems. In: Proceedings of the 46th IEEE Conference Decision Control, pp. 5056–5061 (2007)
5. Saboori, A., Hadjicostis, C.N.: Verification of initial-state opacity in security applications of discrete event systems. Inf. Sci. **246**, 115–132 (2013)
6. Guo, Y., Jiang, X., Guo, C., Wang, S., Karoui, O.: Overview of opacity in discrete event systems. IEEE Access **8**, 48731–48741 (2020)
7. Cassez, F., Dubreil, J., Marchand, H.: Synthesis of opaque systems with static and dynamic masks. Formal Meth. Syst. Des. **40**, 88–115 (2012)
8. Yin, X., Li, S.: Synthesis of dynamic masks for infinite-step opacity. IEEE Trans. Autom. Control **65**(4), 1429–1441 (2020)
9. Mullins, J., Yeddes, M.: Opacity with Orwellian observers and intransitive non-interference. In: Proceedings of the 12th International Workshop on Discrete Event Systems (WODES), France, pp. 344–349 (2014)
10. Yeddes, M.: Enforcing opacity with Orwellian observation. In: Proceedings of the 13th International Workshop on Discrete Event Systems (WODES), Xi'an, China, pp. 306–312 (2016)
11. Hou, J., Yin, X., Li, S.: A framework for current-state opacity under dynamic information release mechanism. Automatica **140**, 110238 (2022)
12. Lin, F.: Opacity of discrete event systems and its applications. Automatica **47**(3), 496–503 (2011)
13. Zhang, B., Shu, S., Lin, F.: Polynomial algorithms to check opacity in discrete event systems. In: Proceedings of the 24th Control and Decision Conference (CCDC), pp. 763–769 (2012)
14. Tong, Y., Ma, Z., Li, Z., Seactzu, C., Giua, A.: Verification of language-based opacity in Petri nets using verifier. In: Proceedings of the 2011 American Control Conference, pp. 757–763 (2016)
15. Basile, F., De Tommasi, G.: An algebraic characterization of language-based opacity in labeled Petri nets. In: Proceedings of the 14th International Workshop on Discrete Event Systems, vol. 51, no. 7, pp. 329–336 (2018)
16. Ma, Z., Tong, Y., Li, Z., Giua, A.: Basis marking representation of Petri net reachability spaces and its application to the reachability problem. IEEE Trans. Autom. Control **62**(3), 1078–1093 (2017)
17. Behinaein, B., Lin, F., Rudie, K.: Optimal information release for mixed opacity in discrete-event systems. IEEE Trans. Autom. Sci. Eng. **16**(4), 1960–1970 (2019)
18. Bérard, B., Mullins, J.: Verification of information flow properties under rational observation. arXiv preprint arXiv:1409.0871 (2014)
19. Zhang, B., Shu, S., Lin, F.: Maximum information release while ensuring opacity in discrete event systems. IEEE Trans. Autom. Sci. Eng. **12**(3), 1067–1079 (2015)
20. Basile, F., De tommasi, G., Motta, C.: Assessment of initial-state-opacity in live and bounded labeled Petri net systems via optimization techniques. Automatica **152**, 110911 (2023)

An Enhanced Interface-Based Probabilistic Compositional Verification Approach

Samir Ouchani[1(✉)], Otmane Ait Mohamed[2], and Mourad Debbabi[3]

[1] CESI LINEACT, Aix-en-Provence, France
souchani@cesi.fr
[2] Hardware Verification Group, Concordia University, Montreal, Canada
otmane.aitmohamed@concordia.ca
[3] CSL Laboratory, Concordia University, Montreal, Canada
mourad.debbabi@concordia.ca

Abstract. In this paper, we aim to advance the state of the art in the verification process of systems, predominantly modeled as Probabilistic Automata (PA). This model accommodates both nondeterministic and probabilistic behaviors. Our primary strategy to address the notorious state space explosion problem inherent in model checking is the adoption of abstraction and compositional verification techniques, culminating in the development of a distributed verification approach centered on the communication interface amongst composed automata. Initially, the abstraction technique refines the system in relation to the requirement under verification and amalgamates states demonstrating comparable behaviors. Not only does it simplify the system, but it also enables a decomposition of global requirements into local ones. This decomposition process facilitates parallel verification and securely allows inference on the global requirement from local results. Moreover, the soundness of our proposed framework has been substantiated, ensuring that it correctly interprets and applies the properties of the system under scrutiny. In the final phase, we leveraged the PRISM model checker to assess the effectiveness of our proposed framework. This evaluation was carried out on three benchmark tests, providing empirical evidence to support the benefits of our approach. Our contribution to the field lies in the novel combination of abstraction and compositional verification techniques in a distributed verification framework, validated through theoretical soundness proofs and practical tests using the PRISM model checker. This result paves the way for more efficient and scalable model-checking processes for Probabilistic Automata.

Keywords: Abstraction · Compositional Verification · Probabilistic Automata · PRISM · PCTL

1 Introduction

Model checking [1,2] is a well-established formal automatic verification technique designed for finite-state concurrent systems. It examines temporal logic specifications and automata-based formalism on system models. Alongside qualitative

B. Ben Hedia et al. (Eds.): VECoS 2023, LNCS 14368, pp. 60–75, 2024.
https://doi.org/10.1007/978-3-031-49737-7_5

model checking, quantitative verification methods based on probabilistic model checkers [3,4] have recently gained traction. Probabilistic verification enables probabilistic interpretation of a given property's satisfiability in systems that intrinsically exhibit probabilistic behavior. Despite its broad adoption, model checking typically requires substantial memory and processing time, which can be attributed to the potentially exponential growth of the system's state space due to the number of variables and concurrent behaviors. Therefore, reducing the complexity of the verification process is paramount for verifying large-scale systems.

Various techniques have been investigated [1–3,5] to address the aforementioned issue in qualitative model checking, which were subsequently extended to the probabilistic case. These solutions broadly aim to enhance the model-checking algorithms by introducing symbolic data structures such as binary decision diagrams, or focusing on model analysis. Predominantly, two classes of solutions are identified in the literature: abstraction and compositional verification. Abstraction provides a compact representation of the global system under verification, while compositional verification bypasses the construction of the whole system parts. Our work delves into both classes.

Abstraction techniques fall into four categories [2]: 1) state merging abstraction, 2) variable abstraction, 3) restriction-based abstraction, and 4) observer automata abstraction. Our proposed framework exploits the first and third categories. Additionally, well-recognized compositional verification techniques [6] include partitioned transition relation, lazy parallel composition, interface processes, and assume-guarantee. We employ the interface processes technique to counteract the state explosion problem in our work.

Contributions. Figure 1 presents an overview of our proposed framework, which accepts a system modeled as a composition of Probabilistic Automata (PA) and a requirement expressed in Probabilistic Computation Tree Logic (PCTL) [4] as input. Initially, the abstraction by restriction disregards the irrelevant propositions concerning a specific requirement. Subsequently, our developed state merging rules aggregate states that depict similar behaviors. To showcase the efficiency of our approach, we employ compositional verification using interface processes to verify local PCTL properties on the resultant PAs separately. Finally, we use the probabilistic model checker PRISM [7] as a probabilistic verification engine.

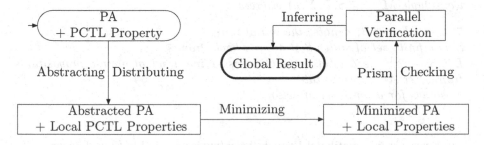

Fig. 1. The Interface-based Probabilistic Compositional Verification.

Related Work. There is a vast literature dealing with the abstraction and compositional verification of probabilistic systems. For instance, [8] introduced a game-based abstraction approach for systems exhibiting both discrete and continuous events, as well as Markov Decision Processes, as described in [9]. Symmetry reduction has been proposed in [10,11]. The partial order reduction is applied for the probabilistic branching time in [12]. In terms of probabilistic compositional verification, [13–15] proposed an assume-guarantee method for verifying the probabilistic safety properties of discrete-time Markov chains. Compositional verification powered by abstraction can be also applied to industrial modeling formalism, like SysML [16]. Also, models were shaped to fit the abstraction and composition, and refined to accelerate the verification process [17]. To our knowledge, several probabilistic model checkers, such as PRISM, which supports symmetry reduction, and LiQuor[1], which includes the partial-order reduction, also support abstraction.

Paper Organization. The remainder of this paper is structured as follows. The subsequent section presents the models for our systems and the specifications for their requirements. The compositional reduction approach we propose is detailed in Sect. 3. Experimental results are presented in Sect. 4, and finally, Sect. 5 concludes the paper.

2   Probabilistic Systems

This section delves into the fundamental characteristics and applications of probabilistic systems, and further examines the methodologies employed in probabilistic modeling. Subsequently, specific focus is dedicated to the precise specification of probabilistic system requirements.

2.1   Probabilistic Modeling

In systems featuring both non-determinism and probabilistic choices, Probabilistic Automata (PAs) present an apt formal model for design and representation. For a clearer understanding, let's look at the formal definition of a PA in Definition 1.

Definition 1 (Probabilistic Automata). *A Probabilistic Automaton (PA) is a quintuple $M = (\overline{s}, S, L, \Sigma, \delta)$ wherein:*

- *$\overline{s}$, a member of S, denotes the initial state,*
- *S is a finite set of states that are reachable from $\overline{s}$,*
- *$L : S \rightarrow 2^{AP}$ is a labeling function assigning a set of atomic propositions from a set AP to each state,*
- *Σ stands for a finite set of actions,*

---

[1] http://www.il.informatik.uni-bonn.de/baier/projectpages/LIQUOR/LiQuor.

– $\delta : S \times \Sigma \to Dist(S)$ *is a probabilistic transition function that, for each state* $s \in S$ *and action* $\alpha \in \Sigma$, *assigns a probability distribution* $\mu \in Dist(S)$. *Here,* $Dist(S)$ *symbolizes the set of convex distributions over* S.

Typically, a system is composed of multiple interacting components. This concept in PAs is manifested through the principle of parallel composition, described in Definition 2.

Definition 2 (Parallel Composition of PAs). *The parallel composition of two PAs:* $M_1 = (\overline{s}_1, S_1, L_1, \Sigma_1, \delta_1)$ *and* $M_2 = (\overline{s}_2, S_2, L_2, \Sigma_2, \delta_2)$, *is represented as a PA* $M = ((\overline{s}_1, \overline{s}_2), S_1 \times S_2, L, \Sigma_1 \cup \Sigma_2, \delta)$ *where:*

- $L(s_1, s_2) = L_1(s_1) \cup L_2(s_2)$,
- *For each pair of probability distributions* $\mu_1 \in \delta_1(s_1, \alpha)$ *and* $\mu_2 \in \delta_2(s_2, \alpha)$, *we define:*

$$\delta((s_1, s_2), \alpha) = \begin{cases} \mu_1 \times \mu_2 & \text{if } \alpha \in \Sigma_1 \cap \Sigma_2, \\ \mu_1 & \text{if } \alpha \in \Sigma_1 \setminus \Sigma_2, \\ \mu_2 & \text{if } \alpha \in \Sigma_2 \setminus \Sigma_1. \end{cases}$$

2.2 Requirements Specification

To verify a Probabilistic Automaton (PA), we apply the Probabilistic Computation Tree Logic (PCTL) to define associated specifications. In the BNF grammar provided below, "ap" represents an atomic proposition, k is an element of the natural numbers set $\mathbb{N}$, p is within the interval $[0, 1]$, and $\bowtie$ signifies the set of relational operators $<, \leq, >, \geq$. The symbols "$\wedge$" and "$\neg$" are logical operators denoting conjunction (AND) and negation (NOT), respectively. Temporal logic operators include "X" (next), "$U^{\leq k}$" (bounded until), and "U" (until). Formally, the PCTL syntax is defined as:

$$\phi ::= \top \mid ap \mid \phi \wedge \phi \mid \neg\phi \mid P_{\bowtie p}[\psi], \tag{1}$$

where

$$\psi ::= X\phi \mid \phi U^{\leq k}\phi \mid \phi U\phi. \tag{2}$$

We can also derive additional operators:

- True logic: $\top \equiv \neg\bot$.
- Disjunction: $\phi_1 \vee \phi_2 \equiv \neg(\neg\phi_1 \wedge \neg\phi_2)$.
- Implication: $\phi_1 \to \phi_2 \equiv \neg\phi_1 \vee \phi_2$.
- Future operator: $F\phi \equiv \top U \phi$ or $F^{\leq k}\phi \equiv \top U^{\leq k} \phi$.
- Globally operator: $G\phi \equiv \neg(F\neg\phi)$ or $G^{\leq k}\phi \equiv \neg(F^{\leq k}\neg\phi)$.
- Probability of always ϕ: $P_{\geq p}[G\phi] = P_{\leq 1-p}[F\neg\phi]$.

To describe a satisfaction relation of a PCTL formula in a given state "s", we introduce the concept of a class of adversaries (Adv) [4]. An adversary is employed to resolve the non-deterministic choices in a PA, meaning a PCTL formula should be satisfied under all possible adversaries. Thus, the satisfaction relation ($\models_{Adv}$) of a PCTL formula is defined as follows, where "s" is a state and "π" is a sequence of states, or path:

- $s \models_{Adv} \top$ is always satisfied.
- $s \models_{Adv} a \Leftrightarrow a \in L(s)$, where $L(s)$ is the labeling function of state s.
- $s \models_{Adv} \phi_1 \wedge \phi_2 \Leftrightarrow s \models_{Adv} \phi_1$ and $s \models_{Adv} \phi_2$, and $s \models_{Adv} \neg\phi \Leftrightarrow s \not\models_{Adv} \phi$.
- $\pi \models_{Adv} X\phi \Leftrightarrow \pi(1) \models_{Adv} \phi$, where $\pi(1)$ is the second state in path π.
- $\pi \models_{Adv} \phi_1 U^{\leq k}\phi_2 \Leftrightarrow \exists i \geq k, \forall j < i : \pi(i) \models_{Adv} \phi_2$ and $\pi(j) \models_{Adv} \phi_1$.
- $\pi \models_{Adv} \phi_1 U\phi_2 \Leftrightarrow \exists k \geq 0 : \pi \models_{Adv} \phi_1 U^{\leq k}\phi_2$.
- $s \models_{Adv} P_{\bowtie p}[\psi] \Leftrightarrow P_{s_{Adv}}(\{\pi | \pi_{Adv} \models \psi\}) \bowtie p$, where $P_{s_{Adv}}$ represents the probability measure over all paths π starting from state s under adversary Adv.

3 Interface-Based Verification Approach

This section provides a comprehensive overview of our methodology for verifying a PCTL property in a probabilistic system. The explanation is structured into two key subsections. The first subsection, i.e., Sect. 3.3, introduces a minimization algorithm that aims at reducing a Probabilistic Automaton (PA) while considering a PCTL property.

Suppose S is a probabilistic system composed of n Probabilistic Automata (PAs), represented as $M_{j:1\leq j\leq n}$. The system S can be denoted by the expression $M_1 \|_{i_1} \cdots \|_{i_{n-1}} M_n$, where "$\|_i$" signifies a composition operation involving synchronization between PAs through a particular interface i. Crucial properties associated with the composition operator "$\|_i$" are commutativity and associativity, as described in Property 1.

Property 1 (Commutativity and Associativity). The operator $\|_i$ exhibits both commutativity and associativity:

1. $M_1 \|_i M_2 \equiv M_2 \|_i M_1$.
2. $M_1 \|_{i_1} (M_2 \|_{i_2} M_3) \equiv (M_1 \|_{i_1} M_2) \|_{i_2} M_3$.

Proof. The proof is reported in the appendix.   □

3.1 Minimization Phase

In an attempt to manage the complexity of model composition, we propose a strategy to reduce the behavior of a model utilizing a minimization operator. This operator is defined in Definition 3 and represented by "$\downarrow$". We define $M' = M \downarrow_{ap}$ as the operation of minimizing the behavior of M to obtain M' with respect to the atomic proposition ap. We also use $\mathcal{L}(ap)$ to denote the set of PCTL formulas that include $ap \in AP$.

Definition 3 (Model Minimization). *The process of minimizing a model M to $M \downarrow_{ap}$ should abide by the following rules:*

1. *Rule 1:* $\forall ap \notin AP_{s_i} : M(s_{i-1} \rightarrow s_i \rightarrow s_{i+1}) \downarrow_{ap} = M(s_{i-1} \rightarrow s_{i+1})$.
2. *Rule 2:* $\forall ap \notin AP_{s_i} : M(s_{i-1} \rightarrow_{p_1} s_i \rightarrow_{p_2} s_{i+1}) \downarrow_{ap} = M(s_{i-1} \rightarrow_{p_1 \times p_2} s_{i+1})$.

3. *Rule 3:* $\forall ap \notin AP_{s_i} \cap AP_{s_i'}$: $M(s_{i-1} \rightarrow_p s_i \rightarrow_{p_1} s_{i+1}; s_i \rightarrow_{1-p_1} s_{i+1}';$
$s_{i-1} \rightarrow_{1-p} s_i' \rightarrow_{p_2} s_{i+1}; s_i' \rightarrow_{1-p_2} s_{i+1}') \downarrow_{ap} = M(s_{i-1} \rightarrow_{p_1 \times p \times \frac{1}{p+p'} + p_2 \times \frac{p'}{p+p'}}$
$s_{i+1}; s_{i-1} \rightarrow_{1-p_1 \times \frac{p}{p+p'} + p_2 \times \frac{p'}{p+p'}} s_{i+1}').$

In this paper, we describe a relation between two Probabilistic Automata (PAs), denoted as M and M' and symbolized as $M\mathcal{R}M'$. This relationship is characterized by the concept of weak simulation, which incorporates the idea of observable actions interspersed between invisible actions. We denote the latter using the symbol "$\downarrow$". Formally, the probabilistic weak simulation relation introduces the concept of observable action "a", which is preceded and followed by sequences of invisible steps. This weak transition is notated as $s \overset{a}{\Longrightarrow} P$, where P is the distribution over states reached from state s through a series of combined steps.

Definition 4 (Probabilistic Weak Simulation). *A probabilistic weak simulation between two Probabilistic Automata (PAs) M_1 and M_2 is a relation $\mathcal{R} \subseteq S_1 \times S_2$ if, and only if:*

1. *Each initial state of M_1 is related to at least one initial state of M_2, and*
2. *For each pair of states (s_1, s_2) such that $s_1 \mathcal{R} s_2$, and for each transition $s_1 \overset{a}{\rightarrow} \mu_1$ in M_1, there exists a weak combined transition $s_2 \overset{a}{\Longrightarrow} \mu_2$ in M_2 such that $\mu_1 \sqsubseteq_\mathcal{R} \mu_2$.*

In the above definition, $\sqsubseteq_\mathcal{R}$ is the lifting of relation $\mathcal{R}$ to probability distributions, achieved by employing a weight function as introduced by Segala [18]. This weight function, denoted by $\triangle$, associates each state in M_1 with a set of states in M_2, each assigned a particular probability. The formal definition of the weight function is provided below.

Definition 5 (Weight Function). *A function $\triangle : S \times S' \rightarrow [0,1]$ is a weight function for the two distributions $\mu_1, \mu_2 \in Dist(S)$ with respect to $\mathcal{R} \subseteq S \times S'$, if and only if:*

1. *If $\triangle(s_1, s_2) > 0$ then $(s_1, s_2) \in \mathcal{R}$,*
2. *For all $s_1 \in S$: $\sum_{s_2 \in S} \triangle(s_1, s_2) = \mu_1(s_1)$, and*
3. *For all $s_2 \in S'$: $\sum_{s_1 \in S} \triangle(s_1, s_2) = \mu_2(s_2)$.*

Below, Proposition 1 establishes that the relation between two Probabilistic Automata, M and M', is a probabilistic weak simulation.

Proposition 1 (Minimization Relation). *Given two Probabilistic Automata, M and M', we denote the probabilistic weak simulation of M by M' as $M \precsim_w M'$, where M' is the result of a reduction process applied to M which abstracts away invisible actions, symbolized by $M' = M \downarrow_{ap}$.*

Proof. The proof is provided in the appendix section. $\square$

Property 2 (Minimization Preservation). Given a property ϕ expressed in the PCTL language $\mathcal{L}(ap)$, and a set of atomic propositions ap that are relevant in the context of M, if the minimized version of M, denoted by $M \downarrow_{ap}$, satisfies ϕ, then the original PA M must also satisfy ϕ. Mathematically, this is expressed as $\forall \phi \in \mathcal{L}(ap), ap \in AP_M : M \downarrow_{ap} \models \phi \Rightarrow M \models \phi$.

Proof. The proof is given in the appendix.   □

Proposition 2 ($\precsim_w$ Composition). *The probabilistic weak simulation relation preserves the composition of PAs: if M_1 is weakly simulated by M'_1, then the composition of M_1 with another PA M_2 is weakly simulated by the composition of M'_1 with the same M_2. Mathematically, this is expressed as $M_1 \precsim_w M'_1 \Rightarrow M_1 \|_i M_2 \precsim_w M'_1 \|_i M_2$.*

Proof. The proof is in the appendix.   □

Definition 6 (Minimization Rule). *Given a composed PA $M_1 \|_i M_2$, the minimization rule prescribes the following transformations:*

- *Construct M'_2 as the minimized version of M_2 with respect to the shared interface i, formally $M'_2 \equiv M_2 \downarrow_{ap(i)}$. Here, M'_2 represents the behavior of M_2 that is observable by M_1.*
- *For any property ϕ expressed in the language $\mathcal{L}(ap(i) \cup AP_{M_1})$, if $M_1 \|_i M'_2$ satisfies ϕ, then $M_1 \|_i M_2$ also satisfies ϕ. Mathematically, $\forall \phi \in \mathcal{L}(ap(i) \cup AP_{M_1}) : M_1 \|_i M'_2 \models \phi \Rightarrow M_1 \|_i M_2 \models \phi$.*

Theorem 1 (Soundness). *The minimization rule, as specified in Definition 6, is sound.*

Proof. The proof of the soundness is given in the appendix.   □

3.2 The Composition Phase

In this section, we detail the process of decomposing a global property into local ones. Definition 7 introduces the decomposition operator "♮", which enables compositional verification by substituting the propositions of a PA with propositions related to its interfaces. This operator utilizes the substitution notation $Q[z/y]$ from the π-calculus, which denotes that in the structure Q, the term z replaces the term y.

Definition 7 (PCTL Property Decomposition). *Let ϕ be a PCTL property to be verified on $M_1 \|_i M_2$. The decomposition of ϕ into ϕ_1 and ϕ_2 is denoted by $\phi = \phi_1 ♮_i \phi_2$, where:*

1. *$AP(\phi) = (AP(\phi_1) \cup AP(\phi_2)) \backslash \{ap(i)\}$, with $ap(i)$ representing the atomic propositions related to interface i,*
2. *$AP(\phi_1)$ is a subset of AP_{M_1},*
3. *$AP(\phi_2)$ is a subset of AP_{M_2},*

4. $\phi_1 = \phi([ap(i)/AP_{M_2}])$,
5. $\phi_2 = \phi([ap(i)/AP_{M_1}])$.

Property 3 demonstrates that the decomposition operator "$\natural$" exhibits commutative and associative properties.

Property 3. For $M_1 \parallel_i M_2$, the decomposition operator $\natural_i$ is both commutative and associative:

1. $\phi_1 \natural_i \phi_2 \equiv \phi_2 \natural_i \phi_1$.
2. $\phi_1 \natural_{i_1} (\phi_2 \natural_{i_2} \phi_3) \equiv (\phi_1 \natural_{i_1} \phi_2) \natural_{i_2} \phi_3$.

Proof. The proof approach for Property 3 is based on Definition 7.   □

Proposition 3. *The decomposition of the PCTL property ϕ using the decomposition operator $\natural$ for the parallel composition $M_1 \parallel_i M_2$ is sound.*

Proof. The proof of Proposition 4 is in the appendix.   □

The key advantage of Proposition 4 is its ability to derive the deduction rule for the interface operator, as outlined in Theorem 2.

Theorem 2 (Compositional Reduction - CR). *Let ϕ be a PCTL property to be verified on M, such that: $M = M_1 \parallel_i M_2$ and $\phi = \phi_1 \natural_i \phi_2$. The following deduction rule applies:*

$$\frac{M_1 \parallel_i M_2 \downarrow_{ap(i)} \vdash \phi_1 \qquad M_2 \vdash \phi_2 \qquad \psi = \phi_1 \natural_i \phi_2}{M_1 \parallel_i M_2 \models \phi}$$

Property 4 (CR-Symmetry). The compositional reduction rule is symmetric.

$$\frac{M_1 \parallel_i M_2 \downarrow_{ap(i)} \models \phi_1 \qquad M_2 \models \phi_2 \qquad \phi = \phi_1 \natural_i \phi_2}{M_1 \parallel_i M_2 \models \phi}$$

Proof. The proof follows the same structure as the proof of Theorem 2.   □

Proposition 4. *The decomposition of a PCTL property ϕ by the decomposition operator $\natural$ for $M_1 \parallel_i M_2$ is sound.*

Proof. The proof of Proposition 4 is in the appendix.   □

3.3   The Verification Phase

Our approach fundamentally relies on the PRISM model checker to ensure the soundness of the probabilistic system under scrutiny, which is modelled as a composition of Probabilistic Automata (PAs). In this section, we delve into defining the syntax and semantics inherent in the PRISM programming language. PRISM has a versatile architecture that can accommodate a range of probabilistic models. These include Discrete-Time Markov Chains (DTMCs), Continuous-Time Markov Chains (CTMCs), Markov Decision Processes (MDPs), Probabilistic

Timed Automata (PTAs), and Probabilistic Automata (PAs). It's noteworthy to mention that within the PRISM framework, PAs are referred to as MDPs. However, in the process of formalizing the approach for this study, our primary focus will be directed towards PAs. The choice of focusing on PAs is due to their ability to model a wide array of complex, probabilistic behaviors that are crucial for our study.

A probabilistic system S described by a PRISM program P comprises a set of n modules ($n > 0$). Each module's state is defined by an evaluation of a set of finite-ranging local variables. The system's global state is the union of evaluations of the local variables V_l and the global variables V_g, denoted as $V = V_g \cup V_l$. The behavior of each module is defined by a set of guarded commands.

Each command dictates the primary behavior changes of P. A command is of the form: [a] g $\rightarrow$ p_1 : $u_1+...+p_m$: u_m or [a] g $\rightarrow$ u. This implies that, for the action 'a', if the guard 'g' holds, then an update 'u_i' is enabled with a probability 'p_i'. Guards are propositional formulas based on expressions' comparisons. An update 'u_i' is a conjunction of assignments to variables: $(v'_j = val_j)\&\cdots(v'_k = val_k)$, where v_i are variables and val_i are values evaluated via expressions, ensuring type consistency.

Definition 8 (PRISM Command). *A PRISM command c is a tuple $c = (a, g, u)$ where:*

- *a is an action label,*
- *g is a predicate over V,*
- *$u = \{(p_i, u_i)|m > 1, i \leq m, \sum_{i=1, p_i>0}^{m} p_i = 1$ and $u_i = \{(v, eval(v))\}\}$ where $eval : V \rightarrow \mathbb{N} \cup \{true, false\}$ assigns an integer or a boolean value to each variable $v \in V$. If $p_i = 1$, we omit the probability.*

A module, which describes the behavior of a system's sub-part, can be considered as a set of commands. Formally, it is defined as follows:

Definition 9 (PRISM Module). *A PRISM module M is a tuple $M = (var, init, cmd)$ where:*

- *var is a finite set of local variables for the module,*
- *init are the initial values of var,*
- *$cmd = \{c_i : 0 \leq i \leq m\}$ is a set of commands defining the module's behavior.*

A system S, comprising n parts, can be described by a PRISM program P containing n modules. The system components are combined using a Communicating Sequential Processes (CSP) expression.

Definition 10 (PRISM System). *A PRISM system is a tuple $P = (var, exp, M_1, \ldots, M_n, sys)$ where:*

- *$var = V_G \bigcup_{i=1}^{n} V_{li}$ is a finite set comprising the union of global and local variables,*
- *exp is a global logic expression,*
- *$M_1, \ldots, M_n$ is a finite set of modules,*
- *sys is a CSP algebraic expression defining the combination of the models.*

4   Experimental Results

We implement our proposed framework on the Probabilistic Broadcast Protocol (PBP), the Randomized Dining Philosophers (RDP), and Leader Election Protocol (LEP) benchmarks[2]. To compare the results of our approach, we verify PCTL properties on Probabilistic Automata (PA) models with and without our method applied. We measure and compare the number of states (#S), the number of transitions (#T), the time needed for the model construction (T_c in seconds), and the time needed for the model verification (T_v in seconds). We undertake this comparison with the aim of presenting empirical results that validate the efficiency and effectiveness of our approach.

For the PBP benchmark, we aim to measure "the minimum probability that the message sent by the base node 0 is successfully received by node j", where j ranges from 1 to 8. This property can be expressed in PCTL as follows:

$$P_{\min} =? \left[G \left((\text{active}_0 \wedge \neg\text{send}_0) \Rightarrow F \left(\neg\text{active}_j \wedge \neg\text{send}_j \right) \right) \right] \tag{3}$$

Following the PBP model and the decomposition rule (Definition 7), we decompose Property 3 into two properties, 4 and 5. Property 4 concerns the atomic propositions of node 0 and the propositions related to the interaction between nodes 0 and j. As per Definition 7, the propositions of Property 5 only belong to node j's propositions.

$$P_{\min} =? \left[G \left((\text{active}_0 \wedge \neg\text{send}_0) \Rightarrow F \left(\text{active}_j \wedge \neg\text{send}_j \right) \right) \right] \tag{4}$$

$$P_{\min} =? \left[G \left((\text{active}_j \wedge \neg\text{send}_j) \Rightarrow F \left(\neg\text{active}_j \wedge \neg\text{send}_j \right) \right) \right] \tag{5}$$

Table 1 shows the verification costs for these properties.

Table 1. Verification Cost for PBP Benchmark

j	1	2	3	4	5	6	7	8
Res(3)	0.246	0.0615	0.246	0.104	0.035	0.0615	0.035	0.0148
Res(4)	1.0	1.0	1.0	1.0	1.0	1.0	1.0	1.0
Res(5)	0.246	0.0615	0.246	0.104	0.035	0.0615	0.035	0.0148

For the RDP benchmark, we aim to verify the proposition "if a philosopher is hungry, then eventually some philosopher eats". Here, "hungry" refers to any action prior to the "eat" action. This property can be expressed in PCTL as follows:

$$\text{"hungry"} \Rightarrow P \geq 1[\text{true } U \text{ "eat"}] \tag{6}$$

---

[2] http://www.prismmodelchecker.org/benchmarks.

This benchmark does not incorporate interfaces, so we confine our experiments to the minimization algorithm. The verification costs of Property 6 are shown in Table 2, where $\#Phil$ denotes the number of philosophers.

Table 2. Verification Cost for RDP Benchmark

	PRISM					CR-Approach				
$\#Phil$	$\#S$	$\#T$	T_c	T_v	Res	$\#S$	$\#T$	T_c	T_v	Res
3	956	3696	0.027	0.379	T	596	2286	0.025	0.135	T
4	9440	48656	0.127	8.357	T	3964	20360	0.000905	4.396	T
5	93068	599600	0.358	124.707	T	36788	233208	0.006481	49.448	T
6	1288574	9879228	1.011	week	T	460336	3475264	0.56	35289.578	T

For the LEP benchmark, we evaluate "the minimum probability that two different processes do not have the same source". For two different processes P_i and P_j, the PCTL property for verification is expressed as follows:

$$P_{\min} =? \left[(P_i \neq P_j) \Rightarrow (\text{source}(P_i) \neq \text{source}(P_j)) \right] \tag{7}$$

Table 3 presents the verification cost of Property 7, where $\#Proc$ is the number of processes. Similar to the RDP benchmark, LEP does not incorporate common interfaces.

Table 3. Verification Cost For LEP Benchmark

	PRISM					CR-Approach				
$\#Proc$	$\#S$	$\#T$	T_c	T_v	Res	$\#S$	$\#T$	T_c	T_v	Res
3	27	108	0.023	0.005	1	8	24	0.0	0.005	1
4	81	432	0.028	0.034	1	16	64	0.020	0.031	1
5	243	1620	0.113	0.249	1	32	160	0.036	0.041	1
6	729	5832	0.154	0.893	1	64	384	0.044	0.43	1
7	6561	69984	0.327	9.994	1	128	896	0.047	0.49	1

The above results demonstrate that our verification framework preserves the verification of PCTL properties while significantly reducing the verification size and time.

5   Conclusion

In this paper, we presented a verification framework aimed at enhancing the scalability of probabilistic model-checking. In particular, we targeted systems modeled as probabilistic automata, which accommodate both nondeterminism and probabilistic choice behaviors. Our proposed framework harnesses probabilistic abstraction to disregard and amalgamate behaviors deemed irrelevant to a specified PCTL property. In addition, we introduced a probabilistic compositional verification mechanism to optimize model-checking efficiency. This mechanism operates by decomposing a global PCTL property into local properties corresponding to the interfaces between PAs. We established the soundness of our algorithms by elucidating the relationship between the abstract and concrete PAs, demonstrating that this relationship upholds the satisfaction of PCTL properties. Considering our reliance on PRISM, we proposed dedicated syntax and semantics for PAs specified within this context. Finally, we substantiated the effectiveness of our approach by applying it to a benchmark.

Looking forward, we aim to extend our approach along several trajectories. First, we intend to integrate our algorithms within the PRISM model checker. Second, we plan to expand our proposed abstraction to address other formalisms such as probabilistic timed and priced automata, stochastic Petri nets, and SysML activity diagrams. Furthermore, we aim to investigate other abstraction approaches, specifically data abstraction targeting system features like time and data. Lastly, we propose to explore strategies to reduce property within the model.

A   Appendix

Property 5 (Commutativity and Associativity). The operator $\|_i$ exhibits both commutativity and associativity:

1. $M_1 \|_i M_2 \equiv M_2 \|_i M_1$.
2. $M_1 \|_{i_1} (M_2 \|_{i_2} M_3) \equiv (M_1 \|_{i_1} M_2) \|_{i_2} M_3$.

Proof. Here, we present a detailed proof of Property 1:

1. The proof of the commutativity property is based on the composition of PAs as described in "Definition 2". The procedure consists of three steps:
    (a) Construction of $A = M_1 \|_i M_2$, which involves defining the composed system where M_1 and M_2 are synchronized on the interface i.
    (b) Construction of $B = M_2 \|_i M_1$, which represents the composed system where the roles of M_1 and M_2 are switched.
    (c) Comparison of the structures of A and B to confirm their equivalence, which supports the commutativity of the $\|_i$ operation.
2. The proof of the associativity property is also based on Definition 2. The demonstration consists of the following five steps:
    (a) Construction of $A_1 = M_2 \|_{i_2} M_3$, defining the composed system where M_2 and M_3 are synchronized on interface i_2.
    (b) Construction of $A = M_1 \|_{i_1} A_1$, representing the system where M_1 is synchronized with the already composed system A_1 on interface i_1.
    (c) Construction of $B_1 = M_1 \|_{i_1} M_2$, defining the composed system where M_1 and M_2 are synchronized on interface i_1.

(d) Construction of $B = B_1 \parallel_{i_2} M_3$, representing the system where M_3 is synchronized with the already composed system B_1 on interface i_2.

(e) Comparison of A and B to establish their equivalence, hence validating the associativity of the $\parallel_i$ operation. $\qquad\square$

Proposition 5 (Minimization Relation). *Given two Probabilistic Automata, M and M', we denote the probabilistic weak simulation of M by M' as $M \precsim_w M'$, where M' is the result of a reduction process applied to M which abstracts away invisible actions, symbolized by $M' = M \downarrow_{ap}$.*

Proof. The proof of Proposition 1 relies on establishing a mapping between states of M and M' through a weight function $\triangle$. This function quantifies each state's contribution in M to its corresponding state in M' based on probabilities.

To minimize M to M', we apply minimization rules, noted as $M' = M \downarrow_{ap}$, which simplify M by eliminating specific transitions.

We then validate that the weight function still accurately maps states from M to M' after minimization. Specifically, we confirm that the sum of weights for each state in M matches its corresponding distribution in M', ensuring behavior consistency between M and M'.

This process proves that the weight function successfully maps states between M and M', thus validating the weak simulation relation and proving the proposition. $\qquad\square$

Property 6 (Minimization Preservation). Given a property ϕ expressed in the PCTL language $\mathcal{L}(ap)$, and a set of atomic propositions ap that are relevant in the context of M, if the minimized version of M, denoted by $M \downarrow_{ap}$, satisfies ϕ, then the original PA M must also satisfy ϕ. Mathematically, this is expressed as $\forall \phi \in \mathcal{L}(ap), ap \in AP_M : M \downarrow_{ap} \models \phi \Rightarrow M \models \phi$.

Proof. The proof for the preservation of PCTL properties through minimization can be obtained through an inductive argument based on the structure of the PCTL properties. The inductive base case can be the satisfaction of ϕ in $M \downarrow_{ap}$, and the inductive step can assume the property holds for a given structure and then prove it for the next level of structure complexity. $\qquad\square$

Proposition 6 ($\precsim_w$ Composition). *The probabilistic weak simulation relation preserves the composition of PAs: if M_1 is weakly simulated by M_1', then the composition of M_1 with another PA M_2 is weakly simulated by the composition of M_1' with the same M_2. Mathematically, this is expressed as $M_1 \precsim_w M_1' \Rightarrow M_1 \parallel_i M_2 \precsim_w M_1' \parallel_i M_2$.*

Proof. The proof of Proposition 2 relies on the previously established Probabilistic Weak Simulation Relation (Proposition 1) and the specific details of the PA composition (Definition 2). More specifically, we must show that each transition in the composed $M_1 \parallel_i M_2$ can be simulated by a corresponding transition in $M_1' \parallel_i M_2$, which in turn relies on the definition of weak simulation. $\qquad\square$

Theorem 3 (Soundness). *The minimization rule, as specified in Definition 6, is sound.*

Proof. The soundness of the minimization rule can be proven by combining the results of Proposition 2 and Property 2. In detail, Property 2 ensures that minimization preserves the PCTL properties, and Proposition 2 guarantees that the weak simulation preserves the composition. Hence, the combination of these two results ensures that the minimization process, which involves both reducing M_2 to M_2' and composing M_1 with M_2', does not affect the satisfaction of ϕ by the composed system, confirming the soundness of the minimization rule.   □

Proposition 7. *The decomposition of the PCTL property ϕ using the decomposition operator ♮ for the parallel composition $M_1 \parallel_i M_2$ is sound.*

Proof. The proof of Proposition 4 is built upon Definition 2 and Definition 7. It proceeds by using structural induction on the structure of PCTL formulas.

As an example, consider the "until" operator "U". Let $\phi = \alpha_1 U \alpha_2$ where $\alpha_1 \in AP_{M_1}$ and $\alpha_2 \in AP_{M_2}$. From here, we can deduce the following:

1. $\phi_1 = \alpha_1 U \alpha(i)$ and $\phi_2 = \alpha(i) U \alpha_2$, as per Definition 7.
2. From the hypothesis, it is assumed that $M_1 \parallel_i M_2 \models \alpha_1 U \alpha(i)$ and $M_1 \parallel_i M_2 \models \alpha(i) U \alpha_2$.
3. According to the semantics of PCTL, we have $M_1 \parallel_i M_2 \models (\alpha(i) U \alpha_2) \wedge (\alpha_1 U \alpha(i))$.
4. Hence, we obtain $M_1 \parallel_i M_2 \models \phi_1 U \phi_2$ based on PCTL semantics.
5. Therefore, it follows that $M_1 \parallel_i M_2 \models \phi_1 ♮_i \phi_2$, which is exactly what Proposition 4 claims.

By adopting a similar proof strategy for the rest of the PCTL operators, we can assert that Proposition 4 is valid.   □

Proposition 8. *The decomposition of a PCTL property ϕ by the decomposition operator ♮ for $M_1 \parallel_i M_2$ is sound.*

Proof. The proof of Proposition 4 relies on Definition 2 and Definition 7, and it proceeds by a structural induction on the PCTL structure. For each $\alpha_1 \in AP_{M_1}$, $\alpha_2 \in AP_{M_2}$, and i in the interface, we consider the until operator "U" and let $\phi = \alpha_1 U \alpha_2$. We can perform the following steps:

1. Define $\phi_1 = \alpha_1 U \alpha(i)$ and $\phi_2 = \alpha(i) U \alpha_2$ based on Definition 7.
2. Assume that $M_1 \parallel_i M_2 \models \phi_1$ and $M_1 \parallel_i M_2 \models \phi_2$.
3. From PCTL semantics, it follows that if both ϕ_1 and ϕ_2 hold, then their conjunction also holds: $M_1 \parallel_i M_2 \models (\phi_1) \wedge (\phi_2)$.
4. Furthermore, again by PCTL semantics, if the conjunction of two properties holds, then their until operation also holds: $M_1 \parallel_i M_2 \models \phi_1 U \phi_2$.
5. Finally, by Proposition 4, we can express the until operation as a decomposition operation: $M_1 \parallel_i M_2 \models \phi_1 ♮_i \phi_2$.

By repeating the above style of proof for the remaining operators in the PCTL structure, we find that Proposition 4 holds.   □

References

1. Clarke, E.M., Grumberg, O., Peled, D.A.: Model Checking. The MIT Press, Cambridge (1999)
2. Bérard, B., et al.: Systems and Software Verification. Springer, Heidelberg (2001). https://doi.org/10.1007/978-3-662-04558-9
3. Baier, C., Katoen, J.P.: Principles of Model Checking. The MIT Press, Cambridge (2008) ·
4. Forejt, V., Kwiatkowska, M., Norman, G., Parker, D.: Automated verification techniques for probabilistic systems. In: Bernardo, M., Issarny, V. (eds.) SFM 2011. LNCS, vol. 6659, pp. 53–113. Springer, Heidelberg (2011). https://doi.org/10.1007/978-3-642-21455-4_3
5. Xin-feng, Z., Jian-dong, W., Xin-feng, Z., Bin, L., Jun-wu, Z., Jun, W.: Methods to tackle state explosion problem in model checking. In: Proceedings of the 3rd International Conference on IITA, NJ, USA, pp. 329–331. IEEE Press (2009)
6. Berezin, S., Campos, S., Clarke, E.M.: Compositional reasoning in model checking. In: de Roever, W.-P., Langmaack, H., Pnueli, A. (eds.) COMPOS 1997. LNCS, vol. 1536, pp. 81–102. Springer, Heidelberg (1998). https://doi.org/10.1007/3-540-49213-5_4
7. Kwiatkowska, M., Norman, G., Parker, D.: PRISM 4.0: verification of probabilistic real-time systems. In: Gopalakrishnan, G., Qadeer, S. (eds.) CAV 2011. LNCS, vol. 6806, pp. 585–591. Springer, Heidelberg (2011). https://doi.org/10.1007/978-3-642-22110-1_47
8. Hahn, E.M., Norman, G., Parker, D., Wachter, B., Zhang, L.: Game-based abstraction and controller synthesis for probabilistic hybrid systems. In: Proceedings of the 2011 Eighth International Conference on Quantitative Evaluation of SysTems. QEST '11, Washington, DC, USA, pp. 69–78. IEEE Computer Society (2011)
9. Kattenbelt, M., Kwiatkowska, M., Norman, G., Parker, D.: A game-based abstraction-refinement framework for Markov decision processes. Form. Methods Syst. Des. **36**(3), 246–280 (2010)
10. Donaldson, A., Miller, A., Parker, D.: Language-level symmetry reduction for probabilistic model checking. In: Sixth International Conference on the Quantitative Evaluation of Systems, 2009. QEST '09, pp. 289–298 (2009)
11. Donaldson, A.F., Miller, A.: Symmetry reduction for probabilistic model checking using generic representatives. In: Graf, S., Zhang, W. (eds.) ATVA 2006. LNCS, vol. 4218, pp. 9–23. Springer, Heidelberg (2006). https://doi.org/10.1007/11901914_4
12. Baier, C., D'Argenio, P., Groesser, M.: Partial order reduction for probabilistic branching time. Electron. Notes Theor. Comput. Sci. **153**(2), 97–116 (2006)
13. Feng, L., Han, T., Kwiatkowska, M., Parker, D.: Learning-based compositional verification for synchronous probabilistic systems. In: Bultan, T., Hsiung, P.-A. (eds.) ATVA 2011. LNCS, vol. 6996, pp. 511–521. Springer, Heidelberg (2011). https://doi.org/10.1007/978-3-642-24372-1_40
14. Feng, L., Kwiatkowska, M., Parker, D.: Automated learning of probabilistic assumptions for compositional reasoning. In: Giannakopoulou, D., Orejas, F. (eds.) FASE 2011. LNCS, vol. 6603, pp. 2–17. Springer, Heidelberg (2011). https://doi.org/10.1007/978-3-642-19811-3_2
15. Feng, L., Kwiatkowska, M., Parker, D.: Compositional verification of probabilistic systems using learning. In: Proceedings of the 2010 Seventh International Conference on the Quantitative Evaluation of Systems. QEST '10, pp. 133–142. IEEE Computer Society (2010)

16. Ouchani, S.: Towards a call behavior-based compositional verification framework for SysML activity diagrams. In: Hierons, R.M., Mosbah, M. (eds.) ICTAC 2019. LNCS, vol. 11884, pp. 216–234. Springer, Cham (2019). https://doi.org/10.1007/978-3-030-32505-3_13

17. Ouchani, S.: Towards a fractionation-based verification: application on SYSML activity diagrams. In: Proceedings of the 34th ACM/SIGAPP Symposium on Applied Computing, pp. 2032–2039 (2019)

18. Segala, R.: A compositional trace-based semantics for probabilistic automata. In: Lee, I., Smolka, S.A. (eds.) CONCUR 1995. LNCS, vol. 962, pp. 234–248. Springer, Heidelberg (1995). https://doi.org/10.1007/3-540-60218-6_17

A Sound Abstraction Method Towards Efficient Neural Networks Verification

Fateh Boudardara[1]($\boxtimes$)(iD), Abderraouf Boussif[1], and Mohamed Ghazel[1,2]

[1] Technological Research Institute Railenium, 180 rue Joseph-Louis Lagrange,
59308 Valenciennes, France
{fateh.boudardara,abderraouf.boussif}@railenium.eu
[2] Univ Gustave Eiffel, COSYS-ESTAS, 20 rue Élisée Reclus,
59666 Villeneuve d'Ascq, France
mohamed.ghazel@univ-eiffel.fr

Abstract. With the increasing application of neural networks (NN) in safety-critical systems, the (formal) verification of NN is becoming more, than essential. Although several NN verification techniques have been developed in recent years, these techniques are often limited to small networks and do not scale well to larger NN. The primarily reason for this limitation is the complexity and non-linearity of neural network models. Abstraction and model reduction approaches, that aim to reduce the size of the neural networks and over-approximate their outcomes, have been seen as a promising research direction to help existing verification methods to handle larger models. In this paper, we introduce a model reduction method for neural networks with non-negative activation functions (e.g., *ReLU* and *Sigmoid*). The method relies on merging neurons while ensuring that the obtained model (i.e., the abstract model) over-approximates the original one. Concretely, it consists in merging a set of neurons that have positive outgoing weights and substituting it with a single abstract neuron, while ensuring that if a given property holds on the abstract network, it necessarily holds on the original one. In order to assess the efficiency of the approach, we perform an experimental comparison with two existing model reduction methods on the ACAS Xu benchmark. The obtained results show that our approach outperforms both methods in terms of precision and execution time.

Keywords: Neural network abstraction · model reduction · Neural network verification · Output range computation

1 Introduction

Due to their performance in dealing with complex problems, neural networks (NN) are increasingly developed and deployed in many areas including autonomous systems, such as autonomous cars and trains [2,19]. Such systems are known as safety-critical systems, where each module must meet some specific safety requirements before its deployment. In the other hand, recent works have

B. Ben Hedia et al. (Eds.): VECoS 2023, LNCS 14368, pp. 76–89, 2024.
https://doi.org/10.1007/978-3-031-49737-7_6

demonstrated the sensitivity and the vulnerability of NN to even minor input's perturbations and adversarial attacks [24]. Consequently, neural networks verification is becoming a popular and attractive research domain. NN verification aims to formally provide guarantees on NN and to ensure that the network behaves as intended. Several NN verification approaches have been introduced to assess the safety and the robustness of NN models [16]. Originally, the NN verification problem is transformed to an optimization problem by encoding the NN behaviour and the property to verify as a linear programming problem, and then apply an adequate solver for verification. Mixed-integer Linear Programming (MILP) and SAT/SMT solvers are intensively exploited and applied to deal with the verification problem of NN [5,7,13,15,18]. Next, several formal methods have been developed supporting different properties and architectures of neural networks [10,11,25]. For instance, techniques based on abstract interpretation [9,21] and interval analysis [26,27] are successfully applied to verify some NN models.

However, the existing NN verification methods face challenges when it comes to scaling up and handling real-world sized networks. The complexity and non-linearity of NN models make the verification process computationally expensive and resource-demanding. As a result, the scalability of these methods becomes a significant concern. To address this issue, model reduction methods, also known as abstraction methods, are seen as a promising research direction to handle larger models. The key insight behind model reduction is to reduce the state-space (number of neurons) of the network by merging a set of neurons, while guaranteeing that the obtained reduced (abstract) model is an over-approximation of original one. In other words, the property at hand holds on the original network N whenever it holds on the reduced network $\overline{N}$ [3,8,17]. Therefore, instead of verifying properties on the large original model, these properties can be checked on the reduced model which is easier and faster to verify, enabling to enhance the scalability of the verification process.

In this paper, we propose a new model reduction method for feed-forward neural networks with non-negative activation functions. A function $\alpha : \mathbb{R} \to \mathbb{R}$ is non-negative, if $\forall x \in \mathbb{R}, \alpha(x) \geq 0$. For instance, *ReLU* and *Sigmoid*, that are broadly applied in NN, are non-negative functions. Concretely, the proposed method consists of merging neurons that have positive outgoing weights. However, in case the set of neurons to be merged have some negative outgoing weights, a pre-processing step is required. This step involves building an initial abstract network by eliminating negative edges. The next step is model reduction, which consists of merging a set of nodes and computing its corresponding incoming and outgoing weights as follows: the incoming weight is the maximum value over the incoming weights of the merged nodes, and the outgoing weight is the sum of the weights of the corresponding nodes on the original network N. This method guarantees that the obtained abstract network's output is always greater than or equal to the original network N, i.e., $\overline{N}(x) \geq N(x)$.

To evaluate its performance, we implemented the approach in Python and carried out a series of experiments on the ACAS Xu benchmark [13]. In addition, we conducted a comparison study with respect to two existing model reduction approaches [3,17]. Based on the experimental results, the proposed method outperforms the two approaches in terms of both abstraction time and output range precision.

The remaining of this paper is organized as follows: Sect. 2 provides an overview of existing works in the field of neural network verification, with a specific focus on model reduction methods. Section 3 presents the background and notations related to neural networks and the NN verification problem. The theoretical development of the proposed approach is provided in Sect. 4. In Sect. 5, we summarize the used experimental configurations along with the obtained results. Finally, we provide some conclusion remarks in Sect. 6.

2   Related Works

Neural network verification is an active research area aiming to ensure the safety and dependability of NN in various applications. The verification of NN consists of applying verification methods to formally prove that the network satisfies a set of required properties [10,25]. In recent years, several approaches have been proposed to address this problem. These approaches relies on different techniques, including SAT/SMT solvers [11,14,18], Mixed-Integer Linear Programming [5,6,15], abstract interpretation [9,22,29], and reachability analysis [26–28].

These techniques are often limited to small networks and do not scale to large networks with practical interest. Thus, abstraction and model reduction methods have emerged as a promising direction towards enhancing the scalability of NN verification. These methods aim to reduce the size of the network while preserving relevant properties, such as the over-approximation relation between the original and reduced networks. Ashok et al. [1] proposed a model reduction method based on applying the *k-mean* clustering algorithm to regroup neurons of the same layer into clusters, and then replace each cluster with a representative node. The average error between the original neuron and its representative node is calculated, and then propagated through the model's layers until the output layer. Moreover, this error is used to over-approximate the real output. Ashok et al. [1] used the verification tool DeepPoly [22] on the MNIST benchmark to check the robustness of the model. In another work, Elboher et al. [8] introduced a method consisting of classifying the neurons according to the sign of their weights (positive or negative) and their direct impact on the output (increasing or decreasing). Next, neurons of the same category are merged and the new weights are calculated by taking the sum of the outgoing weights and the min or max of the incoming weights in such a way that the output of the reduced model is always greater than the one of the original one. To assess the efficiency of their approach, Elboher et al. [8] used the Marabou verifier [14] to check some properties on the ACAS Xu benchmark [12]. Inspired by code refactoring, Shriver et al. [20] established a method to redesign a NN model while preserving its behaviour. The restructuring of the NN model helps further operations, like verification, to be applicable on the refactored model. The proposed approach consists of changing some NN operations and parameters that are not supported by the existing verification tools. An interval weight-based model reduction is introduced by Prabhakar and Afzal [17]. The main idea is to replace weights of the merged neurons by the interval hull of their incoming and the outgoing weights. Thus, the model is called interval neural networks (INN). To solve the verification problem on INN, a MILP encoding of the INN is proposed. A generalization of INN, namely Abstract Neural Networks (ANN) is proposed in [23]. In ANN, the weights of the reduced model are obtained by applying abstract domains, and not limited to intervals as in [17]. Recently, Boudardara et al. [3] proposed a method based on INN that support NN with *ReLU* and *Tanh* activation functions. Please refer to our survey work [4] to get a general overview on the abstraction and model reduction methods for neural networks verification.

Figure 1 depicts an illustrative example demonstrating the application of some of the presented model reduction methods on a small network.

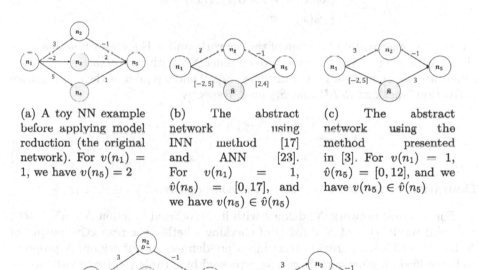

(a) A toy NN example before applying model reduction (the original network). For $v(n_1) = 1$, we have $v(n_5) = 2$

(b) The abstract network using INN method [17] and ANN [23]. For $v(n_1) = 1$, $\hat{v}(n_5) = [0, 17]$, and we have $v(n_5) \in \hat{v}(n_5)$

(c) The abstract network using the method presented in [3]. For $v(n_1) = 1$, $\hat{v}(n_5) = [0, 12]$, and we have $v(n_5) \in \hat{v}(n_5)$

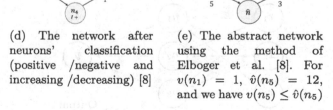

(d) The network after neurons' classification (positive /negative and increasing /decreasing) [8]

(e) The abstract network using the method of Elboger et al. [8]. For $v(n_1) = 1$, $\hat{v}(n_5) = 12$, and we have $v(n_5) \leq \hat{v}(n_5)$

Fig. 1. The application of different model reduction methods on a toy example of NN. $v(n)$ and $\hat{v}(n)$ represents the value of the node s on the original and the abstract networks, respectively.

3   Background

In this paper, we focus on feed-forward neural networks, and we shortly refer to them as neural networks (NN). A NN is a sequence of connected neurons which are grouped in layers. A NN has an input layer, an output layer and one or more hidden layers. The neurons of a layer l_i are connected to all neurons of the successive layer l_{i+1} via weighted edges (see Fig. 2). These connections are denoted by the matrix $W_i \in \mathbb{R}^{|l_i| \times |l_{i-1}|}$, where the weight of the edge connecting a neuron $n_{i-1,k} \in l_{i-1}$ to a neuron $n_{i,j} \in l_i$ is represented as $w^i_{jk} = w(n_{i-1,k}, n_{i,j})$. The propagation of the input values through these layers allows the calculation of the output of the network.

For a NN of L layers, with n inputs and m outputs, we can recursively define its associated function $N : \mathbb{R}^n \to \mathbb{R}^m$ as follows:

$$\begin{cases} N(x) = v_L(x) \\ v_i(x) = W_i \times \alpha(v_{i-1}(x)) + b_i \\ v_0(x) = x \end{cases} \tag{1}$$

where α is an activation function of the network, and v_i is a vector function associated with layer l_i. In this paper, we consider NN with *non-negative* activation functions (see Definition 1). For instance, Eqs. 2 and 3 represent the non-negative activation functions *ReLU* and *Sigmoid*, respectively.

$$ReLU(x) = max(0, x) ; \qquad x \in \mathbb{R} \tag{2}$$

$$\sigma(x) = \frac{1}{1 + e^{-x}} ; \qquad x \in \mathbb{R} \tag{3}$$

Definition 1. *A function* $\alpha : \mathbb{R} \to \mathbb{R}$ *is non-negative if:* $\forall x \in \mathbb{R} : \alpha(x) \geq 0$.

For a neural network N, defined with its associated function $N : \mathbb{R}^n \to \mathbb{R}^m$, a formal verification of N consists of checking whether the respective output of N for a specific input region is within a pre-defined output region. A property to be verified on a network N can be expressed by a tuple $\langle N, Pre, Post \rangle$, where

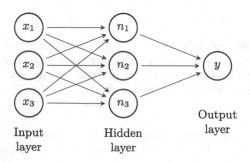

Fig. 2. A neural network with 3 inputs, one hidden layer with 3 neurons, and an output.

Pre and *Post* are the input and the output constraints, respectively. The NN verification problem can be formulated as:

$$\forall x \in \mathbb{R}^n, Pre(x) \implies Post(N(x)) \tag{4}$$

Neural network are known to be complex, and NN verification has been proven to be an NP-hard problem [13]. This poses challenges for verifying large-scale NN. One way to mitigate this is by reducing the size of the network before verification, while ensuring that the obtained network is an over-approximation of the original one. Thus, instead of directly verifying a property on the original large network N, the property can be verified on the reduced model $\overline{N}$, and then the verification results is deduced on the original network N.

It is worth noticing that the over-approximation does not guarantee that the non satisfaction of the property is preserved on the original model. Indeed, if a property does not hold on the abstract network, this does not mean that the property does not hold on the original one. Practically, in this case a counter-example is generated (from the abstract model) and executed on the original one in order to check whether it is really a counter-example. If not, this type of counter-example is referred to as a *spurious counter-example*.

In this paper, we propose a model reduction method for NN with non-negative activation functions. The approach consists of merging nodes while guaranteeing that the output of the reduced network (also called abstract network) $\overline{N}$ is always greater than or equal to the output of the original network N. For the sake of simplicity and clarity, we consider that the network has one output y, and we focus on properties of the following form:

$$\forall x, Pre(x) \implies N(x) < c \tag{5}$$

where $c \in \mathbb{R}$ is a given constant. It is worth noting that many properties can be reduced into one-single output property, as presented in [8]. More details about the approach are provided in the following section.

4   The Proposed Model Reduction Approach

The motivation behind our approach is to reduce the size of the network, which enables faster computation of the output range and improves the scalability for larger NN. The aim of our method is to construct an abstract network, denoted as $\overline{N}$, from the original network N by merging a set of neurons within the same hidden layer, while ensuring the over-approximation of N, i.e.:

$$\forall x \in \mathbb{R}^n : \overline{N}(x) \geq N(x) \tag{6}$$

In this paper, we consider that the network N has one output and we want to verify that $N(x) < c$ for some constraints *Pre* on the input x (see Eq. 5)[1]. So,

---

[1] Many properties of interest can still be accommodated by adding additional neurons to the network [8].

whenever we are able to demonstrate that $\overline{N}(x) < c$, we can directly infer the correctness of the property for the original network N:

$$\forall x, (Pre(x) \implies \overline{N}(x) < c) \implies (Pre(x) \implies N(x) < c)$$

To construct an abstract network $\overline{N}$ from the original network N, we replace a set of neurons s of layer l_i having positive outgoing weights with a single abstract neuron $\hat{n}$. Since neurons have often a combination of positive and negative weights, we begin by eliminating the negative connections of the relevant neurons, i.e., starting from the hidden layer l_i towards the succeeding layers until reaching the last hidden layer of the network N. The abstract neuron is then connected to the previous and next layers through new weighted edges. The calculation of the incoming and outgoing weights for this abstract neuron $\hat{n}$ is computed in a way to ensure that the over-approximation relation presented in Eq. 6 is always satisfied:

- **_Incoming weight:_** the maximum value among the incoming weights of the individual neurons that are being merged.
- **_Outgoing weight:_** the sum of the outgoing weights of the corresponding individual neurons that are being merged.

Formally, let us consider a set of neurons s, which belong to a hidden layer l_i. Each neuron n in the set s has incoming and outgoing weights denoted as $w(n_{i-1,j}, n)$ and $w(n, n_{i+1,k})$, respectively. Here, $n_{i-1,j}$ represents a neuron in the preceding layer l_{i-1}, and $n_{i+1,k}$ represents a neuron in the succeeding layer l_{i+1}. The first step consists of eliminating negative weights to ensure that: $\forall i \le t \le L-1, \forall n_t \in l_t \wedge n_{t+1} \in l_{t+1} : w(n_t, n_{t+1}) \ge 0$. The second step is to replace the set of neurons s by the abstract neuron $\hat{n}$ such that the weights of $\hat{n}$ are calculated as follows:

1. Incoming weights:

$$\forall n_{i-1,j} \in l_{i-1} : w(n_{i-1,j}, \hat{n}) = \max_{n \in s}\{w(n_{i-1,j}, n)\} \tag{7}$$

2. Outgoing weights:

$$\forall n_{i+1,k} \in l_{i+1} : w(\hat{n}, n_{i+1,k}) = \sum_{n \in s} w(n, n_{i+1,k}) \tag{8}$$

Example 1. Figure 3 depicts an example of the model reduction method applied on a small network employing the *ReLU* activation function, where the objective in this example is to merge the set of neurons $s = \{n_1, n_2, n_3\}$ of the original network N (Fig. 3a) and replace it with the abstract neuron $\hat{n}$. The first step involves eliminating the negative outgoing weights of neurons in s. The resulting network of this step is presented in Fig. 3b. Subsequently, the model reduction method is applied on this network to merge the set of neurons s, and calculate the incoming and outgoing weights of the obtained abstract neuron $\hat{n}$ using Eqs. 7 and 8, respectively. The final abstract network is shown in Fig. 3c. Notice that $\overline{N}(x) \ge N(x)$, for all possible values of x.

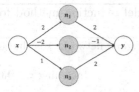
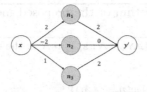

(a) An example network N before abstraction (the original network).

(b) The obtained network after the pre-processing phase applied on the NN presented in Figure 3a (removing negative weights).

(c) The abstract network $\overline{N}$ using the proposed method.

Fig. 3. The application of the proposed model reduction method on a toy example of NN.

Remark 1. Theoretically, the proposed method allows for the merging of all neurons, leading to a network with only one neuron in each hidden layer. However, in practical applications, this may not be beneficial as there is a trade-off to be found between reducing the size of original model and maintaining the precision of the abstract model.

Algorithm 1 provides a summary of the main steps involved in the model reduction procedure applied to a hidden layer l_i. The procedure assumes that all neurons in set o have positive outgoing weights. To apply the model reduction on different hidden layers, a general algorithm is presented in Algorithm 2. The algorithm begins by eliminating negative weights and then, for each set of neurons to be merged on a hidden layer l_i, it invokes the *AbstractOneLayer* procedure (presented in Algorithm 1). The algorithm finally returns the abstract network $\overline{N}$. The procedure *SelectNodes* employed in Algorithm 1 is responsible of selecting the set of nodes to be merged. In this paper, we applied random nodes selection strategy. However, this procedure can be re-implemented to support heuristic-based nodes selection strategies.

In the following, we state the main results for model reduction of NN with non-negative activation function.

Lemma 1. *Let $v_1, v_2, ..., v_n$ be positive numbers, and $w_1, w_2, ..., w_n$ be real numbers. Let $z = \sum_{i=1}^{n} w_i v_i$ and $\overline{z} = \sum_{i=1, w_i \geq 0}^{n} w_i v_i$. Then we have: $\overline{z} \geq z$.*

Proposition 1. *For a neural network $N : \mathbb{R}^n \to \mathbb{R}$ that have a non-negative activation function. Let $\overline{N}$ be the abstract network of N obtained using Algorithm 2. Then we have also $\overline{N}$ defined as $\overline{N} : \mathbb{R}^n \to \mathbb{R}$, and:*

$$\forall x \in \mathbb{R}^n, \overline{N}(x) \geq N(x)$$

Algorithm 1. Pseudo-algorithm of the proposed model reduction method for one hidden layer

---

1: **procedure** ABSTRACTONLAYER(N, s, i)   ▷ N is the original network, s is the set of nodes of layer l_i
2:    **for** $n_{i-1,j} \in l_{i-1}$ **do**   ▷ Incoming weights
3:        $w(n_{i-1,j}, \hat{n}) \leftarrow \max_{n \in s}\{w(n_{i-1,j}, n)\}$
4:    **end for**
5:    **for** $n_{i+1,k} \in l_{i+1}$ **do**   ▷ Outgoing weights
6:        $w(\hat{n}, n_{i+1,k}) \leftarrow \sum_{n \in s} w(n, n_{i+1,k})$
7:    **end for**
8:    replace s with $\hat{n}$
9: **end procedure**

Algorithm 2. Pseudo-algorithm of the proposed model reduction method

---

1: **procedure** ABSTRACT(N)   ▷ N: the original network
2:    $\overline{N} \leftarrow duplicate(N)$ ▷ Create a copy of N
3:    **for** $i \leftarrow 1$ to $L - 1$ in $\overline{N}$ **do**   ▷ Pre-processing: remove negative weights
4:        **for** $n_1 \in l_i$ **do**
5:            **for** $n_2 \in l_{i+1}$ **do**
6:                **if** $w(n_1, n_2) < 0$ **then**
7:                    $w(n_1, n_2) \leftarrow 0$
8:                **end if**
9:            **end for**
10:       **end for**
11:   **end for**
12:   **for** $i \leftarrow 1$ to $L - 1$ in $\overline{N}$ **do**
13:       $s \leftarrow SelectNodes(\overline{N}, i)$
14:       $AbstractOneLayer(\overline{N}, s, i)$
15:   **end for**
16:   **return** $\overline{N}$
17: **end procedure**

The proof of Proposition 1 relies on Lemma 1, which states that removing negative elements from a sum yields to a value greater than the original sum with negative values. Please recall also that the activation function of N of is monotonically increasing and positive.

5   Early Experiments

We developed our model reduction method as a Python tool, which includes a reader for the input network (in the NNET format [12]). This allows users to easily apply our method to neural networks and customize the model reduction parameters. The parameters include the number of the (desired) remaining nodes on each hidden layer after the abstraction and the strategy for node selection. While we utilized a random selection strategy in this first series of experiments, it is possible to integrate different node selection strategies by exploiting some heuristic techniques.

We compared the performance of our proposed method with two existing methods: the method proposed by Prabhakar et al. [17] and a method that we have previously proposed in [3]. In the former method (Prabhakar et al. [17]), the weights of an abstract neuron are defined as the interval hull of the weights of the merged neurons. On the other hand, in the latter method (Boudardara et al. [3]), the incoming weights of an abstract neuron are determined by multiplying the signs of the corresponding outgoing weights with the incoming weights of the set of neurons to be merged. The outgoing weight of the abstract neuron is computed as the sum of the absolute values of the outgoing weights of the merged neurons.

We conducted our experiments on ACAS Xu (Airborne-Collision Avoidance System) benchmark[2] [12]. This benchmark is a collection of 45 feed-forward NN that are trained to provide guidance to the ownship aircraft to avoid a collision with an intruder aircraft. Each network has 5 hidden layers, with 50 neurons in each layer. The network takes 7 inputs including the distance between the two aircraft, their speeds and their directions, and it outputs one of the 5 possible advisories: clear-of-conflict, strong/weak turn to the left, or strong/weak turn to the right.

For purpose of comparison, we adopted the same experimental configuration as [3]. We used the network $ACASXU\_experimental\_v2a\_1\_1.nnet$, then we generated eight abstract models $\overline{N}_i$ by varying the numbers of abstract neurons on hidden layers. The eight configurations have 45, 40, 35, 30, 20, 15, and 10 neurons, respectively. We used the Interval Bound Propagation (IBP) algorithm to calculate the output range for the original network and the abstract ones. Over 50 random runs, we calculated the average abstraction time for each abstract network $\overline{N}_i$, the output range (the first output) and the IBP computation time. We performed a comparison study between our method and two other model reduction techniques proposed by Boudardara et al. [3] and Prabhakar et al [17]. The obtained results are summarized in Figs. 4b, 4a, and 5. In these Figures, "Our" refers to our method, and "Method1" and "Method2" refer to the methods introduced in [3] and [17], respectively.

As depicted in Figs. 4a and 4b, reducing the number of remaining neurons (nodes) significantly decreases the abstraction time and increases the IBP computation time for the two alternative methods [3,17]. In contrast, our proposed method exhibits only minor fluctuations and tends to remain stable when varying the number of neurons of the abstract networks. Moreover, our method is computationally more efficient, with consistently lower abstraction time and IBP computation time compared to the two methods [3,17].

Moreover, as shown in Fig. 5, reducing the number of neurons in the abstract networks leads to an increase in the corresponding upper bound using the three techniques. However, our method is more precise (i.e., with the tightest bounds). The generated abstract networks provides tighter bounds compared to the two others methods [3,17]: the upper bounds obtained on the abstract networks using our method is always less than the upper bounds using the two other methods.

---

[2] Available at https://github.com/NeuralNetworkVerification/Marabou/tree/master/resources/nnet/acasxu.

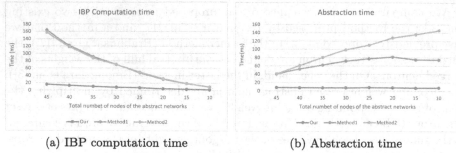

(a) IBP computation time   (b) Abstraction time

Fig. 4. IBP and abstraction time results

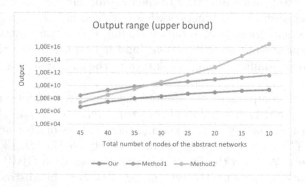

Fig. 5. Output range (upper bound) results

Through this series of experiments, we observe that the proposed method exhibits faster execution time and provides more precise results (tighter bounds) compared to *Method1* [3] and *Method2* [17]. In addition, we can see that the precision of the abstract model is strongly influenced by the number of merged nodes. Specifically, as more nodes are merged, resulting in a higher level of abstraction and more abstract nodes, the upper bound of the abstract models tends to increase.

6   Conclusion

In this paper, we introduced a model reduction method for reducing the size of neural networks and ensuring that the obtained network is an over-approximation of the original one. This leads to enhance the scalability of NN analysis operations such as verification. The introduced method supports feed-forward NN with non-negative activations functions, such as *ReLU* and *Sigmoid*, and provides formal guarantees that the output of the abstract network is always greater than the output of the original one.

We carried out a comparison of our method with two existing abstraction methods [3,17]. The results clearly show that our method outperforms the other approaches, and demonstrates that our method can be used to reduce the size of NN leading to faster operations on the abstract networks, while preserving tighter output bounds.

In future work, we have identified several plans to improve the efficiency of the proposed approach. Mainly, we aim to propose some heuristics for selecting neurons to be merged during the abstraction process, towards enhancing the precision of the constructed abstract networks. Furthermore, in order to assess the scalability and the applicability of our approach, we intend to evaluate the performance of our method on different benchmarks and larger networks.

Acknowledgements. This research work contributes to the french collaborative project TASV (autonomous passengers service train), with Railenium, SNCF, Alstom Crespin, Thales, Bosch, and SpirOps. It was carried out in the framework of IRT Railenium, Valenciennes, France, and therefore was granted public funds within the scope of the French Program "Investissements d'Avenir".

References

1. Ashok, P., Hashemi, V., Křetínský, J., Mohr, S.: DeepAbstract: neural network abstraction for accelerating verification. In: Hung, D.V., Sokolsky, O. (eds.) ATVA 2020. LNCS, vol. 12302, pp. 92–107. Springer, Cham (2020). https://doi.org/10.1007/978-3-030-59152-6_5
2. Badue, C., et al.: Self-driving cars: a survey. Expert Syst. Appl. **165**, 113816 (2021)
3. Boudardara, F., Boussif, A., Meyer, P.J., Ghazel, M.: Interval weight-based abstraction for neural network verification. In: Trapp, M., Schoitsch, E., Guiochet, J., Bitsch, F. (eds.) SAFECOMP 2022. LNCS, vol. 13415, pp. 330–342. Springer, Cham (2022). https://doi.org/10.1007/978-3-031-14862-0_24
4. Boudardara, F., Boussif, A., Meyer, P.-J., Ghazel, M.: A Review of Abstraction Methods towards Verifying Neural Networks. Association for Computing Machinery, New York (2023). https://doi.org/10.1145/3617508. ISSN 1539-9087
5. Cheng, C.-H., Nührenberg, G., Ruess, H.: Maximum resilience of artificial neural networks. In: D'Souza, D., Narayan Kumar, K. (eds.) ATVA 2017. LNCS, vol. 10482, pp. 251–268. Springer, Cham (2017). https://doi.org/10.1007/978-3-319-68167-2_18
6. Dutta, S., Jha, S., Sankaranarayanan, S., Tiwari, A.: Output range analysis for deep feedforward neural networks. In: Dutle, A., Muñoz, C., Narkawicz, A. (eds.) NFM 2018. LNCS, vol. 10811, pp. 121–138. Springer, Cham (2018). https://doi.org/10.1007/978-3-319-77935-5_9
7. Dutta, S., Jha, S., Sankaranarayanan, S., Tiwari, A.: Output range analysis for deep feedforward neural networks. In: Proceedings of the 10th NASA Formal Methods, pp. 121–138 (2018)
8. Elboher, Y.Y., Gottschlich, J., Katz, G.: An abstraction-based framework for neural network verification. In: Lahiri, S.K., Wang, C. (eds.) CAV 2020. LNCS, vol. 12224, pp. 43–65. Springer, Cham (2020). https://doi.org/10.1007/978-3-030-53288-8_3
9. Gehr, T., Mirman, M., Drachsler-Cohen, D., Tsankov, P., Chaudhuri, S., Vechev, M.: AI2: safety and robustness certification of neural networks with abstract interpretation. In: 2018 IEEE Symposium on Security and Privacy, pp. 3–18. IEEE (2018)

10. Huang, X., et al.: A survey of safety and trustworthiness of deep neural networks: verification, testing, adversarial attack and defence, and interpretability. Comput. Sci. Rev. **37**, 100270 (2020)
11. Huang, X., Kwiatkowska, M., Wang, S., Wu, M.: Safety verification of deep neural networks. In: Majumdar, R., Kunčak, V. (eds.) CAV 2017. LNCS, vol. 10426, pp. 3–29. Springer, Cham (2017). https://doi.org/10.1007/978-3-319-63387-9_1
12. Julian, K.D., Lopez, J., Brush, J.S., Owen, M.P., Kochenderfer, M.J.: Policy compression for aircraft collision avoidance systems. In: Proceedings of the 35th Digital Avionics Systems Conference (DASC), pp. 1–10. IEEE (2016)
13. Katz, G., Barrett, C., Dill, D.L., Julian, K., Kochenderfer, M.J.: Reluplex: an efficient SMT solver for verifying deep neural networks. In: Majumdar, R., Kunčak, V. (eds.) CAV 2017. LNCS, vol. 10426, pp. 97–117. Springer, Cham (2017). https://doi.org/10.1007/978-3-319-63387-9_5
14. Katz, G., et al.: The Marabou framework for verification and analysis of deep neural networks. In: Dillig, I., Tasiran, S. (eds.) CAV 2019. LNCS, vol. 11561, pp. 443–452. Springer, Cham (2019). https://doi.org/10.1007/978-3-030-25540-4_26
15. Lomuscio, A., Maganti, L.: An approach to reachability analysis for feed-forward ReLu neural networks. arXiv preprint (2017)
16. Meng, M.H., et al.: Adversarial robustness of deep neural networks: a survey from a formal verification perspective. IEEE Transactions on Dependable and Secure Computing (2022)
17. Prabhakar, P., Rahimi Afzal, Z.: Abstraction based output range analysis for neural networks. In: Advances in Neural Information Processing Systems, vol. 32. Curran Associates, Inc. (2019)
18. Pulina, L., Tacchella, A.: An abstraction-refinement approach to verification of artificial neural networks. In: Touili, T., Cook, B., Jackson, P. (eds.) CAV 2010. LNCS, vol. 6174, pp. 243–257. Springer, Heidelberg (2010). https://doi.org/10.1007/978-3-642-14295-6_24
19. Ristić-Durrant, D., Franke, M., Michels, K.: A review of vision-based on-board obstacle detection and distance estimation in railways. Sensors **21**(10), 3452 (2021)
20. Shriver, D., Xu, D., Elbaum, S., Dwyer, M.B.: Refactoring neural networks for verification. arXiv preprint (2019)
21. Singh, G., Gehr, T., Mirman, M., Püschel, M., Vechev, M.: Fast and effective robustness certification. In: Advances in Neural Information Processing Systems, vol. 31 (2018)
22. Singh, G., Gehr, T., Püschel, M., Vechev, M.: An abstract domain for certifying neural networks. Proc. ACM Program. Lang. **3**(POPL), 1–30 (2019)
23. Sotoudeh, M., Thakur, A.V.: Abstract neural networks. In: Pichardie, D., Sighireanu, M. (eds.) SAS 2020. LNCS, vol. 12389, pp. 65–88. Springer, Cham (2020). https://doi.org/10.1007/978-3-030-65474-0_4
24. Szegedy, C., et al.: Intriguing properties of neural networks. In: 2nd International Conference on Learning Representations, ICLR 2014 (2014)
25. Urban, C., Miné, A.: A review of formal methods applied to machine learning. arXiv preprint (2021)
26. Wang, S., Pei, K., Whitehouse, J., Yang, J., Jana, S.: Efficient formal safety analysis of neural networks. In: Advances in Neural Information Processing Systems, vol. 31 (2018)
27. Wang, S., Pei, K., Whitehouse, J., Yang, J., Jana, S.: Formal security analysis of neural networks using symbolic intervals. In: 27th USENIX Security Symposium (USENIX Security 18), pp. 1599–1614 (2018)

28. Xiang, W., Tran, H.D., Yang, X., Johnson, T.T.: Reachable set estimation for neural network control systems: a simulation-guided approach. IEEE Trans. Neural Netw. Learn. Syst. **32**(5), 1821–1830 (2020)
29. Zhang, H., Weng, T.W., Chen, P.Y., Hsieh, C.J., Daniel, L.: Efficient neural network robustness certification with general activation functions. Advances in Neural Information Processing Systems, vol. 31 (2018)

Towards Formal Verification of Node RED-Based IoT Applications

Ikram Garfatta[1,2]([✉]), Nour Elhouda Souid[1], and Kaïs Klai[1]

[1] University Sorbonne Paris North, LIPN UMR CNRS 7030, Villetaneuse, France
ikram.garfatta@lipn.univ-paris13.fr
[2] University of Tunis El Manar, National Engineering School of Tunis, OASIS,
Tunis, Tunisia

Abstract. The world has been witnessing a proliferation of Internet of Things (IoT) applications in the last decade thanks to the growing awareness of the opportunities they can bring in various domains. However, the widespread adoption of IoT technologies highlights the importance of ensuring the correctness of these applications, which can have an impact on their security and reliability. The work presented in this paper contributes to the efforts addressing the verification in IoT. In this work, we are particularly interested in IoT applications developed using Node-RED, which despite being one of the most used tools by the IoT community still lacks attention when it comes to formal verification of its applications' correctness and security.

We therefore propose a first step towards a formal approach based on the formalization of IoT applications modeled with Node-RED flows that permits their formal verification. This step consists in formally defining Node-RED concepts and proposing a semantically equivalent Petri net model that would serve as a starting point for the development of a model-checker for Node-RED applications.

Keywords: Internet of Things · Petri nets · Formal Verification · Node-RED

1 Introduction

Whether in the form of wearable gadgets, monitors or sensors, smart devices have pervaded almost every aspect of our modern life, especially throughout the last decade. This proliferation has played the main role in the advent of the Internet of Things (IoT) as a concept that has rapidly evolved and been associated with other emerging technologies such as Cloud computing. Its adoption has quickly expanded to range from consumer applications (e.g., for smart homes) to organizational, industrial and other applications (e.g., for transportation, healthcare, agriculture). Faced by the inevitability of the increasing connectivity between the different "things" in our physical and informational world, IoT raises concerns for the privacy of the exchanged data and security of the used applications. In fact,

B. Ben Hedia et al. (Eds.): VECoS 2023, LNCS 14368, pp. 90–104, 2024.
https://doi.org/10.1007/978-3-031-49737-7_7

many IoT-related attacks have been reported over the last years. For instance, in January 2012, hackers were able to exploit a vulnerability in the software of nearly 700 SecureView cameras which allowed them to access and share their live feeds [1]. A CNN report [8] declares that the FDA discovered vulnerabilities in implantable cardiac devices that could allow a hacker to administer inappropriate pacing or shocks to the patients. The fact that such attacks could have fatal consequences proves the necessity to make privacy and security a high priority in the design of IoT systems.

One of the most widely used design tools for IoT application is Node-RED [15]. It is an open-source visual programming tool used for wiring together hardware devices, APIs (Application Programming Interfaces), and online services. It provides a browser-based flow editor that allows users to create and deploy applications by connecting nodes visually. Users can therefore create complex automation tasks and IoT applications using Node-RED without the need for traditional programming. It is particularly popular for building home automation systems, IoT prototypes, and integrating various systems and services together. Node-RED supports a wide range of nodes contributed by the community, which can be easily extended and customized. Additionally, it has a large active user community, providing support, sharing flows, and offering additional functionality through custom nodes and modules.

Despite being widely used by the IoT community, we notice a lack in studies and tools that target the correctness and security of Node-RED applications. This can be traced back to the lack of formal definition of the different elements and concepts of Node-RED.

Through this present work, we aim to take the first step towards a formal verification approach for Node-RED applications, which consists in proposing a formal definition for such applications. More precisely, our final goal is to develop a model-checker dedicated for Node-RED, that would be used to verify the correctness of IoT applications with reference to properties that can be defined by the designer. The aim of this paper is therefore to prepare the input artifact for our end-goal model-checker in the form of a Petri net [12].

The contributions of our work can therefore be presented as follows:

1. We propose a formal definition of the different concepts in Node-RED.
2. We propose a formal representation of Node-RED application as a Petri net model.
3. We formally prove the semantic equivalence between Node-RED applications and our proposed Petri net model.

The rest of the paper is organized as follows. In Sect. 2 we present related work on the verification of IoT applications. Then, some preliminaries will be introduced in Sect. 3. We formalize the syntax and the semantics of Node-RED models in Sect. 4. In Sect. 5, we propose a Petri net representation of Node-RED models and prove the preservation of the semantics between the source (Node-RED) and the target formal model (corresponding Petri net). An example of application of our proposed formal model is presented in Sect. 6. Finally, our conclusions and future perspectives are presented in Sect. 7.

2 Related Work

The verification of different aspects of IoT systems has been addressed in literature. In [14] a taxonomy of formal verification approaches for IoT applications is proposed, in which the authors consider three main formal techniques, namely model checking, process algebra and theorem proving. The survey concludes that security is the most targeted issue by formal verification in IoT and that model checking is the most used formal technique in such a context.

For instance, in [11] the authors propose a model-checking-based approach for IoT security analysis. They start by transforming an IoT model expressed in a formalism that they propose into a probabilistic model and leverage the PRISM tool for its verification with respect to a set of attack trees that they also propose in the form of PCTL formulae expressing functional properties to be checked.

The authors in [5] present an MDE (Model-Driven Engineering) based approach for the formal verification of IoT applications using rewriting logic. This latter technique is leveraged to model and reason about the behavior and properties of IoT systems.

Frama-C has recently been used to verify software in the context of the IoT [2–4,9,10,13], more precisely the modules of Contiki, an open source operating system for the IoT.

While Node-RED itself has been widely adopted and used in practice, formal verification studies specifically focused on Node-RED applications are, to the best of our knowledge, non-existent. However, it's important to note that formal verification techniques and methodologies, in general, can be applied to the underlying components and technologies used within Node-RED applications. For example, if a Node-RED application interacts with a specific IoT protocol or relies on external services, the formal verification techniques applicable to those components can be utilized.

As Node-RED continues to gain popularity and mature as a platform, it is necessary to have more research and studies emerge in the future, specifically targeting the formal verification of Node-RED applications. It is an area that holds potential for further exploration and development, considering the growing importance of reliable and secure IoT applications.

3 Preliminaries

In this section, we introduce the different formal concepts that we will be using throughout this paper.

3.1 Petri Nets

A Petri net [12] is a formal model featuring execution semantics based on mathematics. It is visually represented as a directed bipartite graph containing transitions (represented as rectangles) and places (represented as circles). This formalism has proved to be an efficient means to model and analyse distributed systems and workflows.

Definition 1 (Petri net [12]). *A Petri net is 4-tuple* $\mathcal{N} = \langle P, T, F, W \rangle$ *s.t.:*

- *P is a finite set of places (circles)*
- *T is a finite set of transitions (rectangles) such that* $(P \cup T) \neq \emptyset$ *and* $(P \cap T) = \emptyset$;
- $F \subseteq (P \times T) \cup (T \times P)$ *is a flow relation;*
- $W : (P \times T) \cup (T \times P) \to \mathbb{N}$ *is a mapping assigning a weight to each arc.*

Each node $x \in P \cup T$ of the net has a pre-set and a post-set defined respectively as follows: $^\bullet x = \{y \in P \cup T \mid (y, x) \in F\}$, and $x^\bullet = \{y \in P \cup T \mid (x, y) \in F\}$.

The incidence matrix C associated with the net is defined as follows : $\forall (p, t) \in P \times T : C(p, t) = W(t, p) - W(p, t)$.

A marking of a Petri net $\mathcal{N}$ is a function $m : P \to \mathbb{N}$. The initial marking of $\mathcal{N}$ is denoted by m_0. The pair $\langle \mathcal{N}, m_0 \rangle$ is called a Petri net system. A transition t is said to be enabled by a marking m (denoted by $m \overset{t}{\longrightarrow}$) iff $\forall p \in {}^\bullet t, W(p, t) \leq m(p)$. If a transition t is enabled by a marking m, then its firing leads to a new marking m' (denoted by $m \overset{t}{\longrightarrow} m'$) s.t. $\forall p \in P : m'(p) = m(p) + C(p, t)$. Given a set of markings Q, we denote by $Enable(Q)$ the set of transitions enabled by elements of Q. The set of markings reachable from a marking m in $\mathcal{N}$ is denoted by $R(\mathcal{N}, m)$. The set of markings reachable from a marking m, by firing transitions of a subset $T' \subseteq T$ is denoted by $Sat(m, T')$. By extension, given a set of markings S and a set of transitions T', $Sat(S, T') = \bigcup_{m \in S} Sat(m, T')$. The reachability graph of a marked net $\langle \mathcal{N}, m_0 \rangle$, denoted $\mathcal{G}(\mathcal{N}, m_0)$, is a graph whose nodes are the markings of $R(\mathcal{N}, m_0)$, and the arcs are labeled with the transitions of T of $\mathcal{N}$. The initial node is the initial marking m_0, and a node (marking) m' is the successor of a node m iff $\exists t \in T$ s.t. $m \overset{t}{\to} m'$.

3.2   Labeled Transition Systems

While Petri nets are adequate for the syntactic representation of systems, Labeled Transition Systems are usually used to formally represent their execution semantics.

Definition 2 (Labeled Transition System). *A Labeled Transition System is a tuple* $G = \langle Q, q_0, \Sigma, \to, q_f \rangle$ *where:*

- *Q is a finite set of states;*
- $q_0 \in Q$ *is the initial state;*
- $q_f \in Q$ *is the final state;*
- Σ *is the alphabet of actions;*
- $\to : Q \times \Sigma \to Q$ *is the transition function.*

Let Σ be a finite alphabet. Σ^* is the set of all finite words over Σ including the empty word ϵ. Given two words $u, v \in \Sigma^*$, we denote by $u.v$ the concatenation of u and v defined in the usual way. $|u|$ stands for the length of u ($|\epsilon| = 0$).

In the following, $q \overset{a}{\to} q'$ denotes the fact that $\to (q, a) = q'$, and $q \overset{a}{\to}$ means that $\exists q'$ s.t. $\to (q, a) = q'$. By extending $\to$ to sequences of transitions

$\sigma = a_1 \cdot a_2 \cdot \ldots \cdot a_n$, $q \xrightarrow{\sigma} q_n$ denotes the fact that there exist states $q_1, \ldots, q_n$ s.t. $q \xrightarrow{\sigma_1} q_1 \xrightarrow{\sigma_2} q_2 \ldots \xrightarrow{\sigma_{n-1}} q_{n-1} \xrightarrow{\sigma_n} q_n$. We denote by $Succ(Q', a)$ the successor of a set of states $Q' \subseteq Q$ with the action $a \in \Sigma$ s.t. $Succ(Q', a) = \{q' \in Q$ such that $\exists q \in Q'$ and $q \xrightarrow{a} q'\}$.

The language of a LTS $G = \langle Q, q_0, \Sigma, \rightarrow, q_f \rangle$ is defined by $L(G) = \{\sigma \in \Sigma^*, q_0 \xrightarrow{\sigma} q_f\}$. Furthermore, a language $L_{Q' \subseteq Q}(G)$, is defined as $L_{Q'}(G) = \{\sigma \in \Sigma^*, q_0 \xrightarrow{\sigma} q'$ and $q' \in Q'\}$.

4 Formalization of Node-RED Applications

First created by IBM's Emerging Technology Services team and currently owned by the OpenJS Foundation, Node-RED is a flow-based programming tool. It provides a way to represent an application's behavior as a network of black-boxes or "nodes" (as they are known in Node-RED). Each node serves a specific job: it receives data, processes it, and then transmits the results to other nodes. Data transmission between nodes is handled by the network. In the following, we propose a formal definition for a Node-RED application, by formally defining its syntax and semantics.

4.1 Syntax of a Node-RED Application

In Node-RED, a flow operates by transmitting messages between nodes. These messages are basic JavaScript objects that can have various properties. Typically, a message will have a "msg.payload" property, which is the default property that most nodes will work with. Depending on the type of the node transferring the message, other properties can be required to characterize it (e.g., msg._msgid, msg.parts, etc.). Other properties can also be added by users.

Let $\mathcal{P}$ be the set of such properties. A Node-RED message can then be defined as follows:

Definition 3 (Node-RED message). *A Node-RED message is a tuple $NRM = \langle p_1, p_2, .., p_n \rangle$ such that $\forall i \in [1, n]$, $p_i \in \mathcal{P}$ is a message property and n is the number of its properties. A message NRM has at least one property called payload which represents its content.*

We will be referring to the simple example in Fig. 1 to illustrate the different definitions we propose throughout this section. In this example, the function node fn receives information from 3 input nodes (in blue) and sends out information to 3 output nodes (in green) according to its implemented behaviour described as follows: if fn receives at least 1 message from in_1 and 2 messages from in_2 then it sends out 2 messages on its output port $op4$ and 4 messages on its output port $op5$; if fn receives at least 1 message from in_2 and 2 messages from in_3 then it sends out 1 message on its output port $op4$ and 3 messages on its output port $op5$.

A Node-RED node is the main element in a Node-RED Flow. It is distinguishable and can be either an *input*, *intermediary* or *output* node depending on

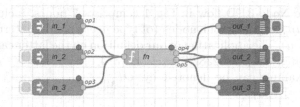

Fig. 1. A simple Node-RED illustrative example

its *type* (see Table 1 for the list of Node-RED node types and their correspondent categories). In the following, we denote by *Type* the set of all node types (i.e., $Type = Input \cup Inter \cup Output \wedge Input \cap Inter \cap Output = \emptyset$). An *input* node is generally used to inject information into a flow. It has no input ports and has at least one output port. An *output* node is generally used to send out information (e.g., to third-party components). It has exactly one input port and no output ports. On the other hand, an *intermediary* node has exactly one input port and at least one output port. Some nodes (e.g., function nodes) can be configured to have more than a single output port and their behaviour (i.e., message relaying) can depend on the source(s) and number of received messages on the input port. Hence, we formally define a Node-RED node as follows:[1]

Definition 4 (Node-RED node). *A Node-RED node nd is a tuple* $\langle id, t, Op \rangle$ *where:*

- *$id \in \mathbb{N}$ is the node's unique identifier.*
- *$t \in Type$ is the node's type*
- *$Op = \{op_i, \forall i \in [1, m]\}$ is the set of the node's output ports (with m the number of these output ports).*

Table 1. Node types in Node-RED

Category	Type
Input	serialin, emailin, inject, cachinput, MQTTinput, httpin, twitterin, Linkin
Output	serialout, emailout, debug, cachoutput, MQTToutput, httpout, twitterout, Linkout
Intermediary	function, template, http request, tcp request, switch, delay, trigger, change, range, csv, html, json, xml, rbe, yml, encrypt, decrypt, file, hmac, sqlinsert, encode, decode, sqldelete, sqlselect, sqlupdate, mongo

In the following, given a set of Node-RED nodes N, we denote by $OP_N = \bigcup_{nd \in N} \{op \in nd.Op\}$ the set of output ports in N.

---

[1] In the following, we denote by $x.y$ the element y of the tuple x.

Example. The Node-RED flow in Fig. 1 comprises 7 nodes, including 3 input nodes (of type *inject*), 3 output nodes (of type *debug*) and 1 intermediary node (of type *function*). The application of our definition on the latter can for instance give the following: $fn = \langle 52382, function, \{op4, op5\}\rangle$. The set of all output ports in this example can be denoted by: $OP_{\{in\_1, in\_2, in\_3, fn, out\_1, out\_2, out\_3\}} = \{op1, op2, op3, op4, op5\}$.

Definition 5 (Node-RED Flow). *A Node-RED flow is a tuple $\langle N, A, R\rangle$ where:*

- *N is the set of Node-RED nodes in the flow, such that $N = N_{in} \cup N_{out} \cup N_{int}$ where:*
  - *N_{in} is the set of Node-RED input nodes such that $\forall nd \in N_{in}$, $nd.t \in Input$ and $nd.Op \neq \emptyset$*
  - *N_{out} is the set of Node-RED output nodes such that $\forall nd \in N_{out}$, $nd.t \in Output$ and $nd.Op = \emptyset$*
  - *N_{int} is the set of Node-RED intermediate nodes s.t., that $\forall nd \in N_{int}$, $nd.t \in Inter$ and $nd.Op \neq \emptyset$.*
  - *N_{in}, N_{out} and N_{int} are pairwise disjoint*
- *$A \subseteq OP_N \times N$ is the flow relation defined as follows:*
  - *$\forall nd \in N_{in}$, $\nexists op \in OP_N$ s.t. $(op, nd) \in A$*
  - *$\forall nd \in N_{inter} \cup N_{out}$, $\exists nd' \in N_{in} \cup N_{inter}$ such that $\exists op' \in nd'.Op \wedge (op', nd) \in A$*
  - *$\forall nd \in N_{inter} \cup N_{in}, \forall op \in nd.Op$, $\exists nd' \in N_{inter} \cup N_{out}$ s.t. $(op, nd') \in A$*
- *R is a set of functions that define the behaviour of Node-RED nodes according to their input.*
  Let $VE_{nd} = \{ve : A \to \mathbb{N}\}$ be a set of functions that define the minimal valid entries for a node $nd \in N$ of the flow as per the definition of the node (in case of a node with a predefined behaviour) or that of the designer (in case of a node whose behaviour is set by the designer).
  R can therefore be defined as follows: $R = \{R_{nd} : VE_{nd} \to (A \to \mathbb{N}), \forall nd \in N\}$.
  For each node $nd \in N$ of the flow, R_{nd} is defined on VE_{nd} such that $R_{nd}(ve)$ is a function assigning to each arc in A an integer value (i.e., $A \to \mathbb{N}$).

Example. The application of our definition on the Node-RED flow F in Fig. 1 gives: $F = \langle N, A, R\rangle$ where:

- $N = \{in\_1, in\_2, in\_3, fn, out\_1, out\_2, out\_3\}$
- $A = \{(op1, fn), (op2, fn), (op3, fn), (op4, out\_1), (op4, out\_2), (op5, out\_2), (op5, out\_3)\}$
- $R = \{R_{nd}, \forall nd \in N\}$ such that:
  - $VE_{in\_1} = VE_{in\_2} = VE_{in\_3} = \{ve_0\}$ where ve_0 is defined such that $ve_0(a) = 0, \forall a \in A$.
    In fact, input nodes have no incoming arcs and therefore have no minimal valid entries.

- $VE_{out\_i} = \{ve_{op_j}, \forall op_j \in OP_N \text{ such that } (op_j, out\_i) \in A\}, \forall i \in \{1, 2, 3\}$, where ve_{op_j} is defined such that $ve_{op_j}(a) = 1$ if $a = (op_j, out\_i)$ and $ve_{op_j}(a) = 0$ otherwise.

  Output nodes will send out information as soon as they receive it and therefore their minimal valid entries would correspond to 1 message on any of the incoming arcs. In our example, we will explicitly have the following:

  * $VE_{out\_1} = \{ve_1\}$ where ve_1 is defined such that $ve_1(a) = 1$ if $a = (op_4, out\_1)$ and $ve_1(a) = 0$ otherwise.
  * $VE_{out\_2} = \{ve_2, ve_3\}$ where ve_2 is defined such that $ve_2(a) = 1$ if $a = (op_4, out\_2)$ and $ve_2(a) = 0$ otherwise; and ve_3 is defined such that $vc_3(a) = 1$ if $a = (op_5, out\_2)$ and $ve_3(u) = 0$ otherwise.
  * $VE_{out\_3} = \{ve_4\}$ where ve_4 is defined such that $ve_4(a) = 1$ if $a = (op_5, out\_3)$ and $ve_4(a) = 0$ otherwise.

- $VE_{fn} = \{ve_5, ve_6\}$ where:

  * $ve_5(a) = \begin{cases} 1 \text{ if } a = (op1, fn) \\ 2 \text{ if } a = (op2, fn) \\ 0 \text{ otherwise} \end{cases}$

  * $ve_6(a) = \begin{cases} 1 \text{ if } a = (op2, fn) \\ 2 \text{ if } a = (op3, fn) \\ 0 \text{ otherwise} \end{cases}$

The valid entries of the function node fn correspond to the behaviours defined in the description of the illustrative example in Fig. 1.

Input nodes inject messages into the flow, message by message. R_nd for such nodes are therefore defined as follows:

- $(R_{in\_1}(ve_0))(a) = \begin{cases} 1 \text{ if } a = (op1, nd) \\ 0 \text{ otherwise} \end{cases}$

- $(R_{in\_2}(ve_0))(a) = \begin{cases} 1 \text{ if } a = (op2, nd) \\ 0 \text{ otherwise} \end{cases}$

- $(R_{in\_3}(ve_0))(a) = \begin{cases} 1 \text{ if } a = (op3, nd) \\ 0 \text{ otherwise} \end{cases}$

Output nodes send messages out of the flow but do not circulate any messages in it. R_nd for such nodes are therefore defined as follows:

- $(R_{out\_1}(ve_1))(a) = 0, \forall a \in A$
- $(R_{out\_2}(ve_2))(a) = 0, \forall a \in A$
- $(R_{out\_2}(ve_3))(a) = 0, \forall a \in A$
- $(R_{out\_3}(ve_4))(a) = 0, \forall a \in A$
- $(R_{fn}(ve_5))(a) = \begin{cases} 2 \text{ if } a = (op4, nd) \\ 4 \text{ if } a = (op5, nd) \\ 0 \text{ otherwise} \end{cases}$

R_{nd} of the function node fn is defined according to the behaviours defined in the description of the illustrative example in Fig. 1.

$$\bullet \ (R_{fn}(ve_6))(a) = \begin{cases} 1 \text{ if } a = (op4, nd) \\ 3 \text{ if } a = (op5, nd) \\ 0 \text{ otherwise} \end{cases}$$

4.2   Semantics of a Node-RED Application

Having set the formal definition of the syntax of Node-RED applications in the previous subsection, we now focus on the formal definition of the semantics of such applications, which provides a formal means to describe their behaviours. To do so, we start by defining what a *state* is for a Node-RED flow (Definition 6) and then we define the dynamics between different states (Definitions 7–9). Finally, we propose a representation of these semantics using a transition system (Definition 10).

Definition 6 (Node-RED State).   *The* state *of a Node-RED flow $F = \langle N, A, R \rangle$ can be characterized as the numbers of messages on its arcs. This can be formally defined as a function: $S : A \mapsto \mathbb{N}$. We note that, similarly to what is conventionally the case for a marking in a Petri net, the function S can also be seen as a vector (of size $|A|$) in which each element represents the number of messages on one of the arcs of the flow.*

Definition 7 (Node-RED Initial State).   *We denote by S_0 the initial state of a Node-RED flow $\langle N, A, R \rangle$ where no messages are circulating between its nodes. Such a state is therefore defined as follows: $\forall a \in A, \ S(a) = 0$.*

Definition 8 (Valid Node-RED Node).   *A non initial node nd of a Node-RED flow $F = \langle N, A, R \rangle$ (i.e., $nd \in N \setminus N_{in}$) is said to be valid in a state S iff it receives from its predecessors a combination of messages that satisfies the minimal requirements defined by its flow relation R_{nd}. This can be formally expressed as follows:*
A node nd is said to be valid under a state S iff $\exists ve \in VE_{nd}$ s.t $S \geq ve$ and is denoted $S \xrightarrow{nd}$.

Definition 9 (Node Execution).   *If a node nd in a Node-RED flow $F = \langle N, A, R \rangle$ is valid under a state S (i.e., $S \xrightarrow{nd}$), then its execution results in a new state S' defined as follows:*
$S' = S - ve + R_{nd}(ve)$ such that $ve \in VE_{nd} \wedge ve \leq S$. This is denoted by $S \xrightarrow{nd/ve} S'$.

Definition 10 (Semantics of a Node-RED flow as a transition system).   *A Node-RED flow $\langle N, A, R \rangle$ is a transition system $\langle Q, q_0, \Sigma, \rightarrow, q_f \rangle$ where:*

- $Q = \{q_s; \forall s \in S\}$
- $q_0 = q_s \in Q$ s.t $s = S_0$
- $\Sigma = \{a_{nd/ve}; \forall nd \in N \text{ and } \forall ve \in VE_{nd}\}$
- $\rightarrow: Q \times \Sigma \rightarrow Q$ s.t $\rightarrow (q_s, a_{nd/ve}) = q_{s'}$ iff $s \xrightarrow{nd/ve} s'$

5   From Node-RED to Petri Nets

Now that we have proposed a formal definition for the syntax and semantics of Node-RED flows, this section will focus on the transformation of such flows into semantically equivalent Petri net models. In fact, such a transformation allows to take benefits from the existing verification tools allowed by Petri net representation. Verifying the correctness of a Node-RED flow would therefore amount to the verification of the correctness of its corresponding Petri net.

5.1   Formalization of a Node-RED Flow

In the following, we propose a Petri net model for a Node-RED flow, which we will later prove to be semantically equivalent. Such a Petri net is obtained by creating a *place* for each arc in the represented flow, a set of *transitions* for each node (a transition for each specified behaviour). These elements are then interconnected according to the definition of the set of functions R of the modeled Node-RED flow.

Definition 11. *A Node Red flow $\langle N, A, R \rangle$ is a Petri net $\langle P, T, F, W \rangle$ where:*

- $P = \{p_a, \forall a \in A\}$
- $T = \bigcup_{nd \in N} T_{nd}$ *where* $T_{nd} = \{t_{ve}^{nd}, \forall ve \in VE_{nd}\}$
- F *is defined s.t.* $\forall nd \in N, \forall ve \in VE_{nd}, \forall a \in A$

$$\begin{cases} (p_a, t_{ve}^{nd}) \in F \text{ iff } ve(a) \neq 0 \\ (t_{ve}^{nd}, p_a) \in F \text{ iff } (R_{nd}(ve))(a) \neq 0 \end{cases}$$

- W *is defined s.t.*

$$\begin{cases} \forall (p_a, t_{ve}^{nd}) \in F, \ W((p_a, t_{ve}^{nd})) = ve(a) \\ \forall (t_{ve}^{nd}, p_a) \in F, \ W((p_a, t_{ve}^{nd})) = (R_{nd}(ve))(a) \end{cases}$$

Example. The application of the transformation on the illustrative example of Fig. 1 yields the Petri net in Fig. 2 that comprises 8 transitions: 3 "source" transitions (in_1, in_2 and in_3) representing the input nodes in the flow, 2 transitions (fn_1 and fn_2) representing the function node (a transition for each specified behaviour for fn) and 4 "sink" transitions (out_1, out_2_1, out_2_2 and out_3) representing the output nodes in the flow (a transition for each link to an output node). It also includes 7 places (pa_1 to pa_7) representing the arcs in the flow. These elements are linked as per the aforementioned formalization. We note that this would result in an unbounded Petri net (the source transitions can always fire in order to simulate real life unbounded resources). However, in order to allow the analysis of the system, we need to make the Petri net bounded. To do so, we add an input place p_{in} that we link to every source transition and that initially contains as many tokens as messages that can be injected into the flow, and an output place p_{out} that we link to every sink transition.

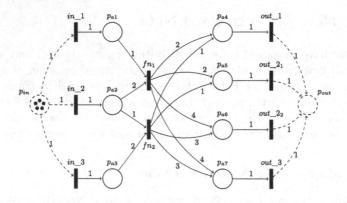

Fig. 2. Petri net of the illustrative example

5.2 Semantics Equivalence/Preservation

In order to ensure that the Petri net resulting from the formalization that we propose for Node-RED applications exhibits an equivalent behaviour to the modeled application, we need to establish the semantics equivalence between the two models.

We recall that the semantics of a marked Petri net $\langle \mathcal{N}, m_0 \rangle$ are represented by its reachability graph $\mathcal{G}(\mathcal{N}, m_0)$ (see Definition 1), which can adequately be represented by a LTS whose states are the set $R(\mathcal{N}, m_0)$ (amongst which, the initial state q_0 corresponds to the initial marking m_0) and alphabet of actions is the set of transitions T. Its transition function is the counterpart of the arcs in the reachability graph (i.e., $\rightarrow (q, a) = q'$ iff $\exists m, m' \in R(\mathcal{N}, m_0)$ that correspond to q and q' respectively, and $\exists t \in T$ that corresponds to a, such that $m \xrightarrow{t} m'$).

Definition 12 (Marking Equivalence). *A state S^N of a Node-RED flow $\langle N, A, R \rangle$ is said to be equivalent to a marking m^P of a corresponding Petri net $\langle P, T, F, W \rangle$ iff $\forall p_a \in P$, $m^P(p_a) = S^N(a)$. We note $S^N \equiv m^P$.*

Definition 13 (Execution Sequence Equivalence). *An execution sequence of length k of a Node-RED flow $\langle N, A, R \rangle$, denoted $\sigma_k^N = nd_i/ve_i \cdot \ldots \cdot nd_j/ve_j$ (with $k = j - i + 1$), is said to be equivalent to an execution sequence of the same length of a corresponding Petri net $\langle P, T, F, W \rangle$, denoted $\sigma_k^T = t_{ve_i}^{nd_i} \cdot \ldots \cdot t_{ve_j}^{nd_j}$, iff $\exists S_1^N, S_2^N, m_1^P$ and m_2^P such that $(S_1^N \equiv m_1^P \wedge S_1^N \xrightarrow{\sigma_k^N} S_2^N \wedge m_1^P \xrightarrow{\sigma_k^T} m_2^P) \implies S_2^N \equiv m_2^P$. We note $\sigma_k^N \equiv \sigma_k^T$.*

Theorem 1. *Let $\mathcal{F}$ be a Node-RED flow and $\mathcal{N}$ the corresponding Petri net as per Sect. 5.1, then $\mathcal{F}$ and $\mathcal{N}$ are semantically equivalent.*

Proof. Let $\mathcal{F}$ be a Node-RED flow and $\mathcal{N}$ the corresponding Petri net as per Sect. 5.1. In order to prove that $\mathcal{F}$ and $\mathcal{N}$ are semantically equivalent we need to prove that: *(I)* $\forall \sigma_k^N, \exists \sigma_k^T$, and *(II)* $\forall \sigma_k^T, \exists \sigma_k^N$, such that $\sigma_k^N \equiv \sigma_k^T, \forall k \in [1, m]$ with m the length of the longest execution sequence. We start by proving *(I)*:

- Let $P(n)$ the statement: $\forall \sigma_n^N, \exists \sigma_n^T$ such that $\sigma_n^N \equiv \sigma_n^T$
- $P(1) : \forall \sigma_1^N, \exists \sigma_1^T$ such that $\sigma_1^N \equiv \sigma_1^T$. This can be derived from the formalization in Sect. 5.1. In fact, the initial marking of $\mathcal{N}$ (m_0^P) corresponds to the initial state S_0^N of $\mathcal{F}$ (see Definition 7). The initial state of a Node-RED flow being a state where no messages are circulating on its arcs, the initial marking of the corresponding Petri net is a marking where no tokens are present in any of its places. Therefore, only *source* transitions are fireable in this initial marking. By definition, these transitions represent *input* nodes, which are the only nodes that can be executed from the initial state of the flow. We can then deduce that the set of fireable transitions ($m_0^P \rightarrow$) corresponds to the set of valid nodes ($S_0^N \rightarrow$). Additionally, the marking m_i^P obtained by firing $t_{ve_i}^{nd_i}$ is equivalent to that obtained by executing nd_i/ve_i ($m_i^P \equiv S_i^N$) since the marking m_i^P is defined as to correspond to the effects of the execution of nd_i considering ve_i in $\mathcal{F}$.
- Assume that $P(k) : \forall \sigma_k^N = nd_1/ve_1 \cdot ... \cdot nd_k/ve_ve_k, \exists \sigma_k^T = t_{ve_1}^{nd_1} \cdot ... \cdot t_{ve_k}^{nd_k}$ such that $\sigma_k^N \equiv \sigma_k^T$ is true for some $k \in [2, m-1]$. We will prove that $P(k+1) : \forall \sigma_{k+1}^N = nd_1/ve_1 \cdot ... \cdot nd_{k+1}/ve_{k+1}, \exists \sigma_{k+1}^T = t_{ve_1}^{nd_1} \cdot ... \cdot t_{ve_{k+1}}^{nd_{k+1}}$ such that $\sigma_{k+1}^N \equiv \sigma_{k+1}^T$ is true.

$$\sigma_{k+1}^N \equiv \sigma_{k+1}^T \implies \exists nd \in N, ve \in VE_{nd}, t_{ve}^{nd} \in T \text{ such that } \sigma_k^N \cdot nd/ve \equiv \sigma_k^T \cdot t_{ve}^{nd} \tag{1}$$

$$\sigma_k^N \equiv \sigma_k^T \iff (S_0^N \xrightarrow{\sigma_k^N} S_k^N \wedge m_0^P \xrightarrow{\sigma_k^T} m_k^T \wedge S_k^N \equiv m_k^T) \tag{2}$$

Analogously to the reasoning in the previous point, we can deduce that:

$$\forall nd \in N, \forall ve \in VE_{nd} \text{ such that } S_k^N \xrightarrow{nd/ve} S_{k+1}^N,$$
$$\exists t_{ve}^{nd} \in T \text{ such that } (m_k^T \xrightarrow{t_{ve}^{nd}} m_{k+1}^T \wedge S_{k+1}^N \equiv m_{k+1}^T) \tag{3}$$

And therefore:

$$\forall \sigma_{k+1}^N = nd_1/ve_1 \cdot ... \cdot nd_{k+1}/ve_{k+1}, \exists \sigma_{k+1}^T = t_{ve_1}^{nd_1} \cdot ... \cdot t_{ve_{k+1}}^{nd_{k+1}} \text{ such that } \sigma_{k+1}^N \equiv \sigma_{k+1}^T \tag{4}$$

The second part (II) is provable following a similar reasoning.

$\square$

6   Example of Application

As application, we consider a healthcare case study (Fig. 3) depicting a mobile medical application that tracks heath indicators of the user[2]. Our use case considers IoT integration with Cloud computing. We use a connected watch, fog nodes, a private and a public Cloud, and a web application, which together form

---

[2] To develop this use case, we used the healthcare case study in [16]; where we changed the factories ensuring cardiovascular diseases and the type of alerts sent to the patients in case of danger.

a medical application. This latter provides continuous monitoring of the vital data of a given patient. Regular or routine measurements could help to detect the first symptoms of heart disease, and make it possible to immediately trigger an alert. The vital information collected by the watch worn by the patient includes blood sugar level, blood pressure, cholesterol level and physical activity.

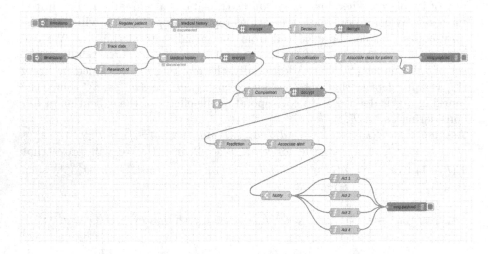

Fig. 3. Node Red flow

The application of our formalization on this Node-RED example yields the Petri net model depicted in Fig. 4.

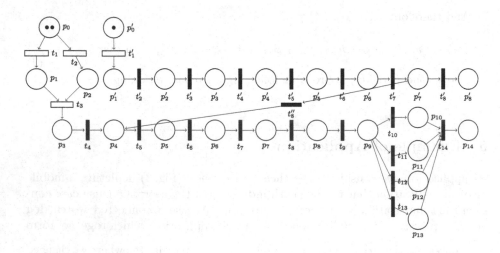

Fig. 4. Use Case Petri Net

7 Conclusion and Perspectives

In this paper we proposed a first step towards closing the gap in the formal verification of Node-RED-based IoT applications. More specifically, we proposed a formalization of both the syntax and the execution semantics of Node-RED flows. Then, we proposed to use Petri nets model as a pivot formal model by giving a way to translate Node-RED flows to a semantically equivalent Petri net. This model would eventually serve as a basis for our end-goal model-checker for Node-RED applications. The formal definition that we propose for Node-RED flows could also serve as a starting point for other researchers to develop their own formal verification approaches.

Besides the development of a generic model-checker, we note that we are particularly interested in the verification of the *opacity* property [7] in IoT applications. Currently, we are working on using the *SOG* technique [6] to check this property and eventually integrate our approach as a plugin in the Node-RED platform that will perform the required steps transparently in the background in order to provide a seamless experience to the users. Further perspectives include the enforcement of the opacity as well as other security properties, using the supervisory and control theory.

Our ongoing research efforts also encompass the formalization of Node-RED applications using Colored Petri Nets (CPN). This parallel approach using CPN adds an additional layer of formalization that provides complementary perspectives which allows the verification of a wider range of properties (e.g., data-related) while keeping the models compact.

References

1. Adhikari, R.: Webcam maker takes FTC's heat for internet-of-things security failure. https://www.technewsworld.com/story/78891.html
2. Blanchard, A., Kosmatov, N., Loulergue, F.: Ghosts for lists: a critical module of Contiki verified in Frama-C. In: Dutle, A., Muñoz, C., Narkawicz, A. (eds.) NFM 2018. LNCS, vol. 10811, pp. 37–53. Springer, Cham (2018). https://doi.org/10.1007/978-3-319-77935-5_3
3. Blanchard, A., Kosmatov, N., Loulergue, F.: Logic against ghosts: comparison of two proof approaches for a list module. In: Hung, C., Papadopoulos, G.A. (eds.) Proceedings of the 34th ACM/SIGAPP Symposium on Applied Computing, SAC 2019, Limassol, Cyprus, 8–12 April 2019, pp. 2186–2195. ACM (2019)
4. Blanchard, A., Loulergue, F., Kosmatov, N.: Towards full proof automation in Frama-C using auto-active verification. In: Badger, J.M., Rozier, K.Y. (eds.) NFM 2019. LNCS, vol. 11460, pp. 88–105. Springer, Cham (2019). https://doi.org/10.1007/978-3-030-20652-9_6
5. Fortas, A., Kerkouche, E., Chaoui, A.: Formal verification of IoT applications using rewriting logic: an MDE-based approach. Sci. Comput. Program. **222**, 102859 (2022)
6. Haddad, S., Ilié, J.-M., Klai, K.: Design and evaluation of a symbolic and abstraction-based model checker. In: Wang, F. (ed.) ATVA 2004. LNCS, vol. 3299, pp. 196–210. Springer, Heidelberg (2004). https://doi.org/10.1007/978-3-540-30476-0_19

7. Hughes, D.J.D., Shmatikov, V.: Information hiding, anonymity and privacy: a modular approach. J. Comput. Secur. **12**(1), 3–36 (2004)
8. Larson, S.: FDA confirms that St. Jude's cardiac devices can be hacked. https://money.cnn.com/2017/01/09/technology/fda-st-jude-cardiac-hack/
9. Loulergue, F., Blanchard, A., Kosmatov, N.: Ghosts for lists: from axiomatic to executable specifications. In: Dubois, C., Wolff, B. (eds.) TAP 2018. LNCS, vol. 10889, pp. 177–184. Springer, Cham (2018). https://doi.org/10.1007/978-3-319-92994-1_11
10. Mangano, F., Duquennoy, S., Kosmatov, N.: Formal verification of a memory allocation module of Contiki with FRAMA-C: a case study. In: Cuppens, F., Cuppens, N., Lanet, J.-L., Legay, A. (eds.) CRiSIS 2016. LNCS, vol. 10158, pp. 114–120. Springer, Cham (2017). https://doi.org/10.1007/978-3-319-54876-0_9
11. Ouchani, S.: Ensuring the functional correctness of IoT through formal modeling and verification. In: Abdelwahed, E.H., Bellatreche, L., Golfarelli, M., Méry, D., Ordonez, C. (eds.) MEDI 2018. LNCS, vol. 11163, pp. 401–417. Springer, Cham (2018). https://doi.org/10.1007/978-3-030-00856-7_27
12. Petri, C.A.: Concepts of net theory. In: Mathematical Foundations of Computer Science: Proceedings of Symposium and Summer School, Strbské Pleso, High Tatras, Czechoslovakia, 3–8 September 1973, pp. 137–146 (1973)
13. Peyrard, A., Kosmatov, N., Duquennoy, S., Lille, I., Raza, S.: Towards formal verification of Contiki: analysis of the AES-CCM* modules with Frama-C. In: Giustiniano, D., Koutsonikolas, D., Banchs, A., Mingozzi, E., Chowdhury, K.R. (eds.) Proceedings of the 2018 International Conference on Embedded Wireless Systems and Networks, EWSN 2018, Madrid, Spain, 14–16 February 2018, pp. 264–269. Junction Publishing, Canada/ ACM (2018)
14. Souri, A., Norouzi, M.: A state-of-the-art survey on formal verification of the internet of things applications. J. Serv. Sci. Res. **11**(1), 47–67 (2019)
15. Technology, I.E.: Node-red (2020). https://nodered.org
16. Zrelli, R., Yeddes, M., Hadj-Alouane, N.B.: Checking and enforcing security through opacity in healthcare applications. In: Braubach, L., et al. (eds.) ICSOC 2017. LNCS, vol. 10797, pp. 161–173. Springer, Cham (2018). https://doi.org/10.1007/978-3-319-91764-1_13

Formal Verification of a Post-quantum Signal Protocol with Tamarin

Hugo Beguinet[1,2], Céline Chevalier[2,3], Thomas Ricosset[1(✉)], and Hugo Senet[1,2]

[1] Thales, Gennevilliers, France
{hugo.beguinet,thomas.ricosset,hugo.senet}@thalesgroup.com
[2] DIENS, École normale supérieure, CNRS, Inria, PSL University, Paris, France
{hugo.beguinet,celine.chevalier,hugo.senet}@ens.fr
[3] CRED, Université Paris-Panthéon-Assas, Paris, France

Abstract. The Signal protocol is used by billions of people for instant messaging in applications such as Facebook Messenger, Google Messages, Signal, Skype, and WhatsApp. However, advances in quantum computing threaten the security of the cornerstone of this protocol: the Diffie-Hellman key exchange. There actually are resistant alternatives, called post-quantum secure, but replacing the Diffie-Hellman key exchange with these new primitives requires a deep revision of the associated security proof. While the security of the current Signal protocol has been extensively studied with hand-written proofs and computer-verified symbolic analyses, its quantum-resistant variants lack symbolic security analyses.

In this work, we present the first symbolic security model for post-quantum variants of the Signal protocol. Our model focuses on the core state machines of the two main sub-protocols of Signal: the X3DH handshake, and the so-called *double ratchet* protocol. Then we show, with an automated proof using the Tamarin prover, that instantiated with the Hashimoto-Katsumata-Kwiatkowski-Prest post-quantum Signal's handshake from PKC'21, and the Alwen-Coretti-Dodis KEM-based double ratchet from EUROCRYPT'19, the resulting post-quantum Signal protocol has equivalent security properties to its current classical counterpart.

Keywords: Secure instant messaging · Signal protocol · Quantum resistant · Formal verification · Tamarin prover · X3DH · Double ratchet

1 Introduction

The Signal protocol is divided into two sub-protocols: X3DH [21], and the double ratchet protocol [20]. The X3DH protocol can be seen as an Authenticated Key Exchange (AKE) protocol. It ensures the authenticity of an initial key shared between two users. It is an asynchronous protocol, which means that there is no need for users to be online at the same time to initialize the protocol. To use the X3DH protocol, each user must first generate a long-term static pair of public and private keys for them to be authenticated, as well as a batch of ephemeral pairs of public and private keys. Both

© The Author(s), under exclusive license to Springer Nature Switzerland AG 2024
B. Ben Hedia et al. (Eds.): VECoS 2023, LNCS 14368, pp. 105–121, 2024.
https://doi.org/10.1007/978-3-031-49737-7_8

long-term public keys and ephemeral key batches are then stored on an honest intermediate server which acts as a buffer. When Bob wants to start a conversation with Alice,
he sends a request to the server, and then receives the Alice's long-term public key and
a fresh Alice's ephemeral public key from her batch. These two public keys enable Bob
to perform the X3DH handshake protocol by sending a message to Alice, which will
enables her to derive their X3DH pre-shared secret key when she is online.

The double ratchet protocol is used to encrypt messages to send through the Signal
protocol with an Authenticated Encryption with Associated Data (AEAD) scheme and
a session key that is shared between the two parties. The session key is renewed each
time a message is sent, using symmetric and asymmetric mechanisms called ratchets.
The double ratchet protocol is initialized with the X3DH pre-shared key as session
key, and an ephemeral public key from the corresponding batch as public key. Then,
to send a message, the public key is used to exchange a fresh secret key, from which
the new session key is derived with the output of a one-way function applied to the
current session key. In addition, a new ephemeral key pair is generated whose public
key is encrypted then sent with the message, using this new session key. This protocol
is repeated for each message sent to ensure strong security properties such as forward
secrecy and post-compromise recovery against passive adversaries.

The current Signal protocol heavily uses the well-known, flexible, and efficient, but
vulnerable to quantum attacks, Diffie-Hellman (DH) key exchange protocol. However,
with the threat of upcoming quantum computers, post-quantum alternatives are subject
to extensive analysis in order to gain assurance in their security. In 2016, the NIST initi-
ated a process to evaluate and standardize quantum-resistant key-establishment and signature schemes, but all remaining candidates in the key-establishment category are key
encapsulation mechanisms (KEMs) like RSA, and not key exchanges like DH. Consequently, the integration of post-quantum KEMs in cryptographic protocols is quite
challenging due to the differences between KEMs and DH, which requires some fundamental adjustments to these protocols to maintain the same security guarantees.

Aside from that, the active area of formal protocol verification is increasingly
accompanying protocol specifications. Designing cryptographic protocols is known to
be hard to get right and hand-written proofs remain highly complex and error-prone.
At the design level, automatic verification aims to manage the complexity of security
proofs and even reveal subtle flaws or as-yet-unknown attacks as the historic example of
the man-in-the-middle attack [16]. Efficient automatic verification tools as Tamarin [17]
or ProVerif [6] have been used to analyze large, real-world protocols. For instance,
ProVerif has been used to analyze TLS 1.3 [4] and Signal [14] and Tamarin as been
used to analyze the 5G AKE protocol [3] and TLS 1.3 [10].

Related Works. The security of the (EC)DH-based Signal protocol has been extensively
studied using hand-written proofs [9]. Those proofs were completed with a symbolic
analysis [14] using the ProVerif prover. Regarding the transition to post-quantum cryptography, there are KEM-based alternatives to the Signal sub-protocols X3DH [7,12]
(the security properties in [12] being closer to that of X3DH, in particular thanks to
the encryption of the signature) and double ratchet [1], with hand-written proofs for
the same security properties as the current Signal protocol. Such KEM-based protocols can be instantiated with post-quantum KEMs from the NIST competition such as

Kyber [2], which will be the first NIST PQC standard for key-establishment. However, those potential replacements for X3DH and double ratchet have so far lacked computer-verified symbolic analyses which results in a limited trust in these protocols. By contrast, some other protocols, such as WireGuard [13] and (KEM)TLS [8,19], already have computer-verified symbolic analyses for post-quantum variants, both using the Tamarin prover.

Contributions. We present the first symbolic proof of a post-quantum variant of the Signal protocol. Our model focuses on the core state machines of the two main sub-protocols of this variant: the Hashimoto-Katsumata-Kwiatkowski-Prest post-quantum X3DH handshake [12] which we refer to as *PQ-X3DH*, and the Alwen-Coretti-Dodis KEM-based double ratchet [1] that we call *KEM-Double-Ratchet*. Then we show, using the Tamarin prover, that these two protocols meet the same security properties as classical X3DH and double ratchet protocols. In addition, we prove the well-formedness of the two models, which informally means that their behavior is as expected.

Our PQ-X3DH Tamarin symbolic analysis ensures the integrity of the two exchanged messages, the authentication of users, the resistance to unknown key-share attacks and replay attacks, and other properties, such as the weak forward secrecy [15] and the key compromise attack resistance, to mitigate the leak of secret information.

With regard to KEM-Double-Ratchet, our Tamarin model ensures the integrity of all the messages, the forward secrecy, and the post-compromise recovery [1]. It is worth noting that in the particular case of Signal, post-compromise recovery is met only if the adversary is passive during the recovering process. While within the double ratchet protocol two parties can exchange a potentially infinite number of messages, we model only three exchanges, which represents the minimum number of exchanges for each security property to hold. A simple induction argument then enables us to generalize these properties to any number of exchanges. To our knowledge, our formal verification model is the first one that covers the post-compromise recovery security property.

Outline. In Sect. 2 we present the two sub-protocols of the considered variant of the Signal protocol and their Tamarin model. Then we present in Sect. 3 the Tamarin formalism used in our symbolic analysis, the different security properties verified, and the results of our formal verification.

2 A KEM-Based Signal Protocol

In this section, we describe the KEM-based variant of the Signal protocol that is the subject of our symbolic analysis. As explained in the introduction, the Signal protocol is separated in two sub-protocols providing different functionalities, we respect this separation for this KEM-based variant in order to facilitate its analysis and clearly identify the contribution of each sub-protocol in the security of the whole protocol. The first sub-protocol named PQ-X3DH is used as authenticated key agreement while the second one named KEM-double-ratchet is used for secure instant messaging by refreshing the session key at each time a message is sent.

2.1 The PQ-X3DH Protocol

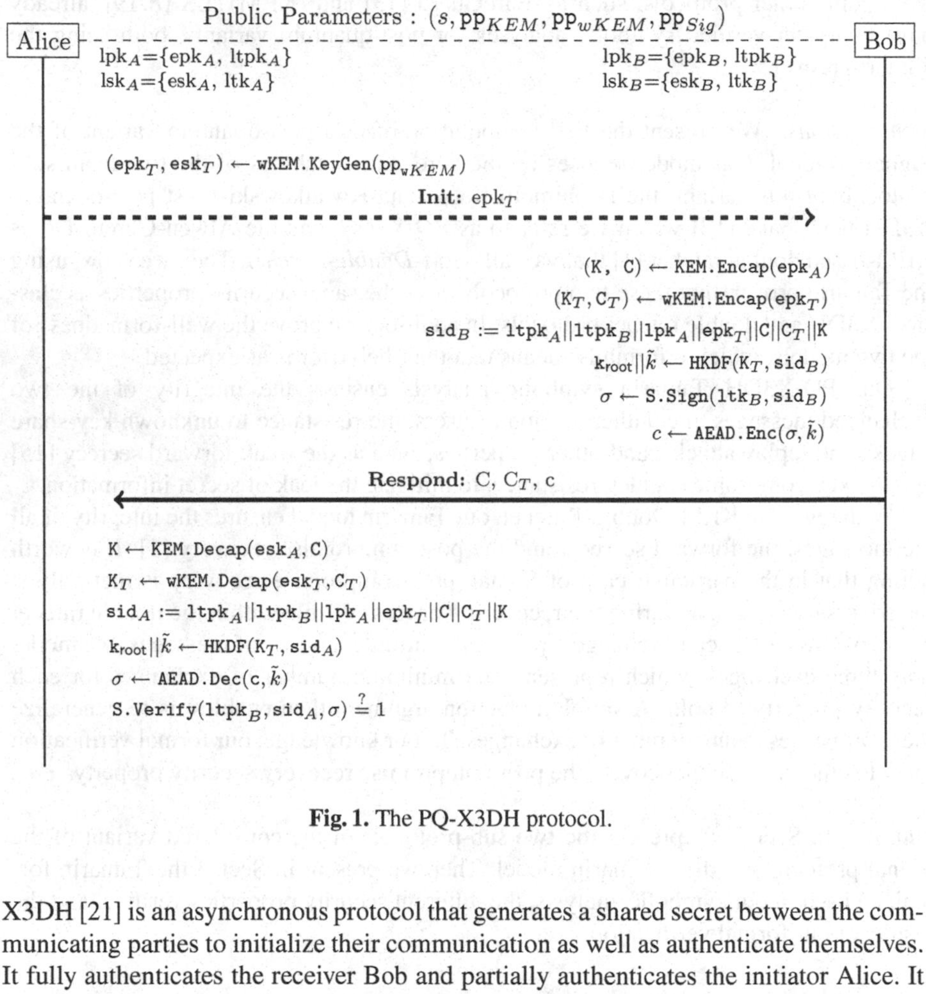

Public Parameters : $(s, \text{PP}_{KEM}, \text{PP}_{wKEM}, \text{PP}_{Sig})$

Alice --- Bob

$\text{lpk}_A = \{\text{epk}_A, \text{ltpk}_A\}$ $\text{lpk}_B = \{\text{epk}_B, \text{ltpk}_B\}$

$\text{lsk}_A = \{\text{esk}_A, \text{ltk}_A\}$ $\text{lsk}_B = \{\text{esk}_B, \text{ltk}_B\}$

$(\text{epk}_T, \text{esk}_T) \leftarrow \text{wKEM.KeyGen}(\text{pp}_{wKEM})$

Init: epk_T

$\cdots\cdots\cdots\cdots\cdots\cdots\cdots\cdots\cdots\cdots\cdots\cdots\cdots\cdots\cdots\cdots\cdots\cdots\rightarrow$

$(\text{K, C}) \leftarrow \text{KEM.Encap}(\text{epk}_A)$

$(\text{K}_T, \text{C}_T) \leftarrow \text{wKEM.Encap}(\text{epk}_T)$

$\text{sid}_B := \text{ltpk}_A||\text{ltpk}_B||\text{lpk}_A||\text{epk}_T||\text{C}||\text{C}_T||\text{K}$

$\text{k}_{\text{root}}||\tilde{k} \leftarrow \text{HKDF}(\text{K}_T, \text{sid}_B)$

$\sigma \leftarrow \text{S.Sign}(\text{ltk}_B, \text{sid}_B)$

$c \leftarrow \text{AEAD.Enc}(\sigma, \tilde{k})$

Respond: C, C_T, c

$\longleftarrow$

$\text{K} \leftarrow \text{KEM.Decap}(\text{esk}_A, \text{C})$

$\text{K}_T \leftarrow \text{wKEM.Decap}(\text{esk}_T, \text{C}_T)$

$\text{sid}_A := \text{ltpk}_A||\text{ltpk}_B||\text{lpk}_A||\text{epk}_T||\text{C}||\text{C}_T||\text{K}$

$\text{k}_{\text{root}}||\tilde{k} \leftarrow \text{HKDF}(\text{K}_T, \text{sid}_A)$

$\sigma \leftarrow \text{AEAD.Dec}(c, \tilde{k})$

$\text{S.Verify}(\text{ltpk}_B, \text{sid}_A, \sigma) \overset{?}{=} 1$

Fig. 1. The PQ-X3DH protocol.

X3DH [21] is an asynchronous protocol that generates a shared secret between the communicating parties to initialize their communication as well as authenticate themselves. It fully authenticates the receiver Bob and partially authenticates the initiator Alice. It is called asynchronous because both parties can initiate the connection while the other is offline. Such property provides flexibility but could completely break the protocol in the case of a malicious server. Apart from such a case the asynchronous protocol is highly secure. We consider here the PQ-X3DH presented in [12] which preserve the security properties of the classical protocol and we focus on the variant of PQ-X3DH that does not use a signature to fully authenticate Alice. The motivation for this change is to allow Alice to deny having taken part in the exchange, in the same way that Bob can deny it thanks to the encryption of his signature.

The PQ-X3DH sub-protocol is presented in Fig. 1. Two key encapsulation mechanisms, KEM and wKEM, are employed as building blocks in this key agreement protocol. wKEM, which is IND-CPA secure, is for ephemeral use. KEM is IND-CCA secure here. Tamarin considers the public-key encryption as ideal (thus IND-CCA), but for an ephemeral use, IND-CPA is sufficient.

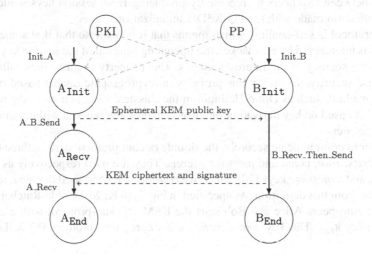

Fig. 2. Graph of the Tamarin PQ-X3DH model.

Tamarin Model. Since Tamarin has no built-in KEM we replace the KEM with an asymmetric encryption scheme encrypting a fresh ephemeral key. The two approaches are equivalent considering the idealization of cryptographic primitives used in Tamarin. Our model for the PQ-X3DH protocol is represented as the state machine in Fig. 2 with nine transition rules:

- PKI and PP: these rules formalize the Public Key Infrastructure (PKI), the Public Parameters (PP). PKI assigns only once a long term key with an ephemeral key to a user. Instead of handling non-replayability with a batch of ephemeral one-time keys we directly use restrictions to ensure the a key can only be used once.
- Init_A and Init_B: each user get from PKI and PP the public parameters and public keys needed for the PQ-X3DH protocol.
- A_B_Send: Alice sends an ephemeral public key to initiate a key encapsulation.
- B_Recv_Then_Send: Bob receives Alice's ephemeral public key, encapsulates two secret keys into two KEM ciphertexts, one with Alice's ephemeral public key and wKEM, the other by using Alice's long-term public key and KEM. Bob also sign the protocol transcript and send his signature encrypted with an AEAD scheme.
- A_Recv: Alice receives Bob's ciphertext and signature and derives a session key that will be used by Alice and Bob to communicate. Then, she decrypts and verifies the signature.
- RevealE: Reveals to the attacker the ephemeral secret keys.
- RevealL: Reveals to the attacker the long-term secret keys.

2.2   The KEM-Double-Ratchet Protocol

The double ratchet protocol (DR for short) is used for securing an ongoing exchange of messages between two peers by repeatedly producing fresh session keys while saving the authentication made with the PQ-X3DH initialization.

This protocol is self-healing, which means that it is made so that if at some point a user's key is intercepted by an attacker, the upcoming renewal of the session key is there to protect the secrecy of the future messages. This property is sometimes called post-compromise security. To satisfy this property, a cryptographic ratchet based on a key exchange method, such as Diffie-Hellman in the classical case, is used in the protocol, and a ratchet based on key derivation functions enables key renewal without interaction between the peers.

In order to communicate securely, the double ratchet protocol derives three types of shared secrets: *root*, *chain* and *message* secrets. They are used respectively as *master*, *derivation* and a *message* keys [20]. Since we consider a KEM-based double ratchet, we deviate a bit from this definition. As specified in Fig. 3, in KEM-Double-Ratchet the two communicating peers Alice and Bob start the KEM-DR sub-protocol with a common pre-shared key k_{root}. This key comes from the key agreement protocol PQ-X3DH.

Tamarin Model. As shown in Fig. 4 we only perform three exchanges of the KEM-double-ratchet protocol. Three exchanges are sufficient to verify all considered security properties as discussed in Sect. 3. Our KEM-DR model has nine transition rules:

- `Init_A` and `Init_B`: each user get a secret preshared key and Bob gets an Alice's KEM ephemeral public key.
- `Send_B1`, `Send_A`, and `Send_B2`: the user encapsulates a fresh secret key with the current KEM public key, derives a new session key, encrypts the message, then sends it encrypted with the KEM ciphertext and a new ephemeral KEM public key.
- `Recv_A1`, `Recv_B`, and `Recv_A2`: the user receives a message, derives the new session key, and verifies the integrity.
- `LeakState`: Reveals to the attacker the current user secrets.

3   Tamarin Formal Verification

In Tamarin, a protocol is seen as a state machine. A state is a multiset of facts, and rules are transitions which shift the state when some conditions are fulfilled. A rule consists of three sets of facts: *premise*, *action facts*, and *conclusion*. If all the premise facts exist, then the rule is applied. Applying a rule means *consuming* premise facts to produce conclusion facts while recording action facts in the protocol *trace*.

Some facts are native in Tamarin such as `In()` and `Out()` to model inputs and outputs of the protocol following the Dolev-Yao model [11]. Moreover, the `Fr()` fact is used to produce fresh or unique variables.

Tamarin proposes a set of *built-ins* cryptographic primitives to model protocols, including symmetric and asymmetric encryption, hash function, and signature. It also allows to define new primitives, via `functions` and `equations` commands. In the

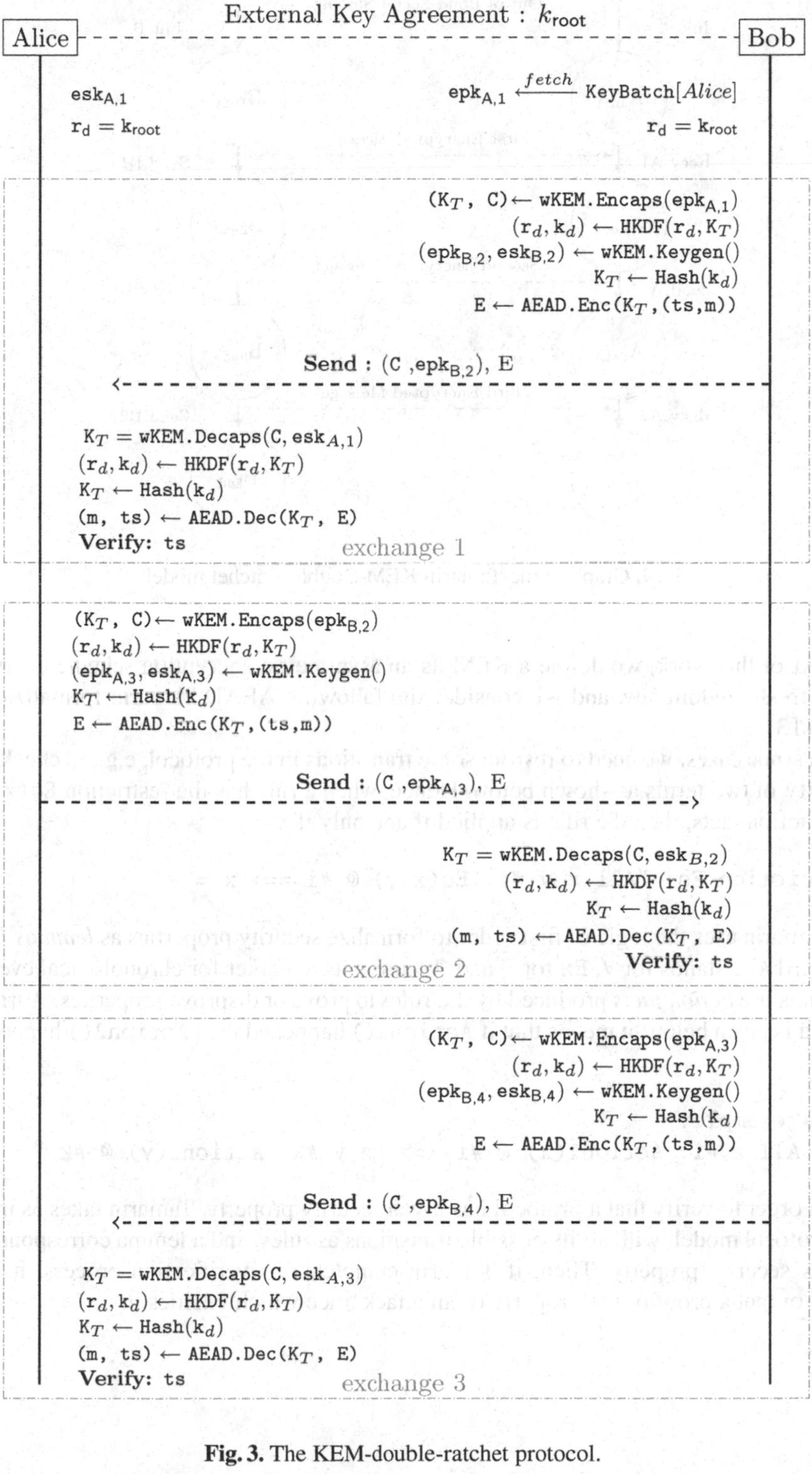

External Key Agreement : k_{root}

| Alice | | Bob |

$\text{esk}_{A,1}$ $\qquad\qquad\qquad\qquad$ $\text{epk}_{A,1} \xleftarrow{fetch} \text{KeyBatch}[Alice]$

$r_d = k_{\text{root}}$ $\qquad\qquad\qquad\qquad\qquad\qquad\qquad$ $r_d = k_{\text{root}}$

$(K_T, \text{ C}) \leftarrow \text{wKEM.Encaps(epk}_{A,1})$

$(r_d, k_d) \leftarrow \text{HKDF}(r_d, K_T)$

$(\text{epk}_{B,2}, \text{esk}_{B,2}) \leftarrow \text{wKEM.Keygen()}$

$K_T \leftarrow \text{Hash}(k_d)$

$\text{E} \leftarrow \text{AEAD.Enc}(K_T, (\text{ts},\text{m}))$

Send : (C ,$\text{epk}_{B,2}$), E

<- -

$K_T = \text{wKEM.Decaps}(C, \text{esk}_{A,1})$

$(r_d, k_d) \leftarrow \text{HKDF}(r_d, K_T)$

$K_T \leftarrow \text{Hash}(k_d)$

$(\text{m, ts}) \leftarrow \text{AEAD.Dec}(K_T, \text{ E})$

Verify: ts $\qquad\qquad$ exchange 1

$(K_T, \text{ C}) \leftarrow \text{wKEM.Encaps(epk}_{B,2})$

$(r_d, k_d) \leftarrow \text{HKDF}(r_d, K_T)$

$(\text{epk}_{A,3}, \text{esk}_{A,3}) \leftarrow \text{wKEM.Keygen()}$

$K_T \leftarrow \text{Hash}(k_d)$

$\text{E} \leftarrow \text{AEAD.Enc}(K_T, (\text{ts},\text{m}))$

Send : (C ,$\text{epk}_{A,3}$), E

- ->

$K_T = \text{wKEM.Decaps}(C, \text{esk}_{B,2})$

$(r_d, k_d) \leftarrow \text{HKDF}(r_d, K_T)$

$K_T \leftarrow \text{Hash}(k_d)$

$(\text{m, ts}) \leftarrow \text{AEAD.Dec}(K_T, \text{ E})$

exchange 2 $\qquad\qquad$ **Verify: ts**

$(K_T, \text{ C}) \leftarrow \text{wKEM.Encaps(epk}_{A,3})$

$(r_d, k_d) \leftarrow \text{HKDF}(r_d, K_T)$

$(\text{epk}_{B,4}, \text{esk}_{B,4}) \leftarrow \text{wKEM.Keygen()}$

$K_T \leftarrow \text{Hash}(k_d)$

$\text{E} \leftarrow \text{AEAD.Enc}(K_T, (\text{ts},\text{m}))$

Send : (C ,$\text{epk}_{B,4}$), E

<- -

$K_T = \text{wKEM.Decaps}(C, \text{esk}_{A,3})$

$(r_d, k_d) \leftarrow \text{HKDF}(r_d, K_T)$

$K_T \leftarrow \text{Hash}(k_d)$

$(\text{m, ts}) \leftarrow \text{AEAD.Dec}(K_T, \text{ E})$

Verify: ts $\qquad\qquad$ exchange 3

Fig. 3. The KEM-double-ratchet protocol.

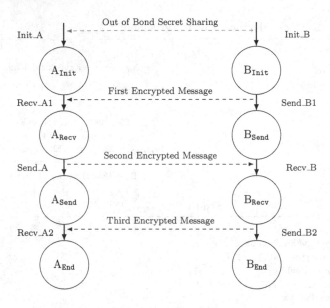

Fig. 4. Graph of the Tamarin KEM-Double-Ratchet model.

context of this work, we define a KEM as an asymmetric encryption scheme encrypting a fresh random key, and we consider the following AEAD Tamarin formalization from [13].

In some cases, we need to restrict some transitions in the protocol, e.g., to check the equality of two terms as shown below. Hence, when a rule has the restriction Eq(x,y) in its action facts, then the rule is applied if and only if $x = y$.

```
restriction Eq: "All x y #i. Eq(x,y) @ #i ==> x = y"
```

Tamarin uses the logic of first order to formalize security properties as *lemmas*. The keyword All stands for ∀, Ex for ∃ and @ represents a marker for chronological events. Lemmas use *action facts* produced by the rules to prove or disprove properties. A trivial lemma is given below, it means that if Action1() happened then Action2() happened too.

```
lemma example:
    " All x #i. Action1(x) @ #i ==> Ex y #k. Action2(y) @ #k "
```

In order to verify that a protocol has given security property, Tamarin takes as input the protocol model, with all its possible transitions as rules, and a lemma corresponding to this security property. Then, if Tamarin completes its verification process, it will either output a proof of the property or an attack trace which falsifies it.

3.1 Security Properties

The security properties verified in our symbolic analysis of PQ-X3DH and KEM-DR are the same properties as those considered in the formal verification of classical X3DH and Double-Ratchet protocols [14].

Integrity. Integrity is an important property for key exchange protocols. It allows the receiver of a message to have the assurance that the message has come unaltered from the intended sender. We separate the integrity of a message that can be verified upon receipt, called instantaneous integrity, and that which can be verified upon receipt of a subsequent message, called delayed integrity.

Authentication. We consider two authentication notions: the *partial authentication* from Definition 1 and the *full authentication* from Defintion 2.

Definition 1 (Partial Authentication). *A user U is partially authenticated to another user V if V can prove that the message she receives comes from the same user as the one with whom she has initialized the session.*

Definition 2 (Full Authentication). *A user U is fully authenticated to another user V if U is partially authenticated to V and V can prove the identity of U.*

Forward Secrecy. Here again we consider two different notions: the *perfect Forward Secrecy* (FS) from Definition 3 and the *weak Forward Secrecy* (wFS) from Definition 4. In this work, we also consider a new notion called *weak state Forward Secrecy* (wsFS) that we define as the wFS property except that the leakage concerns states instead of long term keys.

Definition 3 (perfect Forward Secrecy (FS) [18]). *A protocol is said to have perfect forward secrecy if compromised long-term keys does not compromise past session keys.*

Definition 4 (weak Forward Secrecy (wFS) [15]). *Any session key established by uncorrupted parties without active intervention by the attacker is guaranteed to remain secrete even if the parties to the exchange are corrupted after the session key has been erased.*

Key Compromise Impersonation Resistance. The KCI resistance from Definition 5 is related to the use of long term public/private keys. Since there is no use of long term public/private key in the KEM-DR protocol, the KCI property is only applicable to the PQ-X3DH protocol.

Definition 5 (Key Compromise Impersonation (KCI) Resistance). *Even if an adversary compromises the long term private key of a user U, this adversary can not use this key to impersonate (to U) another user V that is communicating to U.*

Unknown Key-Share Resistance. We recall the definition of a UKS attack in Definition 6. UKS attacks can be seen as implicit impersonation. Thus, in the same way as for the KCI resistance, this property is only applicable to the PQ-X3DH protocol.

Definition 6 (Unknown Key-Share (UKS) attack [5]). *An unknown key-share attack on an AKE protocol is an attack whereby a user U ends up believing she shares a key with V, and although this is in fact the case, V mistakenly believes the key is instead shared with an entity $W \neq U$.*

Post-Compromise Recovery. We recall the post-compromise recovery property in Definition 7. By definition, this property is only applicable when a protocol is iterated repeatedly between the parties, this is the case for KEM-DR but not for PQ-X3DH.

Definition 7 (Post-Compromise Recovery (PCR) [1]). *If the attacker remains passive, i.e., the attacker does not inject any messages, and if users have access to fresh randomness, then the users recover a secure state from a compromised state after a few communication rounds.*

3.2 Tamarin Formalization

Before describing in more detail the Tamarin formalization of the different security properties presented above, we need to define some notations that will be useful later. In the rest of the paper, we use the following notations:

- $\mathcal{L} = \{0, 1, 2\}$ is the set of iteration indices, i.e., the three first exchanges ;
- $\mathcal{M} \subset \{0, 1\}^*$ is the set of messages sent via the Signal protocol ;
- $\mathcal{K} \subset \{0, 1\}^k$ is the set of secret keys where k is the key length ;
- $\mathcal{S} \subset \{0, 1\}^*$ is the set of message indices, i.e., the message numbers ;
- Σ is the set of protocol states.
- Γ is the set of user states.

Moreover, using the Tamarin formalism, we note:

- KU(x): The adversary sent x and therefore has knowledge of x ;
- K(x): The adversary has knowledge of x.

In Table 1, respectively Table 2, we introduce the Tamarin action facts and their abbreviations needed in our symbolic analysis of PQ-X3DH, respectively KEM-DR. These action facts are used to define the Tamarin lemmas corresponding to the security properties.

In Tamarin, the user state is the current set of the secrets of this user. In order to characterize respectively full and partial knowledge of the user's secrets by the attacker, we define the *revealed* state in Definition 8 and the *compromised* state in Definition 9.

Definition 8 (Revealed State). *A state is said to be* revealed *if the adversary has knowledge of every hidden elements of the state.*

Definition 9 (Compromised State). *A state is said to be* compromised *if the adversary has knowledge of any hidden element of the state.*

Table 1. Tamarin action facts for PQ-X3DH, abbreviations and definitions

Action fact	Abbreviation	Definition
SessA	$S_A(A,B,k)$	A accepts the key k as valid to communicate with B
ExplicitAuth	$EA(B,A)$	A explicitly authenticates B
RevealL	$R_L(A)$	The long-term key of A is revealed to the attacker
RevealE	$R_E(A)$	The ephemeral key of A is revealed to the attacker
SendConnect	$SC(A)$	A initiates the PQ-X3DH protocol
RecvConnect	$RC(A,B)$	B receives the initialization message from A
SendSign	$SS(B,A)$	B sends its signature to A
weakFS	$wFS_{A,B}(k)$	Saves k to check its resistance against future reveal
Send/Recv	$Send_{A,n}(m)$	A sends the message m of index n
	$Recv_{B,A,n}(m)$	B checks the integrity of message m of index n from A

Table 2. Tamarin action facts for KEM-Double-Ratchet, abbreviations and definitions

Action fact	Abbreviation	Definition
IntegS/IntegR	$I_{S/R}(n,m,s)$	Sends or receives message m of index n associated With session key s and checks its integrity in reception
FS	$FS(A,B,n,st)$	Saves the current state st associated with the sending of the message of index n between A and B in order to check its resistance against future reveal
Healed	$H_{A,B}(st)$	Checks if the state st has recovered from a previous reveal in the communication between A and B
Reveal	$R(A,n)$	Reveals the secrets of A associated with the message of index n

PQ-X3DH Security Properties. For the sake of clarity, we describe the security properties verified with Tamarin in the usual mathematical formalism. Let $E = A <_t B$ the notation $<_t$ means that E is true if and only if event A occurs before event B. For lack of space, the definitions of the corresponding Tamarin lemmas are presented in the full version of this paper.

Integrity. The integrity is checked on both messages transmitted through the PQ-X3DH protocol. Nothing in this protocol allows an immediate integrity check of the first transmitted message. However, if both parties share the same key at the end of the protocol, then the integrity of this message is ensured in a delayed manner. For this reason, we define the following condition under which the delayed integrity of the first message is assured:

The following properties insure, for any user A, B that have shared a common secret k by respectively sending message m_1 and receiving message m_2 on the first exchange, that $m_1 = m_2$. Which leads with Tamarin formalism too:

$$\forall A, B \in \mathcal{U}, \forall m_1, m_2 \in \mathcal{M}, \forall k \in \mathcal{K}.$$

$$S_A(A,B,k) \wedge S_B(B,A,k) \wedge Send_{A,1}(m_1) \wedge Recv_{B,A,1}(m_2) \implies m_1 = m_2 \,.$$

The integrity of the second message can be immediately verified thanks to the signature. Thus the condition to check the immediate integrity is modeled as: For any user A and B, any message m_1, m_2 if in the second flow of the exchange B sent m_1 and A received m_2 without any corruption of the long term key of B and ephemeral key of A before the reception of the second flow by A then $m_1 = m_2$. Which leads to the following Tamarin formalism:

$$\forall A, B \in \mathcal{U}, \ \forall m_1, m_2 \in \mathcal{M}. \ Send_{B,2}(m_1) \wedge Recv_{A,B,2}(m_2) \wedge$$

$$\wedge \neg (R_E(A) \leq_t Recv_{A,B,2}(m_2)) \wedge \neg (R_L(B) \leq_t Recv_{A,B,2}(m_2)) \implies m_1 = m_2 \,.$$

Authentication. We consider two different notions of authentication depending on the role of the user in the PQ-X3DH protocol. Indeed, the initiator, Alice, does not sign any message and her KEM long term key is provided by a server without guaranteeing its authenticity. In these conditions, Alice can only be partially authenticated according to Definition 1. In the case where the equivalent of a certificate of the Alice's KEM long term key was added, then she could be fully authenticated at the end of the PQ-X3DH protocol. The second user, Bob, signs the message which allows Alice to explicitly authenticates him under the classical conditions of a public key infrastructure. The following condition is for the full authentication of Bob by Alice:

$$\forall A, B \in \mathcal{U}. \ EA(B,A) \leq_t R_L(B) \implies [SS(B,A) \wedge RC(A,B)$$

$$\wedge (SC(A) \wedge SS(B,A) \leq_t EA(B,A)) \wedge (SC(A) \leq_t SS(B,A)) \wedge (RC(A,B) =_t SS(B,A))] \,.$$

This can be described as for any user A and B, if the explicit authentication has been done before any corruption on B's long term key, then the protocol has been honestly executed by A and B.

weak Forward Secrecy. The following condition verifies the wFS property on k_{root} and $\tilde{k}$ keys of the PQ-X3DH protocol in case of future compromise of the initiator's short-term and responder's signing keys.

$$\forall A, B \in \mathcal{U}, \forall k \in \mathcal{K}. \ \neg R_L(B) \leq_t wFS_{A,B}(k_1, k_2) \wedge \neg R_E(A) \implies \neg KU(k) \,.$$

It means that for any user A and B that have agreed on a common key k, if at a certain point no corruption on the long term key of B has happened and if no corruption on the ephemeral key of A has happened then the adversary does not know the common key k.

KCI Resistance. The only possible scenario in which a KCI attack occurs is when the signing long-term key of the responder is compromised, in this case it must be guaranteed that an attacker cannot use this key to impersonate any of the users. Thus we have the following condition for KCI resistance:

$$(\forall A, B, S \in \mathcal{U}, \forall k \in \mathcal{K}. S_A(A,S,k) \wedge R_L(A) \wedge S_B(B,A,k) \implies S = B) \wedge$$

$$(\forall A, B, S \in \mathcal{U}, \forall k \in \mathcal{K}. S_A(A,B,k) \wedge R_L(B) \wedge S_B(B,S,k) \implies S = A) \,.$$

In other word if A or B have shared a key k with a user S and if respectively A or B's long term key has been corrupted and if A or B have agreed with respectively B or A on the key k too, then respectively the user S is B or A and cannot another user.

UKS Resistance. The UKS resistance consists of ensuring that if two users have agreed on a common session key, then they have the assurance that if neither key is compromised then no other user can impersonate either of them.

$$\forall A, B, C, S \in \mathcal{U}, \forall k \in \mathcal{K}. \ S_A(A,S,k) \wedge S_B(B,C,k) \implies S = B \wedge C = A \ .$$

This is a somewhat stronger approach compared to the previous properties that insure that no impersonation will occurs.

Double-Ratchet Security Properties. Regarding the KEM-DR protocol, we verify the classical security properties as well as the post-compromise recovery from [1].

Integrity. For each exchange, we verify that the message sent is indeed the message received thanks to the integrity provided by the AEAD scheme.

$$\forall n \in \mathcal{S}, \forall m_1, m_2 \in \mathcal{M}, \forall k \in \mathcal{K}. \ I_S(n, m_1, s) \wedge I_R(n, m_2, s) \wedge \neg K(k) \implies m_1 = m_2 \ .$$

PCR. As this property ensures that for a corruption during a given exchange it is enough to wait for two exchanges before the session key is secret again, it is necessary to check this condition on three consecutive exchanges. Then this base case allows to prove Theorem 1 by induction.

$$\forall A, B \in \mathcal{U}, \forall st \in \Sigma.$$
$$H_{A,B}(st) \wedge R(B,0) \wedge H_{A,B}(st) <_t R(B,0) \implies \neg K(st) \vee R(B,2) \vee R(A,1) \ .$$

As it can be deduced this properties is proven only on the three first messages. This can be proven using Tamarin for any fixed triplet $(n, n + 1, n + 2)$ of ratchet exchange. However for pure theoretical insurance we prove it using induction using this case as the base case of the induction proof.

weak state Forward Secrecy. Similarly, two consecutive exchanges of the KEM-DR protocol are sufficient to prove by induction the wsFS property in Theorem 2.

$$\forall A, B \in \mathcal{U}, \forall st \in \Sigma.$$
$$FS(A,B,0,st) \wedge R(A,1) \wedge FS(A,B,0,st) <_t R(A,1) \implies \neg K(st) \vee R(B,0) \ .$$

3.3 Formal Verification Results

In Table 3 we present the results obtained from the automatic verification with Tamarin of the security properties considered for the PQ-X3DH and KEM-DR protocols.

Table 3. Results of Tamarin verification for PQ-X3DH and KEM-Double-Ratchet protocols.

Protocols	Integrity		Auth.	Imp. resistance		Forward secrecy			PCR
	Instant	Delayed		KCI	UKS	FS	wFS	wsFS	
PQ-X3DH	✗	✓	✓	✓	✓	✗	✓	NA	NA
KEM-Double-Ratchet	✓	NA	NA	NA	NA	✓	NA	✓	✓

Since the KEM-DR protocol admits an arbitrary number of interactions, properties impacting previous or future states of the protocol require an additional proof in order to holds for any exchange of the protocol. Only the PCR and wsFS properties fall in this case, the others are trivially proven. To be more precise Tamarin allows these propreties to be true for any $k < n$ with n fixed. We therefore propose to extend it to arbitrary n by induction for theoretical purposes.

Theorem 1 (KEM-Double-Ratchet Post Compromise Security). *For all user state* $State_n$ *with* $n > 0$:

$$Compromised(State_n) \wedge \neg\, Revealed(State_{n+1}) \wedge \neg\, Revealed(State_{n+2})$$
$$\implies Healed(State_{n+2})\,.$$

Proof. We prove Theorem 1 by induction for all integer $n > 0$. The base case has been proven using Tamarin. Suppose that the theorem is true for all integer $k < n$, and that:

$$\neg\, Healed(State_{n+3}) \quad \text{with} \quad \neg\, Compromised(State_{n+3})$$

First:

$$Compromised(State_{n+1}) \implies \exists k \leq n + 1, Revealed(State_k)$$

Let name $i = \max\{k \leq n + 2, Revealed(State_k)\}$, if $i < n + 2$ then by definition of i:

$$\neg\, Revealed(State_{i+1}) \wedge \neg\, Revealed(State_{i+2})$$

and by induction hypothesis, the state $i + 2$ is healed which means that the state $n + 3$ is healed too since there is no reveal in between step $i + 1$ and $n + 3$. Now if $i = n + 2$ let remind the definition of an healed state:
By definition of a healed state, for all $n > 2$ we have:

$$Healed(State_n) \iff \exists k < n, \; [Revealed(State_k) \wedge \neg\, Compromised(State_n)]$$
$$\wedge \neg Revealed(State_n)$$

And thus:

$$\neg\, Healed(State_n) \implies \forall k < n, [\neg Revealed(State_k) \vee Compromised(State_n)]$$
$$\vee Revealed(State_n)$$
$$\implies \forall k < n, [\neg Revealed(State_k) \vee \exists j \leq n, Revealed(State_j)]$$
$$\vee Revealed(State_n), \text{ by definition of } Compromised$$

Since we have $i = n + 2$ then: $\texttt{Revealed}(\texttt{State}_{n+2})$. Additionally:

$$\forall k \leq n, \neg\texttt{Revealed}(\texttt{State}_k) \iff \neg\texttt{Compromised}(\texttt{State}_n)$$

Therefore:

$$\neg\texttt{Healed}(\texttt{State}_{n+3}) \implies \neg\texttt{Compromised}(\texttt{State}_{n+1})$$
$$\lor \texttt{Revealed}(\texttt{State}_{n+2}) \lor \texttt{Revealed}(\texttt{State}_{n+3})]$$

Which ends our induction proof.   □

We introduce the notion of *healing ball* in Definition 10 to prove the wsFS property in Theorem 2.

Definition 10 (Healing Ball). *We define the* healing ball B_h *for all user state* $S \in \Gamma$, *as* $B_h(S) = \{\gamma \in \Gamma \mid \texttt{Revealed}(\gamma) \implies \neg \texttt{Healed}(S)\}$.

Theorem 2 (KEM-Double-Ratchet weak state Forward Secrecy). *For all user state* $\texttt{State}_n$ *with* $n \geq 2$:

$$\texttt{Compromised}(\texttt{State}_n) \land (\forall k < n, S \in B_h(\texttt{State}_k), \neg \texttt{Revealed}(S))$$
$$\implies \neg \texttt{Compromised}(\texttt{State}_k).$$

Proof. We prove Theorem 2 by induction for all integer $n > 1$. The base case has been proven using Tamarin. Suppose that the theorem is true for all integer $\ell \leq n$, and that $\texttt{State}_{n+1}$ has been compromised. Then, we have:

$$\texttt{Compromised}(\texttt{State}_{n+1}) \implies \texttt{Revealed}(\texttt{State}_n) \lor \texttt{Revealed}(\texttt{State}_{n+1})$$

and by definition, for all ℓ:

$$\texttt{Revealed}(\texttt{State}_\ell) \implies \texttt{Compromise}(\texttt{State}_\ell)$$

If $\texttt{State}_n$ has been revealed and not $\texttt{State}_{n+1}$, we apply the induction hypothesis. Now suppose that $\texttt{State}_{n+1}$ has been revealed but not $\texttt{State}_n$, we then use the fact that KEM.decaps is supposed ideal by Tamarin and then deterministic, so regarding the backward analysis $\texttt{State}_{n+1}$ is a deterministic function of $\texttt{State}_n$. Finally, if both states have been revealed, then we apply the induction hypothesis.   □

Acknowledgement. We wish to thanks Matthieu Giraud and Renaud Dubois for help on the Tamarin prover as well as helping discussions on the subject and the reviewers for highlighting some typos. First and last authors were supported by ANRT under the program CIFRE N° 2021/0645 and N° 2019/1583.

References

1. Alwen, J., Coretti, S., Dodis, Y.: The double ratchet: security notions, proofs, and modularization for the signal protocol. In: Ishai, Y., Rijmen, V. (eds.) EUROCRYPT 2019. LNCS, vol. 11476, pp. 129–158. Springer, Cham (2019). https://doi.org/10.1007/978-3-030-17653-2_5

2. Avanzi, R., et al.: CRYSTALS-Kyber - Submission to round 3 of the NIST post-quantum project (2021). https://pq-crystals.org/kyber/data/kyber-specification-round3-20210804.pdf

3. Basin, D.A., Dreier, J., Hirschi, L., Radomirovic, S., Sasse, R., Stettler, V.: A formal analysis of 5g authentication. In: Lie, D., Mannan, M., Backes, M., Wang, X. (eds.) CCS, pp. 1383–1396 (2018)

4. Bhargavan, K., Blanchet, B., Kobeissi, N.: Verified models and reference implementations for the TLS 1.3 standard candidate. In: IEEE Symposium on Security and Privacy, SP, pp. 483–502 (2017)

5. Blake-Wilson, S., Menezes, A.: Unknown key-share attacks on the station-to-station (STS) protocol. In: Public Key Cryptography, Second International Workshop on Practice and Theory in Public Key Cryptography, PKC, vol. 1560, pp. 154–170 (1999)

6. Blanchet, B.: Modeling and verifying security protocols with the applied pi calculus and ProVerif. Found. Trends Priv. Secur. 1(1–2), 1–135 (2016)

7. Brendel, J., Fischlin, M., Günther, F., Janson, C., Stebila, D.: Towards post-quantum security for signal's X3DH handshake. In: Dunkelman, O., Jacobson, Jr., M.J., O'Flynn, C. (eds.) SAC 2020. LNCS, vol. 12804, pp. 404–430. Springer, Cham (2021). https://doi.org/10.1007/978-3-030-81652-0_16

8. Celi, S., Hoyland, J., Stebila, D., Wiggers, T.: A tale of two models: Formal verification of KEMTLS via Tamarin. In: Atluri, V., Di Pietro, R., Jensen, C.D., Meng, W. (eds.) ESORICS 2022, Part III. LNCS, vol. 13556, pp. 63–83. Springer, Heidelberg (2022). https://doi.org/10.1007/978-3-031-17143-7_4

9. Cohn-Gordon, K., Cremers, C., Dowling, B., Garratt, L., Stebila, D.: A formal security analysis of the signal messaging protocol. J. Cryptol. 33(4), 1914–1983 (2020)

10. Cremers, C., Horvat, M., Hoyland, J., Scott, S., van der Merwe, T.: A comprehensive symbolic analysis of TLS 1.3. In: CCS, pp. 1773–1788 (2017)

11. Dolev, D., Yao, A.C.: On the security of public key protocols. IEEE Trans. Inf. Theory 29(2), 198–207 (1983)

12. Hashimoto, K., Katsumata, S., Kwiatkowski, K., Prest, T.: An efficient and generic construction for signal's handshake (X3DH): post-quantum, state leakage secure, and deniable. In: PKC, vol. 12711, pp. 410–440 (2021)

13. Hülsing, A., Ning, K.C., Schwabe, P., Weber, F., Zimmermann, P.R.: Post-quantum WireGuard. In: 2021 IEEE Symposium on Security and Privacy, pp. 304–321. IEEE Computer Society Press, San Francisco (2021). https://doi.org/10.1109/SP40001.2021.00030

14. Kobeissi, N., Bhargavan, K., Blanchet, B.: Automated verification for secure messaging protocols and their implementations: a symbolic and computational approach. In: EuroS&P, pp. 435–450 (2017)

15. Krawczyk, H.: HMQV: a high-performance secure Diffie-Hellman protocol. In: Shoup, V. (ed.) CRYPTO 2005. LNCS, vol. 3621, pp. 546–566. Springer, Heidelberg (2005). https://doi.org/10.1007/11535218_33

16. Lowe, G.: Breaking and fixing the Needham-Schroeder public-key protocol using FDR. In: Margaria, T., Steffen, B. (eds.) TACAS 1996. LNCS, vol. 1055, pp. 147–166. Springer, Heidelberg (1996). https://doi.org/10.1007/3-540-61042-1_43

17. Meier, S., Schmidt, B., Cremers, C., Basin, D.: The TAMARIN prover for the symbolic analysis of security protocols. In: Sharygina, N., Veith, H. (eds.) CAV 2013. LNCS, vol.

8044, pp. 696–701. Springer, Heidelberg (2013). https://doi.org/10.1007/978-3-642-39799-8_48
18. Menezes, A., van Oorschot, P.C., Vanstone, S.A.: Handbook of Applied Cryptography. CRC Press, Boca Raton (1996)
19. Schwabe, P., Stebila, D., Wiggers, T.: Post-quantum TLS without handshake signatures. In: 2020 ACM SIGSAC Conference on Computer and Communications Security, Virtual Event, CCS 2020, pp. 1461–1480 (2020)
20. Trevor Perrin, M.M.: The double ratchet algorithm. https://signal.org/docs/specifications/doubleratchet/
21. Trevor Perrin, M.M.: The X3DH key agreement protocol. https://signal.org/docs/specifications/x3dh/

A Comparative Study of Online Cybersecurity Training Platforms

Abdeslam Rehaimi[1]([✉])[iD], Yassine Sadqi[1][iD], and Yassine Maleh[2][iD]

[1] Laboratory LIMATI, FPBM, USMS University, Beni Mellal, Morocco
abdeslam.rehaimi@usms.ac.ma, yassine.sadqi@ieee.org
[2] Laboratory LaSTI, ENSAK, USMS University, Beni Mellal, Morocco
yassine.maleh@ieee.org

Abstract. With the rapidly growing number of cybersecurity training solutions, new opportunities have been introduced for real-world simulated cyber threats to be accessible. It has improved the participant's ability to detect and respond in a timely and effective manner. These platforms vary in technical details. However, all have one common objective to improve cybersecurity understanding and awareness. This paper presents and surveys the ten most popular commercial and open-source cybersecurity training platforms for online learning based on practical training. In addition, a comparative analysis and discussion of platform-specific features based on a proposed software taxonomy that aids in the classification is presented. The findings of this study can be useful to both developers and contributors of cybersecurity training platforms for further improvements or to develop new ones.

Keywords: Capture the Flag · Comparative analysis · Cybersecurity education · Cybersecurity exercises · Cybersecurity training platforms

1 Introduction

With the world's widespread adoption of digital technology in many fields, cyber-attacks have become a major worry for governments, organizations, and individuals as well [1,2]. Cyber threats have become increasingly complex, with attackers using sophisticated methods to infiltrate networks and steal valuable data [3]. The consequences can incur billions of losses [4] and the public exposure of confidential information. The counted severe cyber-attacks grow each year and almost in real-time, presenting a challenge to construct effective detection and prevention systems. A recent report by Microsoft's Digital Security Unit [5] highlights the hybrid war in Ukraine, where more than 40% of cyber-attacks targeted critical infrastructure, resulting in severe consequences for the government, military, economy, and citizens. Despite the urgent need for cybersecurity specialists to combat these threats, there is a significant shortage of trained professionals in the field. This shortage has been highlighted in a recent cybersecurity Workforce Study (ISC)2 research [7], which revealed a significant shortage workforce gap reaching up to 4.07 million in 2019. Shedding a sharp focus on an urgent need for trained cybersecurity specialists to combat threats as they arise [6]. However, the problem that is raised by the literature [8] and also reported by DHS Cyber-Skills Report [9], the industry blames higher education institutions for failing to adequately prepare students with the necessary technical capabilities. Therefore, education and training play a crucial role in equipping individuals with the latest defense techniques to prevent such threats [10,11].

Technology can assist job seekers' skills and knowledge, while it also provides an excellent assessment method for determining applicants' eligibility for cybersecurity job positions [12]. It facilitates engaging in practical training and allows learners to develop advanced problem-solving skills in the field [13]. It also brings opportunities for all levels of learners to see and practice by doing. Great initiatives have been devoted to this context. Researchers and practitioners developed and proposed a variety of cybersecurity training platforms. Capture The Flag (CTF) is one of the most popular examples. It has been introduced as a new way of cybersecurity education. Designed challenges, competition events, and hosted environments made training more accessible, skills enhancing, and an interesting way to learn. Some platforms may also offer certification programs or other professional development opportunities for individuals who want to advance their careers in the field. Moreover, it can also be used by universities, tech giants, and organizations, as well as communities of practitioners that want to learn about best practices for protecting their data and systems assets.

Currently, there are many online platforms that can be either commercial (i.e., cloud-based platforms) or free open source platforms (i.e., self-hosted platforms) [10, 14] Each with its unique software features and characteristics to offer cybersecurity training environments to interested users. Regardless of the technical details, all have one common objective: to enhance cybersecurity understanding and awareness. Subsequently, providing hands-on training and challenges events that simulate real-world cyber threats as closely as possible and respond to the workforce gap as well. This paper presents a survey of the ten most popular self-hosted and cloud-based hosted online cybersecurity training platforms. The main contributions of this work are as follows:

- Identifying design features and functionalities of current cybersecurity training platforms.
- The proposition of a software taxonomy.
- Assessment and comparison of current cybersecurity training platforms based on their features.

This paper is organized into sections: (S1) the introduction; (S2) the related work; (S3) the methodology; (S4) the results and discussion; and (S5) the conclusion and future works.

2　Related Works

Notable works have been conducted by the literature to examine and evaluate cybersecurity training platforms with the aim of identifying the best features and characteristics for creating an ideal platform.

Kucek and Leitner [14], conducted an empirical evaluation to survey and compare eight open-source platforms designed for hosting CTF challenges. In particular, they have evaluated their specific technical features, characteristics, and functionalities. The study aimed to provide a reference for CTF organizers and participants in choosing the right platform and configuring challenges. The authors reported that the majority of open-source platforms can be installed on various operating systems, and it is highly advisable to install them within either Vagrant or Docker for optimal performance and compatibility.

In a similar work, Karagiannis et al. [15], conducted a comprehensive analysis and evaluation of four open-source platforms specifically developed for hosting CTF challenges accompanied by a comparative evaluation. They collected descriptive insights along with undergraduate student's participants through interviews and evaluated the platforms based on criteria related to functionality, extensibility, teaching presence, and flag and challenge management. The conducted work aimed to highlight the distinct features of each platform as well as observe the advantages, disadvantages, characteristics, limitations, and capabilities, focusing on their use as cybersecurity e-learning tools.

On the other side, Raman et al. [16], proposes a framework that focuses on assessing the similarities among CTF events. The authors analyzed ten CTFs and classified them based on challenge types and mapped them to well-known software vulnerabilities and OWASP vulnerabilities. The authors identified factors such as challenge classification, solvability of tasks, periodicity, training, geographical reach, and problem-solving skills. They highlight their notable technical distinctions by assigning weights to these factors using the Analytic Hierarchy Process. Their results suggest the importance of features like challenge classification, levels of difficulty, the training provided before CTF events, and the solvability of tasks as important factors to evaluate and rank CTF events.

In contrast to prior works mentioned above, Swann et al. [17], conducted a comprehensive review of the top cybersecurity gamified learning platforms (i.e., commercial and open-source) available in the literature. They focused on identifying the essential features needed for organizing CTF events. The authors selected 14 widely recognized commercial and open-source (i.e., self-hosted) platforms for evaluation. They categorize the platforms based on the type of challenge format they offer, such as Jeopardy-style challenges and Attack-Defense challenges. The evaluation is based on six key comparison measures, including user experience, coordinator features, scoring system, deployment process, extensibility, and API integration. The authors conclude that PicoCTF is the best self-hosted platform, while TryHackMe, HackTheBox, and RootMe are suitable commercial options.

Knüpfer et al. [18], conducted a study in which they presented a holistic taxonomy framework based on their experience in organizing CTF events related to cybersecurity training and education. The taxonomy primarily emphasizes different key aspects such as the technical dimension, the intended audience, and various additional considerations. The taxonomy is extendable and can be used in further application areas as research on new security technologies.

In this paper, a survey and comparative analysis of the ten most popular commercial and open-source cybersecurity training platforms available in the literature is presented. The study focuses on platform-specific features, services, and technical details and proposes a software and services taxonomy for a comprehensive evaluation of each platform.

3   Methodology

This section outlines the methodology adopted for conducting this work. The process has been carried out to explore, analyze, and report relevant information of selected online cybersecurity training platforms. To survey the selected platforms, six key steps have been followed as shown in Fig. 1. These steps, involve selecting and extracting observed features and characteristics for each platform. Those features and parameters are then used to build a comparison software and services taxonomy that aids in comparison, which is presented in Fig. 2.

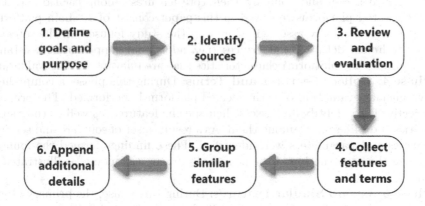

Fig. 1. Proposed Methodology

– **Phase 1: Define Goals and Purpose:** The first phase consists of identifying the goals and the aims (i.e., the purpose of this comparative study). This paper focuses on surveying the specific software features, technical details, and services of the current and most popular cybersecurity online platforms available in the literature. Additionally, providing a comprehensive comparison based on their specific functions, the types of challenges, training modules, and supported configuration options.

- **Phase 2: Identify Sources:** The second phase consists of selecting sources. Thus, a manual lookup has been performed using the widely recognized and adopted search engines by the scientific community. The initial lookup was conducted utilizing popular search engines such as Scopus (https://www. scopus.com/) and Google Scholar (http://scholar.google.com). This initial lookup revealed the existence of two main types of cybersecurity training platforms, particularly open-source (i.e., self-hosted platforms) where the source code is available on the web, and commercial platforms (i.e., cloud-based hosted platforms) that offers some services for free while others are restricted behind a membership subscription. Additionally, a second lookup has been performed over GitHub (https://github.com/) for searching of identified platforms as open-source, based on their popularity (i.e., GitHub stars count) for additional information's collection.
- **Phase 3: Review and Evaluation:** In this phase, a careful evaluation and review to conduct a final selection have been performed. The platforms included in this comparative study were selected based on their popularity and the availability of information about their features online. Considering the wide variety of solutions currently exists, the research exploration, revealed two main types of training platforms which are primarily distinguished as open-source or commercial platforms. Thus, it was important to include both in order to assess and compare their core features among each other. The final selected platforms reviewed in this paper consist of 10 main platforms that were specifically assessed. Moreover, the study focused on the software (i.e., technical details) and services (i.e., additional support and assistance provided by the platform) characteristics that are relevant for the evaluation.
- **Phase 4: Collect Features and Terms:** During this phase, a comprehensive manual evaluation of each selected platform is performed. The primary objective is to identify and assess their specific features, as well as their similarities and differences among them. As a result, a set of software and services features and parameters were identified. These findings formed the foundation for the construction of the proposed software taxonomy, as illustrated in Fig. 2.
- **Phase 5: Group Similar Features:** During this phase, the primary objective is to group similar features identified during the evaluation process. The purpose of this grouping is to construct a software taxonomy that aids in the comparison. As noted by Landwehr et al. [19], a taxonomy serves the purpose of specifying the data to be collected and providing guidelines for recognizing similarities and differences among individuals. Therefore, this phase involves grouping similar features into distinct categories and establishing a hierarchical structure of parameter groupings and clusters within the subject. This systematic approach ensures a clear and organized representation of the parameters used to construct the overall taxonomy.
- **Phase 6: Append Additional Details:** The proposed taxonomy has been further expanded to include additional details, encompassing additional features and parameters. The final taxonomy, depicted in Fig. 2, comprises 11 categories with a total of 33 parameters. These observed parameters com-

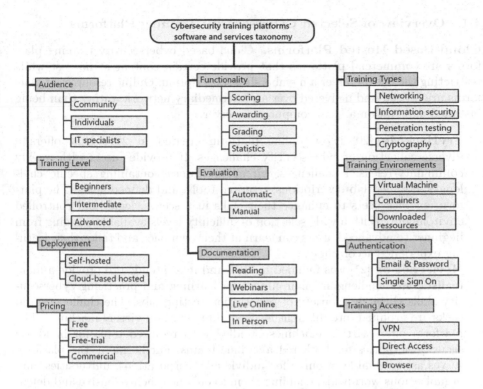

Fig. 2. Cybersecurity training platforms' software and services taxonomy

prehensively describe various aspects of the platforms, including their types, deployment methods, provided support, pricing, target audience, features, challenge types, categories, authentication methods, challenge connections, and access options, among others. The inclusion of these detailed parameters enhances the overall completeness and clarity of the taxonomy. This taxonomy will serve as a framework for the comparative analysis.

4   Results and Discussion

This section, which is broken down into two subsections, summarizes the survey's findings. The selected platforms have been categorized into two main classifications: cloud-based hosted platforms [10] and self-hosted training platforms where the source code is available on the web [14] which are presented in the first subsection. The second subsection, discusses the main findings with a comparison table based on the selected relevant features.

4.1 Overview of Selected Cybersecurity Training Platforms

Cloud-Based Hosted Platforms. Cloud-based cybersecurity training platforms are commercial platforms that provide certain content at no cost while restricting the others under a membership subscription. Online resources of platforms are hosted and delivered over an intermediary network, rather than being installed and run on a local computer or server.

- **TryHackMe** [20] is an online platform created in 2018 that offers a diverse collection of cybersecurity challenges. It provides users with weekly community-released challenges, virtual machines containing specific challenges, detailed lab descriptions, required tools, and defined goals. The platform enables users to enhance their skills in a secure, legal, and controlled environment. With a wide selection of difficulty levels available, ranging from beginner to advanced, users can learn at their own pace and tailor their learning experience accordingly.
- **HackTheBox** [21] was founded in 2017 and it is intended to provide a more realistic and challenging environment for learning and practicing cybersecurity skills through a variety of penetration testing labs. The challenges and tasks are grouped into different levels of difficulty and virtual machines. The platform offers virtual machines bundled with required tools for hands-on security activities for both red and blue teams. Furthermore, the platform serves as a valuable resource for individuals, corporations, universities, and organizations worldwide, enabling them to enhance their offensive and defensive security skills in an engaging and interactive learning environment.
- **Root-Me** [22] is a non-profit organization with the primary goal of educating and raising awareness about hacking and information security. The platform provides the public with access to relevant knowledge and resources. Root-Me is designed for users of all proficiency levels and offers a range of challenges from beginner to expert. It also provides a variety of learning resources, including tutorials and documentation, to help users improve their skills.
- **PentesterLab** [23] is a platform dedicated exclusively to web-based vulnerability testing. It offers guidance to users through various of different concepts related to web application penetration testing. The platform provides a combination of written courses and videos that cover a wide range of topics, starting from basic SQL injections and progressing to advanced concepts. The creators frequently update the content to address newly discovered vulnerabilities and techniques.
- **Virtual Hacking Lab (VHL)** [24] is an e-learning company focusing on practical penetration testing training solutions. They provide comprehensive course materials and easy-to-follow walkthrough guides. VHL offers a wide variety of challenges and exercises to enhance users' cybersecurity skills and allow them to practice penetration testing in a flexible and virtual environment. VHL is designed to be accessible to users of all proficiency levels, with challenges ranging from beginner to advanced.

Self-hosted Platforms. Self-hosted cybersecurity training platforms are platforms that users can install and set up on their own local machines or virtual private servers (VPS). These platforms offer a range of challenging training labs that users can use to practice locally.

- **OWASP Juice Shop (OJS)** [25] is a free and open-source vulnerable web application released under the MIT License. It is constructed using the widely-used MEAN stack, which comprises MongoDB, Express.js, AngularJS, and Node.js. OJS includes a range of common web-based vulnerabilities. Its primary purpose is to facilitate the learning and exploitation of the OWASP Top 10 web-based vulnerabilities, offering challenges at different levels of difficulty.
- **Facebook Capture the Flag (FBCTF)** [26] is an open-source web-based jeopardy-style system developed by Facebook security engineers and released in 2016 under creative commons attribution 4.0. It has been hosted since 2013 to assist with cybersecurity education and training. Moreover, it is meant to be used for organizing CTF competitions that are designed to challenge participants to find and exploit vulnerabilities.
- **CTFd** [27] is an open-source web-based jeopardy-style platform released under Apache license 2.0. Its primary objective is to facilitate the coordination and hosting of Capture the Flag (CTF) competitions, addressing the global demand for cybersecurity awareness worldwide. Notably, the system stands out due to its user-friendly installation process, ease of use, and customizable options, making it an appealing choice for CTF organizers.
- **PicoCTF** [28] is a free and open-source project released under an MIT license. It is developed using the Python programming language alongside JavaScript. It is a platform with original content built on a capture-the-flag framework created by security and privacy experts at Carnegie Mellon University.
- **TinyCTF** [29] is a free and open-source jeopardy-style platform to facilitate the organization of CTF events. It is written with PHP and released under the MIT license. TinyCTF includes a web interface and a scoreboard, providing a comprehensive solution for CTF event management. Additionally, it offers a range of challenges that are user-friendly, featuring clear instructions and hypertext links to guide participants.

4.2 Overview of Selected Features and Parameters

When comparing cybersecurity online platforms, several parameters are relevant to consider. One important parameter is the audience, which can be divided into three categories: community, individuals, and IT specialists. The platform is catered to the specific needs and requirements of each audience group. Another parameter is the training level, which can range from beginners to intermediate and advanced users. The platform offers appropriate training materials and resources for each level of expertise. Deployment is another important parameter, with options including self-hosted platforms or cloud-based hosted platforms.

The choice depends on factors such as scalability and maintenance requirements. Pricing is ranging from free, free trials, and commercial offerings.

The functionality of the platform is another key consideration, including features such as scoring, awarding, grading, and statistics. Scoring refers to the system's ability to assign points or rankings to users based on their performance or achievements. Awarding involves granting rewards, badges, or certifications to users who meet certain criteria. It can be granted both manually and automatically. Grading refers to the platform's ability to assess and evaluate users' progress or knowledge. Statistics involve the collection and analysis of data related to users' performance, progress, or engagement on the platform.

Evaluation methods can be automatic or manual, depending on the platform's capabilities. Automatic evaluation system is built into the platform itself, where the system checks if the user has successfully completed the tasks or challenges. This can be done through various mechanisms such as checking for correct answers, flag submissions, or successful exploitation of vulnerabilities. On the other hand, some platforms may rely on manual evaluation by administrators or moderators. In such cases, the users may need to submit their solutions or flag codes, which are then manually reviewed by the administrators to determine if the tasks have been accomplished efficiently.

Documentation can be provided as reading materials, webinars, live online sessions, and in-person training. Various training types are offered by a platform, such as networking, information security, penetration testing, and cryptography. Additionally, the training environments is provided as virtual machines, containers, or downloaded resources. Authentication options, such as email and password or single sign-on, are used for ensuring secure access to the platform. Finally, the training access options, including VPN, direct access (i.e., using public IP address), or browser-based access are used to access to the training environment for users.

4.3   Comparison of Selected Cybersecurity Training Platforms

Table 1 presents a thorough comparison of the selected platforms discussed in this paper. The comparison is based on the proposed software and services taxonomy depicted in Fig. 1.

Cybersecurity training platforms are online resources that offer a range of training environments and various types of exercises for users to practice and improve their cybersecurity skills. These platforms can be self-hosted, meaning that users install and set up the platform on their own local machines or virtual private servers (VPS), or they can be cloud-based, meaning that the platform is hosted on remote servers and can be accessed from anywhere with an internet connection. Moreover, cloud-based platforms may offer more comprehensive support and documentation, while open-source platforms may rely more on community-driven support and resources. Additionally, cloud-based platforms can be extensible and additional features can be added and unlocked by users with a subscription payment, unlike the limited features of open-source platforms. With this, cloud-based platforms offer more possibilities and advantages of provisioning complete virtual environments such as containers or virtual machines which makes it more popular for users.

Table 1. Cybersecurity training platforms comparison

		TryHackMe	HackTheBox	Root-Me	PentesterLab	Virtual Hacking Lab	OWASP Juice Shop	FBCTF	CTFd	PicoCTF	TinyCTF
Deployment		Cloud-based hosted					Self-hosted				
Pricing		Free-trial	Free-trial	Free-trial	Commercial	Commercial	Free	Free	Free	Free	Free
Audience	Community	Y	Y	Y	Y	Y	N	Y	N	N	N
	Individuals	Y	Y	Y	Y	Y	Y	Y	Y	Y	Y
	IT Specialists	Y	Y	Y	Y	Y	Y	Y	Y	Y	Y
Training Level	Beginners	Y	Y	Y	Y	Y	Y	Y	Y	Y	Y
	Intermediate	Y	Y	Y	Y	Y	Y	Y	Y	Y	Y
	Advanced	Y	Y	Y	Y	Y	Y	Y	Y	Y	Y
Functionality	Scoring	Y	Y	Y	Y	Y	Y	Y	Y	Y	Y
	Awarding	Y	Y	Y	Y	Y	N	N	N	Y	N
	Grading	Y	Y	Y	Y	Y	Y	N	N	Y	N
	Statistics	Y	Y	Y	Y	Y	Y	Y	Y	Y	Y
Evaluation	Automatic	Y	Y	Y	Y	Y	Y	Y	Y	Y	Y
	Manual	N	Y	N	Y	Y	N	N	N	N	N
Documentation	Reading	Y	Y	Y	Y	Y	Y	Y	Y	Y	Y
	Webinars	N	N	N	N	N	N	N	N	Y	N
	Live Online	N	Y	N	N	N	N	N	N	N	N
	In Person	Y	N	N	N	N	N	N	N	N	N
Training Types	Networking	Y	Y	Y	N	Y	N	N	N	N	Y
	Information security	Y	Y	Y	Y	Y	Y	N	N	Y	Y
	Penetration Testing	Y	Y	Y	Y	Y	N	N	N	Y	Y
	Cryptography	Y	Y	Y	N	N	N	N	N	Y	Y
Training Environments	Virtual Machine	Y	Y	Y	N	Y	N	N	N	N	N
	Containers	Y	Y	N	N	Y	N	N	N	N	N
	Downloaded resources	Y	Y	Y	Y	Y	Y	N	Y	Y	N
Training Access	VPN	Y	Y	Y	N	Y	N	N	N	Y	N
	Direct Access	Y	Y	Y	N	Y	N	N	N	N	N
	Browser	Y	Y	Y	Y	Y	Y	Y	Y	Y	Y
Authentication	Email & password	Y	Y	Y	Y	Y	Y	Y	Y	Y	Y
	Single Sign On	Y	N	N	N	N	Y	Y	N	N	N

5   Conclusion and Future Works

Hands-on training opens up new opportunities for learners of all types and levels to gain practical experience through active engagement. It allows individuals to practice and enhance their skills, ensuring they can effectively defend against emerging threats. There are numerous online platforms available that provide practical training opportunities by simulating real-world cyber threats as closely as possible. Consequently, responding to the workforce gap. This paper surveys and examines the ten most popular cloud-based and self-hosted cybersecurity online training platforms currently available. Furthermore, a comparative analysis based on their specific technical features and details is presented. Moreover, a proposed software and services taxonomy consisting of 11 features and 33 parameters is presented. This taxonomy serves as a comprehensive framework for analyzing and evaluating the platforms to perform the comparison. Future research is needed to compare the compatibility and extensibility of the current cybersecurity online platforms with the NIST NICE cybersecurity workforce framework [30]. Moreover, design an improved cybersecurity training platform and explore its impacts on enhancing learners' performance.

References

1. Cabaj, K., Kotulski, Z., Ksiezopolski, B., Mazurczyk, W.: Cybersecurity: trends, issues, and challenges. EURASIP J. Inf. Secur. (2018). https://doi.org/10.1186/s13635-018-0080-0
2. Maleh, Y., Maleh, Y.: Understanding cybersecurity standards. In: Maleh, Y., Maleh, Y. (eds.) Cybersecurity in Morocco. SpringerBriefs in Cybersecurity, pp. 13–27. Springer, Cham (2022). https://doi.org/10.1007/978-3-031-18475-8_2
3. Chakir, O., et al.: An empirical assessment of ensemble methods and traditional machine learning techniques for web-based attack detection in industry 5.0. J. King Saud Univ. - Comput. Inf. Sci. 35, 103–119 (2023). https://doi.org/10.1016/j.jksuci.2023.02.009
4. Ghafur, S., Kristensen, S., Honeyford, K., Martin, G., Darzi, A., Aylin, P.: A retrospective impact analysis of the WannaCry cyberattack on the NHS. NPJ Digit. Med. 2, 98 (2019). https://doi.org/10.1038/s41746-019-0161-6
5. Microsoft's Digital Security Unit: an overview of Russia's cyberattack activity in Ukraine. 21 (2022)
6. AlDaajeh, S., Saleous, H., Alrabaee, S., Barka, E., Breitinger, F., Raymond Choo, K.-K.: The role of national cybersecurity strategies on the improvement of cybersecurity education. Comput. Secur. 119, 102754 (2022). https://doi.org/10.1016/j.cose.2022.102754
7. (ISC2): 2019 Cybersecurity Workforce Study (2019). https://www.isc2.org/-/media/ISC2/Research/2019-Cybersecurity-Workforce-Study/ISC2-Cybersecurity-Workforce-Study-2019.ashx
8. Mouheb, D., Abbas, S., Merabti, M.: Cybersecurity curriculum design: a survey. In: Pan, Z., Cheok, A.D., Müller, W., Zhang, M., El Rhalibi, A., Kifayat, K. (eds.)

Transactions on Edutainment XV. LNCS, vol. 11345, pp. 93–107. Springer, Heidelberg (2019). https://doi.org/10.1007/978-3-662-59351-6_9

9. CyberSkills: CyberSkills Taks Force Report. https://www.dhs.gov/publication/homeland-security-advisory-council-cyberskills-task-force-report. Accessed 28 Nov 2022

10. Chicone, R., Burton, T.M., Huston, J.A.: Using Facebook's open source capture the flag platform as a hands-on learning and assessment tool for cybersecurity education. Int. J. Concept. Struct. Smart Appl. **6**, 18–32 (2018). https://doi.org/10.4018/IJCSSA.2018010102

11. Carlson, L., Sullivan, J.: Hands-on engineering: learning by doing in the integrated teaching and learning program. Int. J. Eng. Educ. **15**(1), 20–31 (1999)

12. Trippe, D.M., Moriarty, K.O., Russell, T.L., Carretta, T.R., Beatty, A.S.: Development of a cyber/information technology knowledge test for military enlisted technical training qualification. Mil. Psychol. **26**, 182–198 (2014). https://doi.org/10.1037/mil0000042

13. Triejunita, C.N., Putri, A., Rosmansyah, Y.: A systematic literature review on virtual laboratory for learning. In: 2021 International Conference on Data and Software Engineering (ICoDSE), pp. 1–6. IEEE (2021). https://doi.org/10.1109/ICoDSE53690.2021.9648451

14. Kucek, S., Leitner, M.: An empirical survey of functions and configurations of open-source capture the flag (CTF) environments. J. Netw. Comput. Appl. **151**, 102470 (2020). https://doi.org/10.1016/j.jnca.2019.102470

15. Karagiannis, S., Maragkos-Belmpas, E., Magkos, E.: An analysis and evaluation of open source capture the flag platforms as cybersecurity e-learning tools. In: Drevin, L., Von Solms, S., Theocharidou, M. (eds.) WISE 2020. IAICT, vol. 579, pp. 61–77. Springer, Cham (2020). https://doi.org/10.1007/978-3-030-59291-2_5

16. Raman, R., Sunny, S., Pavithran, V., Achuthan, K.: Framework for evaluating capture the flag (CTF) security competitions. In: International Conference for Convergence for Technology-2014, pp. 1–5. IEEE (2014). https://doi.org/10.1109/I2CT.2014.7092098

17. Swann, M., Rose, J., Bendiab, G., Shiaeles, S., Li, F.: Open source and commercial capture the flag cyber security learning platforms - a case study. In: 2021 IEEE International Conference on Cyber Security and Resilience (CSR), pp. 198–205. IEEE (2021). https://doi.org/10.1109/CSR51186.2021.9527941

18. Knüpfer, M., et al.: Cyber taxi: a taxonomy of interactive cyber training and education systems. In: Hatzivasilis, G., Ioannidis, S. (eds.) MSTEC 2020. LNCS, vol. 12512, pp. 3–21. Springer, Cham (2020). https://doi.org/10.1007/978-3-030-62433-0_1

19. Landwehr, C.E., Bull, A.R., McDermott, J.P., Choi, W.S.: A taxonomy of computer program security flaws. ACM Comput. Surv. **26**, 211–254 (1994). https://doi.org/10.1145/185403.185412

20. TryHackMe. https://tryhackme.com. Accessed 03 Jan 2023

21. Hack The Box. https://www.hackthebox.com/. Accessed 03 Jan 2023

22. Root Me. https://www.root-me.org/. Accessed 03 Jan 2023

23. PentesterLab. https://pentesterlab.com/. Accessed 03 Jan 2023

24. Virtual Hacking Labs. https://www.virtualhackinglabs.com/. Accessed 03 Jan 2023

25. OWASP Juice Shop. https://owasp.org/www-project-juice-shop/. Accessed 03 Jan 2023

26. FBCTF (2023). https://github.com/facebookarchive/fbctf

134   A. Rehaimi et al.

27. LLC, K.C.// Ctf.: CTFd. https://ctfd.io/. Accessed 03 Jan 2023
28. picoCTF. https://picoctf.org/. Accessed 03 Jan 2023
29. TinyCTF. https://github.com/balidani/tinyctf-platform
30. CISA: NICE Cybersecurity Workforce Framework. https://www.cisa.gov/nice-cybersecurity-workforce-framework. Accessed 03 Jan 2023

White-Box Mutation Testing of Smart Contracts: A Quick Review

Afef Jmal Maâlej[(✉)] and Mariam Lahami

ReDCAD Laboratory, National School of Engineers of Sfax, University of Sfax,
BP 1173, 3038 Sfax, Tunisia
{afef.jmal,mariam.lahami}@redcad.org

Abstract. Once being deployed on the blockchain, smart contracts cannot be altered, requiring more testing. A fault-based testing technique called mutation testing (MT) can significantly increase the utility of a test for smart contracts. MT is a type of white-box testing which is mainly used for unit testing. In fact, certain statements of the source code are changed to check if the test cases are able to find errors in source code. The main objective of MT is ensuring the quality of test cases in terms of robustness in the way that it should fail the mutated source code. In this paper, our goal is to identify and classify the main applications of mutation testing of smart contracts by providing a quick review on the application perspective of mutation testing based on a collection of several papers. In particular, we analysed in which quality assurance processes mutation testing of smart contracts is used, which mutation tools and which mutation operators are employed.

Keywords: White-Box testing · Mutation Testing · Blockchain · Smart Contract

1 Introduction

Blockchain is a modern technology that has revolutionized the way society interacts and trades [18]. It might be described as a network of distributed, decentralized blocks that store data with digital signatures. This approach was initially used to develop digital currencies like Bitcoin and Ethereum. However, recent research and commercial studies have concentrated on the chances that blockchain offers in a variety of other application fields to benefit from this technology's key qualities, such as decentralization, persistency, and anonymity. Healthcare [13], internet of things [15,17] and vehicles [12,14] are just a few of the industries that employ blockchain.

In this context, smart contracts are computer programs implementing business logic that manage the data or assets on a blockchain environment. Although they have been introduced several years ago, the development of smart contracts is still challenging for developers. The latter usually produce vulnerable code which can lead to huge monetary losses. Therefore, it is essential to ensure

B. Ben Hedia et al. (Eds.): VECoS 2023, LNCS 14368, pp. 135–148, 2024.
https://doi.org/10.1007/978-3-031-49737-7_10

that smart contracts do not contain such vulnerabilities. The most important verification and validation technique for detecting both semantic errors and vulnerabilities is software testing. Testing smart contracts is even more crucial than testing regular programs, since their source code once deployed on the blockchain cannot be altered or changed due to their immutable nature. Furthermore, it is highly demanded to evaluate the quality of the tests and improve their adequacy. A powerful approach that can perform such assessments is *Mutation Testing* (MT). Indeed, this test technique consists on injecting faults into a given program to check the fault-detection capabilities of test suites [16].

A wide range of papers make use of this mature fault-based software testing technique to detect functional bugs and vulnerabilities in smart contracts because it is widely studied for over four decades. Thus, several approaches and tools are introduced in order to increase confidence on smart contracts [8,19,21]. However, we noticed the absence of surveys that include work done on mutation testing of smart contracts and give researchers new trends and challenges in this emerging research line.

Therefore, this paper presents a quick review that surveyed the most relevant studies related to MT of smart contracts dated from 2019. Particularly, we tackle the following main research questions:

- **RQ1:** What are the methodologies, approaches and tools based on mutation testing to verify smart contracts ?
- **RQ2:** Which mutation operators are mostly used by the studied approaches?

The answers to these questions help researchers to understand the studied topic, to identify the challenges in this research area and their solutions and also to discuss future directions. To do so, we first chose four well-known scientific and electronic databases (ScienceDirect Elsevier[1], ACM Digital Library[2], SpringerLink[3] and IEEE Xplore[4]) with the aim of extracting the most relevant papers related to our research topic. Second, we used the following search keywords which were the same in all databases: *"Mutation Testing AND Smart contract" OR "Mutation Testing AND Blockchain"*. Then, the selection of articles was performed by removing irrelevant articles after checking their titles and their abstracts and after being fully read we selected **14** as primary studies.

The remainder of this paper is organized as follows. Section 2 provides key concepts related to mutation testing and smart contracts. Related reviews and surveys are discussed in Sect. 3. Next, we investigate in Sect. 4 the most relevant researches on mutation testing applied in the context of smart contract verification. Finally, in Sect. 5, we conclude with a summary of paper contributions, and we identify possible areas of future research.

---

[1] https://www.elsevier.com.
[2] https://portal.acm.org.
[3] https://www.springerlink.com.
[4] https://www.ieee.org/web/publications/xplore/.

2   Background Materials

2.1   Mutation Testing

The use of mutation testing in software testing has the potential to improve software quality. Indeed, it is defined as a testing technique that injects faults into a program by creating several versions, each one contains one semantic fault. These faulty programs are named *mutants*. The generation of mutants is called mutation and that semantic fault is called mutation operator (MO). There are several traditional mutation operators that depend usually on programming languages such as deleting a statement, replacing boolean expressions, replacing arithmetic, and replacing a variable [24].

As highlighted in Fig. 1, the mutation testing process can be explained simply in following steps:

1. Given a program P and a set of test cases T.
2. Produce the mutant $P1$ from P by inserting only one semantic fault into P.
3. Execute T on both P and $P1$ and save results as R and $R1$.
4. Compare the output of mutant program $R1$ to the expected output R:
   (a) If $R1$ is not equal to R (i.e., $R1 \neq R$), the test cases detect the faults and the mutant is killed.
   (b) If $R1$ is equal to R (i.e., $R1 = R$), this can be due to the inefficiency of the test cases or the equivalence[5] of the mutant to the original program.
5. Calculate the mutation score (MS) which is the number of killed mutants divided by the total number of mutants, multiplied by 100. A mutation score of 100% means the test was efficient.

The process of adding test cases, examining expected output, and executing mutants continues until the threshold proposed by the tester is satisfied.

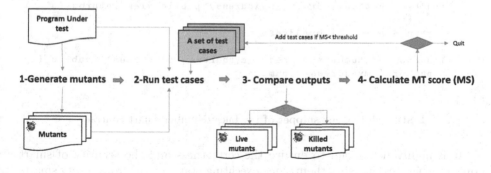

Fig. 1. Mutation Testing process.

---

[5] An equivalent mutant is a mutant, which is functionally equivalent to the original program.

2.2   Smart Contracts

Smart Contracts (SCs) are one of the most interesting features that have been introduced by several blockchain platforms with the purpose of managing digital assets and attaching business logic code to transactions. A SC is seen as a special program that was designed to be deployed on the distributed ledger, the blockchain. Without the need of third parties, SC is executed when some events occur allowing for making irreversible transactions. In the case of Ethereum[6], blockchain developers make use of a Turing complete language called Solidity[7] to implement Ethereum smart contracts. Similarly to JavaScript, the solidity language supports features like user-defined types, libraries and inheritance. By using the *solc*, the solidity compiler, smart contracts are compiled to the Ethereum Virtual Machine (EVM) bytecode.

As highlighted in Listing 1.1, a code snippet of a smart contract is given. A solidity smart contract is a collection of code (i.e., its functions) and data (i.e., its state variables) which is stored in a particular address on the Ethereum blockchain. In the first line, we specify the compiler version, then the keyword contract declares the contract with its name. In line 3, a state variable called "numbers" is declared as *mapping(address => uint)*. Mapping data structure in solidity acts like a hash table in which data are stored in the form of key-value pairs. Mappings are used here to associate each Ethereum address with its lucky number. Next, several functions are defined either to modify the state variable "numbers" by adding a new address with is associated lucky number or to read the lucky number of a given address.

```
1   pragma solidity ^0.8.17;
2   contract LuckyNumber {
3     mapping(address => uint) numbers;
4     function setNum(uint _num) public {
5       numbers[msg.sender] = _num;
6     }
7     function getNum(address _myAddress) public view returns (uint)
          {
8       return numbers[_myAddress];
9     }
10    function addNumbers(address _myaddress, uint _num)  public {
11      numbers[_myaddress]=_num;
12    }
13  }
```

Listing 1.1. Code snippet of the LuckyNumber smart contract.

It is highly demanded to ensure the correctness and the security of smart contracts before deploying them since executing transactions from boggy smarts contracts can lead to significant financial loss. Meanwhile, testing is one of the most important verification and validation techniques for ensuring software qual-

---

[6] https://ethereum.org/en/.
[7] https://solidity.readthedocs.io/.

ity. Especially, mutation testing was widely applied in the context of smart contract to check test suite adequacy and their ability to detect defects as more as possible.

3 Related Reviews

Many researchers are now interested in applying mutation testing technique to enhance software quality especially in the context of Blockchain oriented applications. Indeed, we have found recent surveys and methodical literature reviews that concentrate on dressing a literature review either on static testing [20] or dynamic testing of smart contracts [21].

A systematic review was introduced in [20] and it presented static analysis tools for Ethereum blockchain smart contracts. In this review, authors surveyed 86 papers that are published between 2016 to 2021. Among them only one paper dealt with mutation testing, that introduced the Musc tool [23].

A comprehensive survey on blockchain testing was presented in [22]. The authors mentioned academic articles on the subject of testing blockchains. Since it concentrated on static testing, dynamic testing, and formal verification, it had more scope than our work. It included only 6 papers that dealt with mutation testing.

Similarly, authors in [21] published a survey in which they provided a classification of 20 studies according to the accessibility of smart contract code. Among these papers (written from 2017 to 2021), only 6 of them focused on mutation testing and showed that this testing technique has a good effect on smart contract quality.

To the best of our knowledge, there are no current surveys that give thorough investigations connected to the issue of mutation testing of smart contracts and fully list the quantity and quality of relevant research results. Except the survey in [25] which investigated efforts on mutation testing tools while giving the pros and cons of them. The studied tools are only five: MuSC [23], SuMo [4], Deviant [5], Vertigo [10] and RegularMutator [11].

Compared to all these cited surveys, our review focuses on recent research effort by identifying methodologies and tools in this emerging field, assessing them, and highlighting both their difficulties and the unexplored areas that need more study.

4 Mutation Testing of Smart Contracts

In this section, we describe the different 14 selected papers dealing with white-box mutation testing of smart contracts. Figure 2 illustrates the year-wise analysis of the studied papers. It is clear that the increasing interest of academic research on mutation testing is rising over the years. The trend of using this technique to check the quality of test suites has a constant evolution from 2019 until 2022. Also, Fig. 3 highlights the classification of the selected primary studies by types.

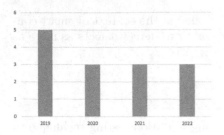

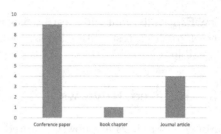

Fig. 2. Year-wise analysis of the selected studies.

Fig. 3. Analysis of the selected primary studies by type.

First of all, the authors provide in [4] a mutation testing approach and an associated fully working tool for Solidity smart contracts. For simulating a variety of conventional and Solidity-specific vulnerabilities, SuMo includes a complete set of mutation operators. Seven of the eleven innovative mutation operators were created with a focus on Solidity's distinctive features by means of the research of the Solidity documentation and the available tools. SuMo introduces mutation operators in particular that focus on the overloading mechanism. The SafeMath library, global blockchain variables, function modifiers, cryptographic global functions, enums, return values, and explicit conversions are other areas where SuMo adds additional operators.

ReSuMo [3] provides a regression testing and mutant selection technique to the SuMo tool [4] to accelerate mutation testing on evolving projects without affecting the accuracy of testing results. During a regression mutation testing initiative, ReSuMo chooses a selection of smart contracts to mutate and a subset of test files to run again using a static, file-level technique. ReSuMo continually updates the results of mutation testing while taking into account the results of the previous program version; this allows it to accelerate mutation testing on evolving projects without reducing the mutation score. The authors should concentrate on examining additional fine-grained regression mutation testing methodologies in order to increase ReSuMo's efficacy, particularly for small and tightly-coupled smart contract projects. The tester would then be able to define a preferred level of computation granularity.

The authors specifically address in [27] the EtherFuzz mutation fuzzy testing technique to find TOD (Transaction-Ordering Dependent) vulnerabilities in smart contracts. They create test cases for the intelligent contract using the ABI (Application Binary Interface), test the byte code of the contract using TOD to find vulnerabilities, then they change the tested data to create new test cases. After recording the execution of the smart contract, the fuzzy test process is regulated until the vulnerability is identified.

The study in [26] proposes five mutation operators specifically for integer overflow vulnerability and applies mutation testing to the integer overflow vulnerability test in Ethereum smart contracts. According to the empirical research, mutation operators are able to produce these vulnerability mutants and assess the appropriate testing tools. The experiment choice of ERC20 token smart contracts, however, could skew the findings in one direction.

Besides, the authors of [6] present AGSOLT (Automated Generator of Solidity Test Suites). They use two search algorithms to automatically construct test suites for standalone Solidity smart contracts, taking into account some of the specific challenges of the blockchain. However, the used data set is not typical of Solidity smart contracts in general, although showing each of the characteristics that are indicative of the identified blockchain specific issues.

In [7], the authors provide a tool called TestSmart that can create a set of efficient test cases for Ethereum smart contracts automatically. It is made up of a module to generate test suites, a module for generating mutants, and a module to select test cases based on the mutants. The generation of the test suite was performed using the Manticore tool. An expansion of the Universal Mutator was used for mutant generation; it comprises the mutation operators previously introduced for Solidity smart contracts. The test cases against the mutants were examined using the Manticore API. The inability to generate test cases with transactions generated neither by the contract owner nor the attacker is a significant weakness of Manticore.

The authors suggest in [11] applying mutational analysis to enhance Solidity smart contracts reliability. They developed a RegularMutator tool for mutation analysis after finding widespread errors in the source code of existing contracts. However, it took around 50 h of machine time to complete the experiments. Actually, mutation analysis is computationally challenging, which prevents it from being useful in some contexts. Additionally, a large number of mutants that survived the experiment need to be manually checked and analysed.

In addition, the authors of [9] evaluate the efficiency of large-scale smart contract mutation testing. They select among the available specific mutation operators for smart contracts, assess their effectiveness in regards to killability, and identify critical vulnerabilities that can be exploited by the mutations. The authors only take into account a replay test suite, which is less efficient than other testing methods and can yield a higher mutation score. The objective of this work was to develop a mutation-based test quality assurance approach that can also act as a starting point for other testing techniques, even though there are better testing methods.

In [2], the authors provide a mutation-based testing system for smart contracts written in the Solidity programming language. They reviewed a comprehensive list of known Solidity smart contract faults and developed 10 classes of mutation operators that were designed based on the actual errors. Furthermore, they added mutation operators to the Universal Mutator tool, enabling it to automatically produce mutants for Solidity-written smart contracts.

The development of a mutation testing framework and its application to the field of smart contracts were both studied by the authors in [10]. They demonstrated how developers may use mutation testing to evaluate the effectiveness of their test suite and make improvements to it in order to make it more efficient.

They also produced a tool called Vertigo, which should identify the precise tests that cover the line on which the mutant causes a syntactic change rather than executing the complete test suite for each mutant. The final result of tests that do not include this line should not be impacted by the modification.

The authors describe in [1] a fully automated method, called SolAnalyser, for Solidity smart contract vulnerability detection that combines static and dynamic analysis. The proposed SolAnalyser tool can be expanded to handle different vulnerability types and allows the automatic detection of 8 different vulnerability classes that are currently underrepresented in existing technologies. In addition, the authors included a fault seeding tool that introduces various vulnerabilities into smart contracts. However, by enhancing the quality of the generated inputs, SolAnalyser precision can further be improved.

The challenge of Ethereum smart contracts test generation was described by the authors of [28] as a Pareto minimization problem. Minimizing uncovered branch coverage, time costs, and gas costs are three objectives that are taken into consideration. Then, in order to identify test suites, the authors suggest a multi-objective strategy based on randomness and NSGA-II (a representative multi-objective genetic algorithm).

The authors of [23] introduce MuSC, an Ethereum Smart Contract (ESC) mutation testing tool. It facilitates autonomous processes including building test nets, deploying them, and running tests, besides it has the capacity to quickly produce large numbers of mutants. With regard to the Solidity ESC programming language, MuSC implements a number of unique mutation operators in particular. As a consequence, it can expose the defects of smart contracts to a certain degree. However, there are several issues that need to be enhanced, like handling errors.

Deviant, a mutation testing tool for Solidity smart contracts, is presented in [5]. It generates mutants of a particular Solidity project automatically and analyses each mutation against the specified tests to determine its efficiency. Deviant offers mutation operators for all of Solidity's special features in accordance with the Solidity fault model, in addition to conventional programming constructs, that simulate various problems in Solidity smart contracts. Using Deviant, the authors evaluated the effectiveness of the tests for three Solidity projects. The findings show that these tests have not yet attained high mutation scores and that a test suite that meets the requirements of Solidity smart contracts for statement and branch coverage does not always guarantee the highest level of code quality.

We highlight that all the previously introduced papers are depicted in Table 1 such as:

- Column **Paper:** refers to the surveyed paper.
- Column **Tool:** refers to the name of the proposed testing tool (if it exists).
- Column **Testing objective:** refers to the aim behind performing mutation testing.

- Column **Number of MO:** refers to the number of adopted mutation operators in each paper (if mentioned), considering the known real bugs made by smart contract developers.
- Column **MS calculation:** refers to the mutation score calculation or not for each paper.
- Column **Number of vulnerabilities:** refers to the number of weaknesses that malicious actors can exploit in smart contracts (if mentioned).
- Column **Year:** refers to the publication year of each paper.

Table 1. Surveyed approaches on white-box mutation testing of smart contracts.

Paper	Tool	Testing objective	Number of MO	MS calculation	Number of vulnerabilities	Year
[3]	ReSuMO	Regression testing	44	Yes	Not mentioned	2022
[27]	EtherFuzz	Security testing	14	No	1	2022
[26]	No proposed tool	Security testing	5	Yes	1	2022
[4]	SuMo	Functional testing	44	Yes	6	2021
[6]	AGSolT	Functional testing	Not mentioned	No	Not mentioned	2021
[7]	TestSmart	Security testing	57	Yes	Not mentioned	2021
[11]	RegularMutator	Security testing	6	Yes	3	2020
[9]	ContractMut	Scalability testing	14	Yes	7	2020
[2]	Extension of the Universal Mutator tool	Security testing	57	No	8	2020
[10]	Vertigo	Functional testing	6	Yes	Not mentioned	2019
[1]	SolAnalyser	Security testing	Not mentioned	No	8	2019
[28]	No proposed tool	Performance testing	3	No	Not mentioned	2019
[23]	MuSC	Security testing	15	Yes	Not mentioned	2019
[5]	Deviant	Functional testing	61	Yes	Not mentioned	2019

To respond the first research question **RQ1** and as presented in Table 1, both [26] and [28] did not propose testing tools as an automation of their solutions, while the other approaches implemented their frameworks in form of different mutation tools, even for the majority source codes are open on GitHub.

Besides, each surveyed approach focuses on a specific testing objective using mutation testing. It could be about:

- *Regression testing* [3]: concerns testing existing software applications to make sure that a change has not broken any existing functionality.
- *Security testing* [1, 2, 7, 11, 23, 26, 27]: concerns a cybersecurity technique that organizations use to identify, test and highlight vulnerabilities in their security posture.
- *Functional testing* [4–6, 10]: concerns a type of testing that seeks to establish whether each application feature works as the software requirements.

- *Scalability testing* [9]: concerns a testing of a software application to measure its capability to scale up or scale out in terms of any of its non-functional capability.
- *Performance testing* [28]: concerns evaluating how a system performs in terms of responsiveness and stability under a particular workload.

Besides, the authors of [6] and [1] did not mention explicitly the number of introduced mutation operators, whereas this latter criterion varies widely from 3 to 61 mutation operators among the other publications. In fact, it is up to the tester to choose the scope or specificity of the operators. Some authors prefer to introduce a specific operator for every singular change, others choose to group together similar changes into one operator. Note that the power of mutation testing is very much dependent on its mutation operators, and the operators that can mimic the real bugs can select more effective test cases.

As a response to **RQ2**, and based on a collection of most repeated bugs that may happen in the implementation of a smart contract in Solidity programming language, the majority of researchers categorize them to two groups:

1) Classic Bugs: these bugs occur in almost any programming language, from which we can mention arithmetic issues or logical bugs (inside conditions).

2) Solidity Bugs: these faults are mostly related to the Solidity programming languages, and the distributed nature of blockchain and smart contracts. Hence, it is noticed that classical mutation operators designed for general-purpose programming languages, e.g. JavaScript, are not sufficient for the Ethereum platform, and other mutation operators need to be designed to simulate the Solidity specific bugs. So, mutation operators are divided as well into two groups: **(i)** Classic mutation operators, and **(ii)** Solidity mutation operators.

In addition, 9 out of 14 papers calculate the mutation score for a set of test cases, which corresponds to the percentage of mutants killed by these scenarios, and is a metric for evaluating the effectiveness of test cases.

50% of studied works mentioned the number of treated vulnerabilities, among basically eight well-known vulnerabilities that are reported frequently in the smart contract weakness classification (SWC) registry[8]. It is about: integer overflow/underflow, division by zero, timestamp dependency, authorisation through tx.orgin, unchecked send, repetitive call function and finally out of gas.

The assessment of the selected studies is based on several criteria highlighted in Table 2. Then, the obtained results are introduced in Table 3. Only four studies achieved 100% on quality evaluation [6, 9, 10, 27]. A wide range of papers are greater than 80%.

---

[8] https://swcregistry.io/.

Table 2. Quality criteria

ID	Criteria
QC1	Are the study context and objectives appropriately described?
QC2	Is the proposed approach described in detail?
QC3	Are the study findings discussed?
QC4	Is the effectiveness of the proposed approach evaluated on at least an example of case study?
QC5	Are the proposed approach limitations outlined and discussed?
QC6	Does the study include a positioning among existing related works?

Table 3. Quality assessment scores of the selected and analysed studies

Paper	QC1	QC2	QC3	QC4	QC5	QC6	Quality %
[3]	1	1	1	1	0	1	83.34%
[27]	1	1	1	1	1	1	100%
[26]	1	1	1	1	0	1	83.34%
[4]	1	1	1	1	0	1	83.34%
[6]	1	1	1	1	1	1	100%
[7]	1	1	1	1	0	1	83.34%
[11]	1	0	1	1	0	1	66.67%
[9]	1	1	1	1	1	1	100%
[2]	1	1	1	1	0	1	83.34%
[10]	1	1	1	1	1	1	100%
[1]	1	1	1	1	0	1	83.34%
[28]	1	1	1	1	0	0	66.67%
[23]	1	1	1	1	0	0	66.67%
[5]	1	1	1	1	0	1	83.34%

5   Conclusion

In this quick review, we investigated the state of art related to mutation testing of smart contracts. We included **14** studies published from 2019 to 2022 and we analysed them to provide researchers relevant information about the used mutation operators and the calculation of mutation score. Moreover, a deep classification of these studies were discussed while giving their strengths and weaknesses.

Up to our best knowledge, existing surveys focused on static analysis and dynamic testing. Our survey has a significant contribution in the literature since it was the first one that dealt specifically with mutation testing of smart contracts. Definitely, more refinement should be accorded in the future to review the latest studies on mutation testing of smart contracts and more meaningful research questions should be proposed.

In conclusion, the study's findings showed that most research publications come from conference proceedings and all of them focused on Ethereum smart contracts written in Solidity language. We think that further research and development are needed in order to advance the state of the art in this research line. For instance, we can investigate the application of mutation testing techniques on others programming languages used for smart contracts (e.g., Serpent, Vyper, Go, etc.) and also other blockchain platforms like HyperLedger Fabric.

References

1. Akca, S., Rajan, A., Peng, C.: SolAnalyser: a framework for analysing and testing smart contracts. In: Proceedings of the 26th Asia-Pacific Software Engineering Conference (APSEC), pp. 482–489 (2019)
2. Andesta, E., Faghih, F., Fooladgar, M.: Testing smart contracts gets smarter. In: Proceedings of the 10th International Conference on Computer and Knowledge Engineering (ICCKE), pp. 405–412. The Organization (2020)
3. Barboni, M., Casoni, F., Morichetta, A., Polini, A.: ReSuMo: regression mutation testing for solidity smart contracts. In: Vallecillo, A., Visser, J., Pérez-Castillo, R. (eds.) QUATIC 2022. CCIS, vol. 1621, pp. 61–76. Springer, Cham (2022). https://doi.org/10.1007/978-3-031-14179-9_5
4. Barboni, M., Morichetta, A., Polini, A.: SuMo: a mutation testing strategy for solidity smart contracts. In: Proceedings of the IEEE/ACM International Conference on Automation of Software Test (AST), pp. 50–59 (2021). https://doi.org/10.1109/AST52587.2021.00014
5. Chapman, P., Xu, D., Deng, L., Xiong, Y.: Deviant: a mutation testing tool for solidity smart contracts. In: Proceedings of the IEEE International Conference on Blockchain (Blockchain), pp. 319–324 (2019). https://doi.org/10.1109/Blockchain.2019.00050
6. Driessen, S., Nucci, D.D., Monsieur, G., van den Heuvel, W.: AGSoLT: a tool for automated test-case generation for solidity smart contracts. CoRR **abs/2102.08864** (2021). https://arxiv.org/abs/2102.08864
7. Fooladgar, M., Arefzadeh, A., Faghih, F.: TestSmart: a tool for automated generation of effective test cases for smart contracts. In: Proceedings of the 11th International Conference on Computer Engineering and Knowledge (ICCKE), pp. 476–481 (2021). https://doi.org/10.1109/ICCKE54056.2021.9721448
8. Hammami, M.A., Lahami, M., Maâlej, A.J.: Towards a dynamic testing approach for checking the correctness of ethereum smart contracts. In: Kallel, S., Jmaiel, M., Zulkernine, M., Hadj Kacem, A., Cuppens, F., Cuppens, N. (eds.) CRiSIS 2022. LNCS, vol. 13857, pp. 85–100. Springer, Cham (2022). https://doi.org/10.1007/978-3-031-31108-6_7
9. Hartel, P., Schumi, R.: Mutation testing of smart contracts at scale. In: Ahrendt, W., Wehrheim, H. (eds.) TAP 2020. LNCS, vol. 12165, pp. 23–42. Springer, Cham (2020). https://doi.org/10.1007/978-3-030-50995-8_2

10. Honig, J.J., Everts, M.H., Huisman, M.: Practical mutation testing for smart contracts. In: Pérez-Solà, C., Navarro-Arribas, G., Biryukov, A., Garcia-Alfaro, J. (eds.) DPM/CBT -2019. LNCS, vol. 11737, pp. 289–303. Springer, Cham (2019). https://doi.org/10.1007/978-3-030-31500-9_19

11. Ivanova, Y., Khritankov, A.: RegularMutator: a mutation testing tool for solidity smart contracts. Procedia Comput. Sci. **178**, 75–83 (2020)

12. Jabbar, R., Fetais, N., Kharbeche, M., Krichen, M., Barkaoui, K., Shinoy, M.: Blockchain for the internet of vehicles: how to use blockchain to secure vehicle-to-everything (V2X) communication and payment? IEEE Sens. J. **21**(14), 15807–15823 (2021)

13. Jabbar, R., Fetais, N., Krichen, M., Barkaoui, K.: Blockchain technology for healthcare: enhancing shared electronic health record interoperability and integrity. In: 2020 IEEE International Conference on Informatics, IoT, and Enabling Technolo gies (ICIoT), pp. 310–317. IEEE (2020)

14. Jabbar, R., Kharbeche, M., Al-Khalifa, K., Krichen, M., Barkaoui, K.: Blockchain for the internet of vehicles: a decentralized IoT solution for vehicles communication using ethereum. Sensors **20**(14), 3928 (2020)

15. Jabbar, R., Krichen, M., Kharbeche, M., Fetais, N., Barkaoui, K.: A formal model-based testing framework for validating an IoT solution for blockchain-based vehicles communication. In: 15th International Conference on Evaluation of Novel Approaches to Software Engineering, pp. 595–602. SCITEPRESS-Science and Technology Publications (2020)

16. Jia, Y., Harman, M.: An analysis and survey of the development of mutation testing. IEEE Trans. Software Eng. **37**(5), 649–678 (2011). https://doi.org/10.1109/TSE.2010.62

17. Krichen, M.: Strengthening the security of smart contracts through the power of artificial intelligence. Computers **12**(5), 107 (2023)

18. Krichen, M., Ammi, M., Mihoub, A., Almutiq, M.: Blockchain for modern applications: a survey. Sensors **22**(14), 5274 (2022)

19. Krichen, M., Lahami, M., Al-Haija, Q.A.: Formal methods for the verification of smart contracts: a review. In: 15th International Conference on Security of Information and Networks, SIN 2022, Sousse, Tunisia, 11–13 November 2022, pp. 1–8. IEEE (2022). https://doi.org/10.1109/SIN56466.2022.9970534

20. Kushwaha, S.S., Joshi, S., Singh, D., Kaur, M., Lee, H.N.: Ethereum smart contract analysis tools: a systematic review. IEEE Access **10**, 57037–57062 (2022). https://doi.org/10.1109/ACCESS.2022.3169902

21. Lahami, M., Maâlej, A.J., Krichen, M., Hammami, M.A.: A comprehensive review of testing blockchain oriented software. In: Proceedings of the 17th International Conference on Evaluation of Novel Approaches to Software Engineering, ENASE 2022, Online Streaming, 25–26 April 2022, pp. 355–362. SCITEPRESS (2022)

22. Lal, C., Marijan, D.: Blockchain testing: challenges, techniques, and research directions. CoRR **abs/2103.10074** (2021). https://arxiv.org/abs/2103.10074

23. Li, Z., Wu, H., Xu, J., Wang, X., Zhang, L., Chen, Z.: MuSC: a tool for mutation testing of ethereum smart contract. In: Proceeding of 34th IEEE/ACM International Conference on Automated Software Engineering (ASE), pp. 1198–1201 (2019)

24. Nguyen, Q.V., Madeyski, L.: Problems of mutation testing and higher order mutation testing. In: van Do, T., Thi, H.A.L., Nguyen, N.T. (eds.) Advanced Computational Methods for Knowledge Engineering. AISC, vol. 282, pp. 157–172. Springer, Cham (2014). https://doi.org/10.1007/978-3-319-06569-4_12

25. Sujeetha, R., Preetha, C.A.S.D.: Analysis on mutation testing tools for smart contracts. IJETT J. **70**, 280–289 (2022)
26. Sun, J., Huang, S., Zheng, C., Wang, T., Zong, C., Hui, Z.: Mutation testing for integer overflow in ethereum smart contracts. Tsinghua Sci. Technol. **27**(1), 27–40 (2022). https://doi.org/10.26599/TST.2020.9010036 https://doi.org/10.26599/TST.2020.9010036
27. Wang, X., Sun, J., Hu, C., Yu, P., Zhang, B., Hou, D.: Etherfuzz: mutation fuzzing smart contracts for TOD vulnerability detection. Wireless Commun. Mob. Comput. **2022** (2022). https://doi.org/10.1155/2022/1565007
28. Wang, X., Wu, H., Sun, W., Zhao, Y.: Towards generating cost-effective test-suite for ethereum smart contract. In: Proceedings of the IEEE 26th International Conference on Software Analysis, Evolution and Reengineering (SANER), pp. 549–553 (2019)

Blockchain-Based Trust Management for IoMT Environment

Mariem Fourati[✉], Amel Meddeb-Makhlouf, and Faouzi Zarai

New Technologies and Communication Systems Research Unit, ENET'COM, Sfax, Tunisia
mariem.frt@gmail.com, {amel.makhlouf,
faouzi.zerai}@enetcom.usf.tn

Abstract. Nowadays, many services keep evolving and can be used in different environments. One of the challenging environments is the Internet of Things, which makes people's lives easier. Nevertheless, securing these systems is a big challenge. To address this challenge, several methods have been proposed to establish a trust level for entities considering different characteristics, basically the direct observations and feedbacks. In this paper, we present a trust computation model that considers not only the collected observations from different nodes, but also the collected medical data. In this contribution, we choose to work with ECG data. In our model, a decentralized propagation method is adopted where we use a private blockchain to track different trust updates. The results show the time required to compute the trust.

Keywords: IoT · Trust · Healthcare · ECG · Blockchain

1 Introduction

The IoT (Internet of Things) proposes a wireless network composed of a collection of nodes communicating with each other. In the past few years, this network has led to a huge exchange of information between different sensors and environments facilitating, as a result, the access to distinct services such as the healthcare service called IoMT (Internet of Medical Things) based on medical sensors collecting miscellaneous medical data. This allows remote patient monitoring and offers different customized services. The major problem in this environment consists of having security threats and cyber-attacks [1–3]. Those threats affect one or many security objectives such as integrity and availability [4]. Consequently, it can cause data alteration and service damaging. Thus, researchers focus on mechanisms to boost security in the IoMT environment.

One of those mechanisms is the trust-based systems where each network must ensure a certain level of trust between network nodes to avoid any malicious behavior. Trust can be defined as having belief that something does not represent a danger [5]. In the healthcare IoT, the doctor must guarantee a minimum of trust towards the data received from the patient such as ECG (Electrocardiogram) data. To limit the dangers on the IoMT and to offer a better service to patients and doctors, we propose a trust system using features to compute trust level and to share it using a decentralized network i.e. blockchain. Thus, our main objectives are:

B. Ben Hedia et al. (Eds.): VECoS 2023, LNCS 14368, pp. 149–162, 2024.
https://doi.org/10.1007/978-3-031-49737-7_11

- Deploying a system that controls trust between patient and medical side,
- Considering the medical data (i.e., ECG attributes) as an additional factor in the trust level,
- Deploying a blockchain network that brings interesting features like decentralization and traceability to store trust variations.

Our paper is organized as Follows: Sect. 2 introduces the related works, which motivates our work detailed in Sect. 3. The performance evaluation of the proposed solution is presented in Sect. 4, while Sect. 5 concludes the paper.

2 Related Work

Recent researches worked on designing trust systems ensuring confidence between entities. They designed different approaches related to different domain of application in IoT. But they are always based on the same trust management system architecture [6–8].

The contribution [9] treats the case of SMP (Smart Marketplace) that calculates a participant trust per resources. It is calculated according to feedbacks, past experiences, and the degree of commitment. There are three important components in the commitment feature: Resource availability, successful transactions rate and the turnaround time that describe the responding time to a request.

In the IoT systems, regardless the application domain, numerous contributions were proposed. Xu. And Junbin in [10] designed a framework of BBTM (Blockchain-based Trust Management Method) that focuses on reliability in trust management to energy-limited nodes in IoT network. The fundamental metric used is the feedback. The evaluation is ensured by mobile edge that is rewarded according to their results. In [11], the authors designed a trust system included in an ABAC (Attribute Based Access Control) authorization system that supervises Service Provider and Service Consumer. The storage is divided into two parts: private storage for sensitive data and public storage for nodes' scores. The TRS (Trust and reputation system) is based on experiences and feedbacks. Another blockchain-based trust model presented by Tu. et al. [12] where the architecture is composed of devices connected to gateways. Both direct and indirect reputation are based on gateways' evaluations. They also implemented a dynamic Evaluation Mechanism that adapts the used time interval between trust calculations.

In the IoMT and healthcare, we present the trust mechanism BFT-IoMT [13] that aims to mitigate Sybil attacks based on a fuzzy logic. The algorithm uses essentially the node's MAC address and energy. An approach based on Deep learning: NeuroTrust was proposed in [14]. In fact, authors propose to divide the trust features into two types: direct and indirect. Direct evaluation calculates trust using the packet delivery ratio, the compatibility between different nodes, and reliability. For nodes without previous observations, the solution appeals to indirect evaluation that includes the shared experience by neighboring nodes. In [15], the authors designed TrIDS that calculates trust level using beta reputation model to exploit it in the intrusion detection system. The IDS is deployed in Medical Cyber-physical Systems. The trust level is computed based on rules checking the existence of intrusions and alerts. This is done using behavior monitoring and collection to create intrusive profiles. Based on binomial Distribution, the Binomial Distribution-Based Trust Management Algorithm [5] aims to protect the WBAN system through devices' reputation and information encryption. The reputation level is based on cooperation occurrence between nodes as well as the cooperation probability.

Those proposals used both direct observations and indirect recommendations but disregard the control over medical signals transmitted via the WSN (Wireless Sensor Networks).

Table 1. Related work Overview

Paper	Trust Metrics			Trust Propagation		Application field
	Direct observations	Indirect recommendations (feedbacks)	Service/Health related data	Centralized	Decentralized	
T-smart [9]	✔	✔			✔	Smart Marketplace
BBTM [10]	✔	✔			✔	IoT
Trust-based Blockchain Authorization for IoT [11]		✔			✔	IoT
Blockhain-based Trust and Reputation Model [12]	✔	✔			✔	IoT
BFT-IoMT[13]	✔				✔	IoT healthcare
NeuroTrust [14]	✔	✔		✔		IoT healthcare
TrIDS [15]	✔			✔		Smart healthcare
Binomial Distribution-Based Trust [5]	✔			✔		IoT healthcare
Trust-Based Decision Making for Health IoT Systems [16]	✔	✔	✔	✔		IoT healthcare

Authors in [16] considered the medical aspect of the patient and proposed a trust computation process that takes into consideration not only user's localization ratings' but also loss health possibility. Through this protocol design, they can make decisions related to only the trustworthy users. But they used as a trust propagation mechanism a centralized cloud.

The previously studied related works are resumed in Table 1. They proposed trust computing solutions based on different features. These works analyses user's behaviors and history. Nevertheless, these works do not consider the network-based intrusions and anomalies detected from patient medical data that can be corresponded to executed attacks, which affects the patient life. Added to that, some works uses a centralized trust storage which can affect data availability if there are no security mechanisms implemented.

To overcome these drawbacks, our approach proposes a different way to estimate the trust level by using not only direct sensors' related observations but also medical attributes to evaluate the trustworthiness of a patient in the network. Moreover, to track attackers, we propose to store trusts levels into a private Blockchain.

3 Proposed Solution

In this section, we propose to ameliorate the existent trust systems by introducing (1) other features in the trust computing; (2) formulas considering attacks aiming the patient data and (3) traceability of the trust updates via the blockchain technology. Hence, we develop in the following the calculating trust solution.

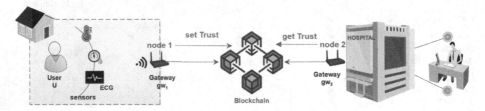

Fig. 1. System Architecture

3.1 Architecture

Our system architecture is derived from [14], where we have two main sides: the user side and the medical supervision side. The user side contains nodes and sensors collecting both health data and surrounding environment data like the humidity and temperature. Those sensors gather the information that will be sent to the gateway (see Fig. 1). The medical sensors can collect multiple health data: ECG measures, blood pressure, temperature. In our approach we will consider ECG features.

The medical side represents the hospital or the medical organization inspecting the patient data. It englobes the medical personal that can access medical patient data.

This architecture aims to ensure trust between entities constituting the IoT system. In fact, the hospital side must trust the data of every patient. In fact, before the doctor can consult collected data, the gateway gw_2 retrieves trust level from the Blockchain. If it is trusted, the data will be allowed to access. The trust level is stored in the blockchain network. As a result, the user U and the organization must have a connected blockchain node to guarantee the connectivity and the visibility of the transactions in the ledger. Added to that, they will be able to set the trust value and get it. In our solution, the gateway will be the blockchain node.

As described in Fig. 2, the gateway collects information from different sensors and performs attributes' pre-processing before invoking the features and the final score in the smart contract.

The trust is then stored in a deployed smart contract in the blockchain network.

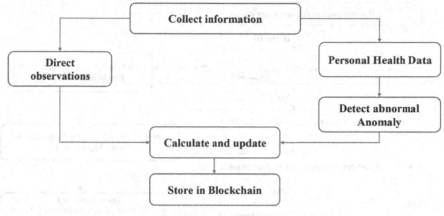

Fig. 2. General Process

3.2 Trust Management Model

We propose to implement a trust solution based on different metrics. The gateway handles the trust mechanism, composed of data reception, computation and sending data to the blockchain. The global algorithm is detailed in the organigram in Fig. 3.

The patient that wants to access the network is always controlled. In fact, if it is his first access, he will be accepted and each time interval the trust is updated. The first decrease in the trust will not eliminate him from the network. However, successive decrease that led to a trust value less than the defined threshold will result the rejection.

If the device that wants to join the system is rejected before, then it will be accepted and monitored during some time interval, to estimate his good faith.

Let $w1$ and $w2$ present weights with: $w1 + w2 = 1$ and $w1 < w2$, since we want to take into consideration the trust history. Trust threshold is a value defined by the network administrator. It defines the limit that helps deciding when the user is either trusted or not.

3.3 Trust Computation

The trust metrics are divided into direct observations and medical information. The metrics associated to direct observations are energy consumption rate and packet transmission ratio. Those features are collected from every node connected to a person. Trust is calculated every interval Δt that is defined by the administrator.

The energy feature presents the energy consumption rate of a sensor. The consumption is controlled, so if there is any suspicious deviation in the energy use, it will be tracked as a sign of malicious behavior like the DoS (Denial of Service) attack [17]. This consumption differs from a sensor nature to another. In fact, the user U is connected to numerous sensors. Hence, we collect the energy rate of every node i connected to him. Then, we calculate the normalized energy value consumed per sensor i as detailed in Eq. (1).

$$e_i = \frac{energy\ rate_i}{100} \tag{1}$$

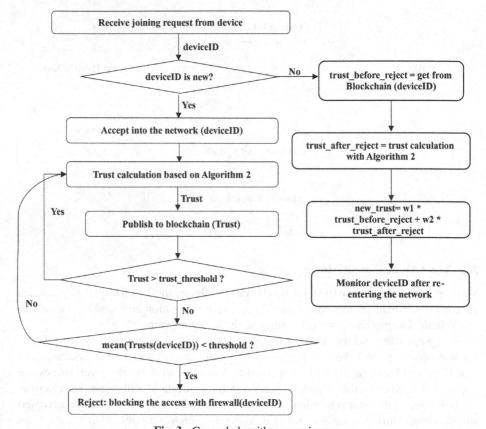

Fig. 3. General algorithm organigram

The patient's energy consumption value will be the average of different energy values e_i (Eq. (2)). An important increase in the energy consumption leads to a decrease in the trust level.

$$e = 1 - \frac{\sum_i e_i}{i} \qquad (2)$$

The packet ratio is inspired from [14] which is defined as described in (3).

$$PDR = \frac{\sum received\ packets\ gw1}{\sum total\ sent\ packets\ gw1} \qquad (3)$$

In our network, healthcare sensors present a fundamental information source. Those data can be affected either by normal noise (for example noise caused by patient movement) or by intrusion. It is necessary to detect anomalies accruing from intrusions to include this information in the trust score. As the medical data is miscellaneous, and each body sensor can return a specific data form, we will focus on the ECG signals. ECG or Electrocardiography is used to track the electric signal of the human body heart [18]. ECG signals are characterized by different attributes such as QRS interval and heart beats. Any changes in the characteristics of the signal reflects a disease or an instability in the human body. Many works like [19] described the different diseases patterns in ECG signals that can appear on the patient data.

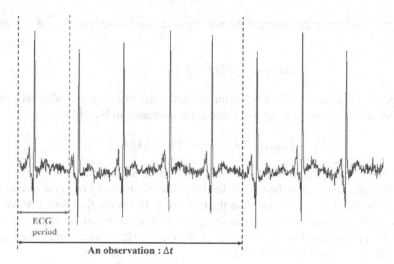

An observation : Δt

Fig. 4. Relation between observation and ECG period

We propose in this work to detect, in each time interval Δt, the existing security related anomalies in the ECG data. A detected value is declared as anomaly if it deviates from the normal pattern of the disease. In other words, any value that exceeds the normal threshold is considered as anomaly.

A time interval Δt is an observation that include n ECG periods as detailed in Fig. 4. With n is the periods' number per observation that is fixed by the system's administrator.

ECG data is analyzed by the gateway. In fact, the received ECG value is compared to the normal disease threshold. The output of this operation is dissected into two categories according to the deviation: normal or abnormal behavior. The number of detected anomalies in an observation is used in the trust equation. Anomalies rate is described in Eq. (4).

$$Arate = \frac{NB_{anomalies}}{NB_{periods}} \tag{4}$$

Added to that, we consider the margin between detected ECG value in the period and the defined threshold th_n for a malicious behavior. Therefore, we calculate this deviation $D_{ECGperiod}$ in every medical period as explained in Eq. (5).

$$D_{ECGperiod} = \text{value} - th_n \tag{5}$$

Based on (6), the final signal deviation $D_{\Delta t}$ considered in the trust formula is expressed by the mean of different deviations values issued from (5).

$$D_{\Delta t} = mean(D_{ECGperiod}) \tag{6}$$

With (7), the related trust for those medical signals is the weighted combination of Eqs. (4) and (6) where the trust increments when the anomalies' number decrements.

$$T_{ECG} = 1 - (w_{ECG} * Arate + (1 - w_{ECG}) * D_{\Delta t}) \tag{7}$$

The trust value for the interval Δt will be as defined in (8). α, β, and γ represent weights.

$$T(\Delta t) = \alpha * PDR + \beta * T_{ECG} + \gamma * e \tag{8}$$

Since a node cannot deflect behavior suddenly, the instant trust value will include the old one with the use of weights (λ and μ) as indicated in Eq. (9).

$$T_{patient} = \lambda T(\Delta(t - 1)) * \mu T(\Delta t) \tag{9}$$

The whole trust calculation process is described in Algorithm 1.

All the collected patient data related either to the environment or to the medical state is handled by the gateway to calculate the trust level. If it is the first time that we affect a trust level to the patient, we note this information in the distributed ledger. Otherwise, we retrieve the current state from the blockchain network, we recalculate the trust and we publish the transaction in the ledger.

Every medical entity wishing access to the patient data must be sure that the patient data are reliable. That's why, the system recovers the trust value from the blockchain. If it is classified as trusted, then the system will allow access to the doctor. If not, it will be rejected and not taken into consideration.

Algorithm 1. Trust Computation Algorithm
*1: **for** each observation Δt*
*2: **for** each device i*
3: Get data collected in time interval
4: Standardize energy_rate_i by equation (1)
*5: **if** device **i** is a medical sensor **then***
*6: **for** each medical period ECG_period*
*7: **if** classified as anomaly*
8: NBanomalies++
9: calculate deviation $D_{ECGperiod}$ with equation (5)
10: T_{ECG} calculated by equation (7)
11: PDR calculated by equation (3)
12: new Trust $T(\Delta t)$ calculated by equation (8)
13: Patient trust $T_{patient}$ calculated by equation (9)

3.4 Blockchain Network

The blockchain technology consists of different nodes that share a distributed ledger to ensure transactions storage. One of the most interesting characteristics of this network is decentralization and traceability. The blockchain network can be either public or private [20].

In our proposed solution, we adopted the private blockchain because we will implement it into a healthcare ecosystem that contains known nodes. We propose to create the blockchain (as described in Fig. 5) consisting of nodes. Those nodes represent different gateways connected to the network either a medical professional or a person.

The used blockchain platform is GoQuorum. It is a permissioned blockchain based on the Ethereum network. The major difference between GoQuorum and Ethereum is the used consensus protocol. In fact, to achieve consensus, this permissioned network does not rely on proof of work algorithms. Instead, it is based on different consensus algorithms in particular Raft, algorithms based on Byzantine fault tolerance and Clique PoA [21]. To implement the blockchain, we should select a consensus algorithm. According to [22], achieving consensus in the raft consensus algorithm is faster than other algorithms. Thus, we have chosen raft as consensus algorithm.

As Fig. 5 shows, the network is composed of several nodes. Every node is a gateway connected either to a medical side or a simple user. Therefore, the number of nodes vary according to gateways' number. To identify an entity into the blockchain network, we use the account address generated by the GoQuorum network. As the blockchain is based on cryptography, each entity must have a key pair.

After creating network and nodes, the connected account aims to save or retrieve a value from the blockchain. Hence, the node must call the adequate function from the smart contract. In fact, the smart contract is a self-executing program that ensures treatment via transactions.

The relative smart contract to our system contains methods that allows a node to invoke either a store action or a retrieve action. Once the smart contract developed with the solidity programming language, it should be compiled then deployed into the blockchain network. This is a one-time but a fundamental action to make the methods' call possible. Indeed, the output of the contract deployment is the contract address that each node should indicate to perform a transaction.

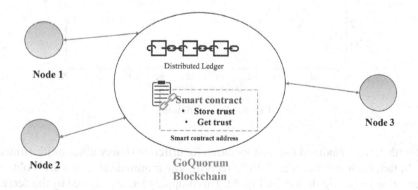

Fig. 5. Blockchain architecture

4 Performance Evaluation

Two parts are evaluated in this part: trust calculation algorithm and blockchain deployment and calls. Those experiments are executed on a terminal with 8 GB RAM and an intel Core i7 CPU.

To evaluate the trust approach, we have used Matlab to run the proposed algorithm. PDR data and energy is generated randomly within the defined intervals. We supposed that the total number of sensors in the connected home is 5. So, we have 5 different values for PDR and energy rate.

ECG trust weight is fixed to $w_{ecg} = 0.4$. Weights in the trust associated to the patient are defined as: $\alpha = 0.3$, $\beta = 0.3$, and $\gamma = 0.4$. Weights between instant and previous patient trust is fixed to $w1 = 0.4$ and $w2 = 0.6$.

Used ECG data [23] called Cardiac Arrhythmia Database, contains different ECG characteristics like QRS interval, P interval, t interval and heart rate. Also, it contains tags for different arrythmia diseases. We based our evaluation on associated values to normal ECG, ECG containing tachycardia and abnormal ECG values.

First, we calculated the needed time to execute this process in the gateway. The duration of this algorithm was 0.0032 s.

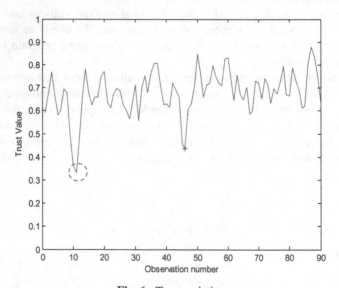

Fig. 6. Trust variation

After that, we visualized the trust variation for different observations as illustrated in Fig. 6. In fact, each value reflects 5 ECG records. The minimal value of trust is obtained at observation 11 (as highlighted in Fig. 6). This dropping value is caused by the decrease in ECG trust and an increase of energy consumption. Indeed, in this time interval, ECG data reflects values exceeding the normal threshold.

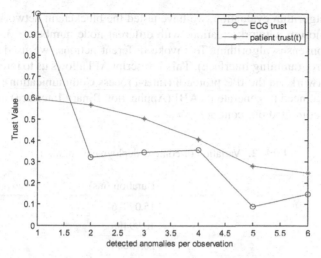

Fig. 7. Effect of ECG data and anomalies on patients' trust

Also, we tested anomalies' direct effects on the trust values. That is why we represented the trust according to intrusion number (Fig. 7). We can obviously notice that any decrease in ECG trust score led to a decrease of the patient trust degree.

Finally, we studied the effect of period number per observation on the processing time. As it is shown in Fig. 8, we have obtained a decreasing curve. In one hand, incrementing the period's number in one observation led to an amelioration in the QoS of our model since the rate of exchanging data decreases. In the other hand, this increase affects the system security, as the update interval will be higher. Therefore, the system's security efficiency is affected.

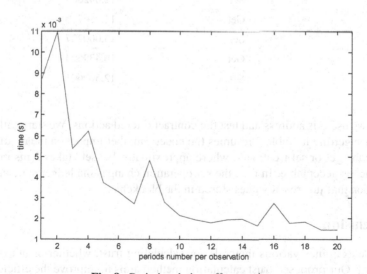

Fig. 8. Period variation effect on time

After the algorithm evaluation, we have tested the blockchain network. We started with the GoQuorum network creation, with different node number $\geq$ 3. We selected RAFT as a consensus algorithm. To invoke different actions, we used web3js API (Application Programming Interface). This Javascript API allows us to interact with our GoQuorum network via the IPC protocol (Inter-Process Communication). To consume this contract, we need to generate its ABI (Application Binary Interface) and bytecode. Therefore, we compiled our contract.

Table 2. Variation of contract deployment duration

Nodes' number	Duration (ms)
3	15,09316
5	16,99486
7	20,13085

First, we deployed our smart contact to obtain the contract address. Table 2 shows the different durations taken by the deployment process according to nodes' number. It is interesting to see that the deployment does not introduce an important overhead in term of time (in ms) compared to the execution algorithm (in s).

Table 3. Variation of actions duration

Nodes' number	Action	Duration (ms)
3	Get	11,056433
	Set	12,042064
5	Get	11,7667
	Set	13,000227
7	Get	10,439524
	Set	12,569601

Then, we use this address and test the contract offered actions. We start with storing a value, then getting it. Table 3 resumes the nodes' number impact on the required time to execute the get or set treatment, where approximatively "set" takes 2 ms more than "get", which is acceptable. In fact, the set operation changes the ledger state unlike the get operation that just reads values stored in the blockchain.

5 Conclusion

This article examines various methods for calculating trust, whether or not related to medical IoT. Our proposed trust calculation method aims to improve the efficiency and safety of medical-based patient monitoring systems. It relies on direct observations and medical data. Each trust update is stored in a transaction on the private blockchain to track identified attackers.

We studied the approach performance with ECG data and defined the threshold based on tachycardia disease. Our model is applied on different medical data; we just have to adapt the deviation calculation module to our input medical data. Our evaluation showed the different effects of data on the trust score. The overhead in terms of processed time is also evaluated, where our solution is not time consuming, which is interesting regarding the proposal benefits.

In the future, we plan to improve the model in several ways: (1) increase the security of the gateway as it manages data collection and processing, and (2) include a comparison of our solution with others to validate the performance of our work. In addition, it is interesting to make the system smarter by using machine learning to study the impact of variations in medical data on trust.

References

1. Xiong, W., Legrand, E., Åberg, O., Lagerström, R.: Cyber security threat modeling based on the MITRE enterprise ATT&CK Matrix. Softw. Syst. Model. **21**(1), 157–177 (2022). https://doi.org/10.1007/s10270-021-00898-7
2. FBASHI: Fuzzy and Blockchain-Based Adaptive Security for Healthcare IoTs | IEEE Journals & Magazine | IEEE Xplore. https://ieeexplore.ieee.org/abstract/document/9703287
3. Sengupta, J., Ruj, S., Das Bit, S.: A comprehensive survey on attacks, security issues and blockchain solutions for IoT and IIoT. J. Netw. Comput. Appl. **149**, 102481 (2020). https://doi.org/10.1016/j.jnca.2019.102481
4. Pelekoudas-Oikonomou, F., et al.: Blockchain-based security mechanisms for IoMT edge networks in IoMT-based healthcare monitoring systems. Sensors **22**(7), Art. no. 7 (2022). https://doi.org/10.3390/s22072449
5. Singh, S., Chawla, M., Prasad, D., Anand, D., Alharbi, A., Alosaimi, W.: An improved binomial distribution-based trust management algorithm for remote patient monitoring in WBANs. Sustainability **14**(4), Art. no. 4 (2022). https://doi.org/10.3390/su14042141
6. Sharma, A., Pilli, E.S., Mazumdar, A.P., Gera, P.: Towards trustworthy internet of things: a survey on trust management applications and schemes. Comput. Commun. **160**, 475–493 (2020). https://doi.org/10.1016/j.comcom.2020.06.030
7. Ahmed, A.I.A., AbHamid, S.H., Gani, A., Khan, S., Khan, M.K.: Trust and reputation for internet of things: fundamentals, taxonomy, and open research challenges. J. Netw. Comput. Appl. **145**, 102409 (2019). https://doi.org/10.1016/j.jnca.2019.102409
8. Fortino, G., Fotia, L., Messina, F., Rosaci, D., Sarné, G.M.L.: Trust and reputation in the internet of things: state-of-the-art and research challenges. IEEE Access **8**, 60117–60125 (2020). https://doi.org/10.1109/ACCESS.2020.2982318
9. Waleed, M., Latif, R., Yakubu, B.M., Khan, M.I., Latif, S.: T-smart: trust model for blockchain based smart marketplace. J. Theor. Appl. Electron. Commer. Res. **16**(6), Art. no. 6 (2021). https://doi.org/10.3390/jtaer16060132
10. Wu, X., Liang, J.: A blockchain-based trust management method for internet of things. Pervasive Mob. Comput. **72**, 101330 (2021). https://doi.org/10.1016/j.pmcj.2021.101330
11. Putra, G.D., Dedeoglu, V., Kanhere, S.S., Jurdak, R., Ignjatovic, A.: Trust-based blockchain authorization for IoT. IEEE Trans. Netw. Serv. Manage. **18**(2), 1646–1658 (2021). https://doi.org/10.1109/TNSM.2021.3077276

12. Tu, Z., Zhou, H., Li, K., Song, H., Yang, Y.: A blockchain-based trust and reputation model with dynamic evaluation mechanism for IoT. Comput. Netw. **218**, 109404 (2022). https://doi.org/10.1016/j.comnet.2022.109404

13. Ali, S.E., Tariq, N., Khan, F.A., Ashraf, M., Abdul, W., Saleem, K.: BFT-IoMT: a blockchain-based trust mechanism to mitigate sybil attack using fuzzy logic in the internet of medical things. Sensors **23**(9), Art. no. 9 (2023). https://doi.org/10.3390/s23094265

14. Awan, K.A., Din, I.U., Almogren, A., Almajed, H., Mohiuddin, I., Guizani, M.: NeuroTrust—artificial-neural-network-based intelligent trust management mechanism for large-scale internet of medical things. IEEE Internet Things J. **8**(21), 15672–15682 (2021). https://doi.org/10.1109/JIOT.2020.3029221

15. Singh, A., Chatterjee, K., Satapathy, S.C.: TrIDS: an intelligent behavioural trust based IDS for smart healthcare system. Clust. Comput. **62**(2), 903–925 (2023). https://doi.org/10.1007/s10586-022-03614-2

16. Al-Hamadi, H., Chen, I.R.: Trust-based decision making for health IoT systems. IEEE Internet Things J. **4**(5), 1408–1419 (2017). https://doi.org/10.1109/JIOT.2017.2736446

17. Li, W., Meng, W., Kwok, L.F.: Surveying trust-based collaborative intrusion detection: state-of-the-art, challenges and future directions. IEEE Commun. Surv. Tutor. **24**(1), 280–305 (2022). https://doi.org/10.1109/COMST.2021.3139052

18. Merdjanovska, E., Rashkovska, A.: Comprehensive survey of computational ECG analysis: databases, methods and applications. Expert Syst. Appl. **203**, 117206 (2022). https://doi.org/10.1016/j.eswa.2022.117206

19. ECG Disease Patterns. https://medschool.co/tests/ecg-disease-patterns

20. Guo, H., Yu, X.: A survey on blockchain technology and its security. Blockchain: Res. Appl. **3**(2), 100067 (2022). https://doi.org/10.1016/j.bcra.2022.100067

21. Mazzoni, M., Corradi, A., Di Nicola, V.: Performance evaluation of permissioned blockchains for financial applications: the ConsenSys Quorum case study. Blockchain: Res. Appl. **3**(1), 100026 (2022). https://doi.org/10.1016/j.bcra.2021.100026

22. Comparing proof of authority consensus protocols | ConsenSys GoQuorum (2023). https://docs.goquorum.consensys.net/concepts/consensus/comparing-poa

23. Cardiac Arrhythmia Database. https://www.kaggle.com/datasets/bulentesen/cardiac-arrhythmia-database

Command & Control in UAVs Fleets: Coordinating Drones for Ground Missions in Changing Contexts

Moussa Amrani[✉][iD], Abdelkader Ouared[iD], and Pierre-Yves Schobbens[iD]

Faculty of Computer Science/NaDI, Rue Grandgagnage, 21, 5000 Namur, Belgium
{Moussa.Amrani,Abdelkader.Ouared,Pierre-Yves.Schobbens}@unamur.be

Abstract. Save-And-Rescue missions often present risks for first responders when their mission occurs in hazardous or risky environments. Thanks to significant advances in robotics and Artificial Intelligence, deploying a swarm of Unmanned Aerial Vehicles (UAVs) (also known as drones) for these missions, has become a promising direction to facilitate first responders' work. However, despite these recent advances, this remains a difficult challenge because of the ever changing environment and operation conditions the drones evolve in. Ideally, drones should collaborate and share information about the situation, and eventually report back to the humans involved when key decisions have to be taken, freeing up time and human resources for other challenging and crucial tasks.

Command & Control (C2) is a military concept that studies how a set of entities and resources may be best deployed, organised, and driven towards the achievement of tasks at the service of a high-level objective. With the recent increase in distributiveness and variety of information, C2 found new interesting application areas (disaster relief and financial operations; mass vaccination campaigns; etc.)

This paper explores the meaning of implementing C2 in UAV fleets for deployment in large ground missions such as Save-And-Rescue, as a way to systematically implement human-to-drones and drones-to-human communications. We capture in a metamodel the specification of a C2 system that describe how teams of drones work collaboratively, based on a C2 approach. We show how the C2 System may evolve when change is detected, while keeping the C2 System coherent.

1 Introduction

Save-and-Rescue missions often present risks for first responders when happening in hazardous environments (e.g. rugged mountains, large-area fires, floods, etc.) Deploying Unmanned Aerial Systems (UAVs) on those fields is therefore becoming a norm. Relying on an UAV fleet equipped with onboard intelligence opens the way to semi-autonomous tasks execution, resulting in enhanced response times and better efficiency for responders, improving in fine the rescue mission's outcome. This intelligence requires a careful design of the many interactions and communications: humans communicate mission goals and tasks to drones, and with other humans as well; while drones report their progress, difficulties, and results to humans, and sporadically need feedback to appropriately react to unexpected events.

Command & Control (C2) [3,17] is a military concept that studies how a set of entities and resources may be best deployed, organised, and driven towards the achievement of missions realising a high-level objective. With the increase in distributiveness and variety of information, C2 found new interesting application areas: e.g., disaster relief and financial operations [8]; mass vaccination campaigns [10,12]; etc. NATO attempted in recent years to promote and deliberately implement C2 in its own large-scale operations [13]. Various C2 domains describe scenarios with increasing complexity raising from the dynamic nature of the environment, the entities' interactions, and the very nature of the humans involved. This is known as C2 Agility: the ability for task-performing entities to effectively detect changes, and adapt accordingly, in a timely fashion [18].

C2 advocates the use of so-called *approaches*, i.e. guidelines for defining how entities involved in performing a mission may coordinate, communicate and interact in a "fractal" way [3], meaning that those guidelines are adopted at any level of decomposition for the teams involved. These C2 approaches define three central components: who is in charge of the internal and external communications (the so-called *leader* in a team, and the *point/person of contact*, or PoC, for different teams); how the communication is organised among members; and what the communication consists of.

In this paper, we explore how it may be possible to apply NATO's notion for C2 in the context of a fleet of drones deployed to complete a Save-and-Rescue mission, i.e. organising the drones into so-called teams that operate under designated C2 approaches. After explaining what C2, C2 Approaches and C2 Agility consist of in the NATO vision (cf. Sect. 2), we propose a metamodel (cf. Sect. 3) enabling the creation and edition of C2 Systems, defined as collaborating teams under C2 Approaches, from which it becomes possible to simulate the System (cf. Sect. 5), and in particular to interactively force changes on the drones environment to observe C2 Agility (cf. Sect. 4).

2   Command & Control in a Nutshell

Command & Control, often abbreviated as C2, is a set of features and processes, based on humans, physical and informational systems aimed at *solving problems* at large scale. We briefly review in this section the appropriate literature on how C2 emerged, what it precisely is, and organically consists of, and why it requires agility, i.e. the ability to *react* to change, which inevitably occurs during mission.

2.1   Command & Control (C2)

Despite being clearly grounded into military's doctrinal and operational vocabulary, the terms *command*, *control*, and the expression *Command & Control*, do not have a consistent meaning or a clear, common understanding. As stated by

[16], only humans may command, because they may demonstrate the ability to exercise their knowledge, experience, intuition, innovative thinking, dedication, motivation, etc. to take the decisions associated with Command and live with the consequences. Since C2 plays a crucial role for organising military operations, it progressively integrated information and communication technologies for handling the difficulties of contemporary missions and challenges, opening the door for multiple concepts enriching the original C2 concept with Intelligence (C2I), Surveillance and Reconnaissance (C2ISR), and even more advanced and focused technologies designed for Target Acquisition and Reconnaissance.

To understand what C2 is, it is helpful to explain what it is intended for, and how it is structured. For the military context, there exists three definitions. The US Department of Defense, in its Dictionary of Military and Associated Terms, defines C2 as *"the exercise of authority and direction by a properly designated commander over assigned and attached forces in the accomplishment of a mission. Command and Control functions are performed through an arrangement of personnel, equipment, communications, facilities, and procedures employed by a commander in planning, directing, coordinating, and controlling forces and operations in the accomplishment of the mission."*[1]. The NATO Glossary defines C2 as *"the functions of commanders, staffs, and other Command and Control bodies in maintaining the combat readiness of their forces, preparing operations, and directing troops in the performance of their tasks. The concept embraces the continuous acquisition, fusion, review, representation, analysis and assessment of information on the situation; issuing the commander's plan; tasking of forces; operational planning; organizing and maintaining cooperation by all forces and all forms of support; organizing command and control; preparing subordinate command and control bodies and forces for combat operations; supervising and assisting subordinate commanders, staffs and forces; the direct leadership of troops during performance of their combat missions"*[2]. [20] define C2 as *"a set of organisational and technical attributes and processes that employ human, physical, and information resources to solve problems and accomplish missions"*.

What is interesting in these definitions is their commonalities enlighting a list of operating concepts: (i) C2 is a list of *functions*; (ii) intended, as a ultimate objective, to help accomplish *missions* (iii) which may be seen as composed of *tasks* assigned to some *entities* (or, *"forces"*). Before going deeper into the functions constituting C2, it may be interesting to first focus on what is intended as *Control* and *Command*, and precisely identify their relationships and interactions. According to [16], **Control** is composed of *"those [Control] structures and processes devised by* Command *to enable and manage the risks"* associated to missions; while **Command** is *"the creative expression of human will necessary to accomplish the mission"*.

---

[1] Dictionary of Military and Associated Terms, Joint Publication I-02, Retrieved on March 2021, http://www.dtic.mil/doctrine/jel/doddict/data/.

[2] NATO Glossary, Retrieved on March 2021, available at https://www.nato.int/docu/glossary/eng/15-main.pdf.

The authors provide interesting insights on how and why those components (Control, and Command) are interdependent and both necessary. When facing a mission, there are an infinite possibility for performing it, considering the various interest factors (costs, resources, etc.) Defining a Control structure reduces the problem space to a more manageable space that fixes the set of possibilities, but also directly influences the possible course of actions. In this reduced problem space, Control procedures define regulated processes that allow control structures to effectively perform work. Command, then, requires to study the specificities of this framework, and to exercise the human mind and creativity to devise solutions to accomplish the mission with the best possible outcomes. Just like control in cyber-physical systems, Control in the C2 sense requires to monitor structures, but also processes; however, in C2, Control goes beyond because it also require to carry out and adjust procedures according to pre-established plans. On the other hand, Command is the act of enabling command and managing risk using the existing structures and processes: this would require to create new, and to modify existing control structures and processes when necessary, but also to initiate and terminate control as well as defining the conditions for initiation and termination.

Note that C2 is a "fractal" concept [3], meaning that it applies to various granularity levels. Therefore, Control structures and processes range over a large variety of artefacts that may fundamentally differ in their formality and rigidity: in the military context, this would include at the most formal and rigid end of the spectrum the equipment (including software and communication technologies) and tangible resources (including humans), to the less rigid end of organisational structures and doctrine. Therefore, when applied at an organisation level, C2 determines the organisation's purpose, priorities and ultimately, capabilities, shaping the horizon of possible actions; when applied at the missions level, C2 is concerned by how to best use an organisation's assets (people, systems, material and their relationships) to achieve the organisation's goals.

2.2   C2 Functions and Approaches

C2 does not represent an end to itself, but is rather a means towards creating value, which, in the military context, is often understood as accomplishing, or completing, a (set of) mission(s). Therefore, C2 designates a set of interrelated, but distinct functions that apply to organisations at different scales. Many definitions, including the ones provided above issued by military (inter-)national organisations, seem rather regulatory in nature, and limited in their applicability to the military context. In order to focus on concepts and approaches of C2 in general, the NATO System Analysis and Studies (SAS) Panel proposed to clarify two important questions: *why* one does C2; and *what functions* an instantiation of C2 needs to accomplish to achieve its purposes [17, Chap. 2]. Similar to [3], the Panel notices that due to the fractal nature of C2, the purpose of applying C2 at the mission level is to *employ the assets of an organisation—its people, systems, materiel and relationships with others—in pursuit of mission-specific goals and objectives.* Any instantiation of C2 should at least propose the

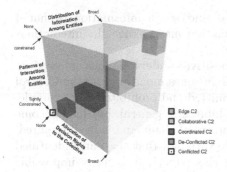
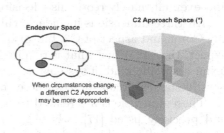
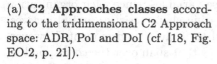

(a) **C2 Approaches classes** according to the tridimensional C2 Approach space: ADR, PoI and DoI (cf. [18, Fig. EO-2, p. 21]).

(b) **C2 Approach Manœuver:** a change in the endeavour space triggers a change in the most appropriate C2 Approach. (from [18, Fig. EO-4, p. 22]).

Fig. 1. C2 Approaches definition according to NATO (reproduced from [18])

following functions[3] [3]: (i) Establish intent, i.e. the goal or the objective of a mission; (ii) Determine roles, responsibilities and relationships; (iii) Establish rules and constraints (e.g. schedules, etc.); and (iv) Monitor and assess the situation and progress. As a consequence, C2 should be seen as determining "*bounds for decisions*" rather than enforcing decisions themselves. The latter is indeed unrealistic in situations where frequent changes in the problem space where a mission takes place prevents uniform and monolithic solutions in intents, organisations, command and control. As observed earlier, decisions (and Command) requires creativity and willingness to cope with the uncertainty and scale of complex problems.

Given a mission, many possible approaches to accomplish those C2 functions may be envisioned. The Panel [17] defined precisely three dimensions for C2 Approaches. The **Allocation of Decision Rights (ADR)** designates the way authority and responsibilities are distributed within an entity, i.e. which decisions are assigned to which entities, and when (under which circumstances) and how to take them. The **Patterns of Interactions (PoI)** relate to the info-structure available, as well as doctrine, culture and other factors, and covers the "reach" (number and variety of participants), "richness" (breadth and quality of the content involved), and interaction quality (medium, availability, continuity, etc.). Finally, the **Distribution of Information (DoI)** designates the nature of information that is shared and transmitted among entities, but also who is responsible for it and when transmission is supposed to occur. Those dimensions are obviously far from being independent: the way decisions rights are allocated

---

[3] The authors add leading-related functions associated with Command, such as "inspiring, motivating, engendering trust, training, educating", etc. However, these functions have little interest for our purpose of applying C2 for a Cyber-Physical System such as a drone swarm.

directly influences how interactions operate, and which information is shared and transmitted; on the other hand, information may change the interactions and even ultimately reorganise decision rights.

All three dimensions include so-called "positive" understandings enforced by the Command aspect of C2, but also "negative" ones monitored by the Control aspect: they all define what is required, permitted and prohibited. For example, using a specific kind of systems may be prohibited in general, but may become possible under circumstances where the approval of Command is itself required.

These dimensions are related to multiple variables that the Panel identified and precisely listed [17] (which go beyond this paper). It is likely impossible to capture all possible combinations of these variables, since each organisation likely has its own structure, works with specific characteristics and objectives, and has to perform particular tasks related to a given environment. However, the Panel defined several C2 Approach *classes* that span over the corresponding tridimensional space; thus encompassing similar combinations of these variables, corresponding to a specific way of considering each of the three dimensions: *Conflicted, Deconflicted, Coordinated, Collaborative* and *Edge* (cf. Fig. 1a). We elaborated and operationalise these classes in Sect. 3.2.

2.3   C2 Agility and C2 Approach Manœuver

Hypothetically, there exist a most appropriate C2 Approach for a particular mission conducted in specific circumstances. However, as time passes and circumstances change, entities have to adapt and evolve to complete missions: this so-called *C2 Agility* may be performed at two scales. First, when changes are relatively circumscribed, entities may choose to organise and behave differently to cope with new elements; however, when those prove to be insufficient, a change in the C2 Approach may be required, triggering a change at a larger scale.

The so-called *endeavour space* captures the changes occurring during missions, as a theoretical construction representing the set of possible futures, according to three changing dimensions: "*Self*", *i.e.*, changes occurring inside the entities themselves, *e.g.*, added and lost capacity, degradation of system's performances due to physical damage or system failure; modification of teams; breach of information security; etc.; *Mission*, *i.e.*, changes affecting the mission itself, *e.g.*, completion time, scope, ground conditions, etc.; and finally *Environment*, *i.e.*, changes affecting elements outside of the entities and the mission, *e.g.,*. operating conditions (weather, terrain, etc.) Small changes in the endeavour space may be anticipated with changes in the *Self*, showing that an entity stays successful in completing a mission with agility. However, larger, or simultaneous changes, may require C2 Approach *Agility* that requires three steps: first, *detection*, i.e. understanding that such a large-scale change occurred; then *analysis* to recognise that the current C2 Approach no longer operates well under new circumstances; second, *selection*, i.e. figuring out which C2 Approach becomes more relevant; and third, *transition* to the new C2 Approach in a timely manner. These steps are referred to as *C2 Manœuver*, as illustrated in Fig. 1.

3   A Metamodel for *Control & Command*

We now explore the possibility of articulating Control & Command (C2) strategies in the context of drone swarms, that are deployed from a Control Centre to perform Save-And-Rescue Missions, according to the following use case.

A *Mission Officer* receives a *Mission Description* that needs to be translated into a *Mission Specification* aimed at being handled by a swarm. This Specification is send to a Drone Engineer, who will prepare the drones fleet accordingly: which drones need to be equipped with what kind of workload (video, night vision and/or thermal cameras, GPS, different payloads, etc.) A drone may come in various sizes, autonomy, speed/altitude flight capability, with various software variations, etc. This aspect is described in our settings with a Feature Model [6]: a description of the material and the drone, their characteristics, and their possible combinations (e.g., a thermal camera weighs 8 kg, requiring a drone capable of at least carrying this weight). This results in a series of constraints that are easily solvable once the Feature Model has been elaborated [9].

To simplify the description, we consider that a Mission Specification consists of a list of tasks that are independent of each other, i.e. the completion of one Task does not influence the completion of others. Furthermore, we consider that each Task is handled by one Drone at a time: each Drone is assigned a list of tasks so that all tasks constituting the Mission Specification are initially covered. Knowing which hardware is available in the Control Centre, the Drone Engineer comes with an initial proposal of a C2 System that is able to cover the Mission Specification's list of tasks (or revisit it, if necessary). This C2 System covers the following aspects: (i) Drones are organised into teams that will collaborate towards fulfilling the Mission Specification. Each drone receives an initial valid configuration. (ii) All teams operate under a specific C2 Approach.

We further interpreted the notions of NATO's C2 notions of ADR (Allocation of Decision Rights), PoI (Patterns of Interactions) and DoI (Distribution of Information) as follows. For ADR, each entity explicitly designates a *leader*, who may for example keep track of the failed tasks and try to allocate them to other drones, assuming a direct communication is possible. The PoI is encoded into a communication topology that enables communication channels between entities. The DoI is left as future work, as the detail of the information raises many questions regarding format, security, communication channels, etc.; however, we capture components directly influencing the mission.

We describe in Sect. 3.1 a candidate metamodel for creating, editing and deploying C2 systems, as entities organised along C2 Approaches. We then discuss how those C2 Approaches may translate topologically into the C2 system in Sect. 3.2.

3.1   Metamodel Description

Figure 2 describes a possible metamodel for capturing C2 Systems, as envisioned by NATO [18]. The root element is C2System: it describes the system in its entirety: which teams of drones are deployed to perform a mission, as specified by the set of tasks it is composed of.

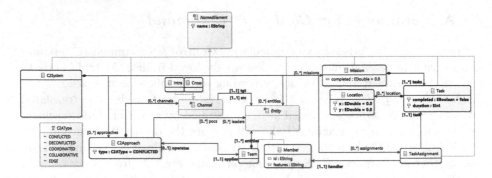

Fig. 2. A Metamodel to specify and edit C2 Systems

A C2System is composed of a set of Entities that are composite aggregations of drones (named Members) organised into Teams. A Member is uniquely defined in the swarm by an id, and integrates a set of HW/SW features that are valid according to a predefined Feature Model. The features attribute is a String encoding of the list of atomic features present in the Member. We assume the ability for the Drone Engineer to check the hardware and software constraints resulting from a candidate configuration of teams. The Engineer may eventually benefit from recommenders that would help in choosing particular equipments, or reaching the best combination(s) fitting a given Mission Specification.

A C2System is created to respond to a particular Mission defined as a list of Tasks. For now, we consider Tasks are independent from each others, atomic, and specified with a completion duration and a geographical Location. They may later be detailed with richer features.

A C2System is always defined with a specific C2Approach, as defined by [18], enforcing the C2 characteristic elements: The *ADR* for each Entity is captured as a leader in a non-composite Entity; and as a poc(s) for a composite one. The *PoI* is captured by the C2AType, whose examples of organisation patterns are described in Table 1, following the NATO classification [18]. We abstract for now from the *DoI*, since it requires further investigation and captures detailed behaviour of the C2System. Note that the *PoI* is freely defined at each Entity composition level, as depicted in the examplar model of Fig. 3.

By using Model-Driven Engineering techniques [21], defining such a metamodel leads to the automatic generation of an editor to create *instances* of a C2 System, as demonstrated by a sample system in Fig. 3. Note that the metamodel described in Fig. 2 is tailored for creating systems, rather than analysis or any other activities surrounding C2 systems. To that end, we explicitly distinguished Intra and Cross communication Channels that may have been amalgamated on a first approach. On our sample C2 system, these Channels are visually represented differently, and the Leader is represented as a dark circle, as opposed to other Members. Note that our editor enforces the correlation between the C2Approach declared for a Team (under the reference operates) and the actual topology depicted for it.

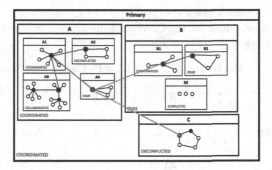

Fig. 3. A Simple C2System with a top-level Team Primary: it is composed of three sub-Teams A, B (themselves further decomposed), and C (containing only drones). Each Team operates under a particular C2Approach refered to by its C2AType (in blue text), defining the communication topology (cf. Table 1).

3.2   C2 Approaches

The PoI (*Patterns of Interactions*) are a crucial part for defining an appropriate C2 Approach. Based on first ideas and insights by [2], we argue that it is possible to explicitly describe PoIs in a rigorous way. Table 1 depicts and summarises the PoIs and links them with their visual representation as C2AType, and illustrates them on teams from C2 System of Fig. 3. Furthermore, we described what we intended as "patterns" in Table 1: each name associated to a C2AType translates into a specific structure that clearly identifies (i) one (or several) leaders ($\#L$) and/or Point of Contacts (PoCs) ($\#\mathbf{PoCs}$), depending on the composite nature of each Entity; and (ii) a mathematical structure capturing the *Topology* intended by the PoI pattern.

CONFLICTED designates a situation where team members maintain no communication at all: each member evolves completely independently from the others, and no coordination is expected. This kind of situation is sometimes encountered in hostile fields where communication signals may be intercepted and used as exploits to retrieve information that may be lethal. In Figure 3, only Team B3 operates under this approach. This C2 Approach does not require any specification, since it does enforce no pattern at all.

DECONFLICTED corresponds to a situation where communication is kept at minimal: each team member communicates with exactly two other members, thus forming a *ring* between members; a specific member is elected (or chosen) as a *leader* for ensuring external communication with other teams. Since this C2A approach is more common, Teams C and A2 operates under this approach in Fig. 3. This pattern enforces a *ring*, which is defined with one leader/poc, and an ordering of the entities constituting the team (modelled as a function producing a list from the set of entities).

COORDINATED designates a situation where communication becomes more affordable and centralised, allowing each member to directly and solely com-

Table 1. Patterns of Interactions (PoIs), as part of C2 Approach. The terms in the first column are used as values for the **C2AType** enumeration in Fig. 2. The column *Ex.* illustrates the PoI using the model of Fig. 3.

PoI Name	Pattern	Ex.	#L	#PoCs	Topology
CONFLICTED		B3	0	0	$\emptyset$
DECONFLICTED		A2, C	1	1	[Entity $\rightarrow$ $\langle$Entity$\rangle$]
COORDINATED		A1 B1 A Primary	1	1	$\emptyset$
COLLABORATIVE		A3	n	n	(leader $\cup$ pocs) $\rightarrow$ $\wp$(Entity)
EDGE		A4 B2 B	0	0	$\emptyset$

municate with the leader. This leads to a *star*-like topology, and is adopted by Teams A1, B1, A and Primary itself. This C2 Approach enforces a *star* pattern, which only requires one leader/poc that connects all other entities.

COLLABORATIVE describes a situation where team members need to more toroughly coordinate their efforts, leading to an intermediate topology: a number of small clusters operate as if they were **COORDINATED**, i.e. they solely refer to their (sub-)leader, but leaders are allowed to communicate with each other, resulting in *clusterised starred* topologies, as operated by A3. This C2 Approach enforces a *clustered-starred* pattern, which requires identifying multiple leaders/pocs, and a function mapping each to the entities connected to it.

EDGE describes a situation where everyone is reachable, allowing each member to communicate with any other member. For coordination and centralisation purposes, this C2 Approach still defines a leader. This C2 Approach is adopted by A4, B2 and B. This C2 Approach enforces a *full* connection between members, which does not require further specification.

Note that for Save-And-Rescue, the communication channels have to be supported by an underlying network that will handle message passing. This may be achieved through classic networks (e.g. Global System for Mobile communication, or military communication networks), or ensured with an additional drone (typically flying at higher altitudes) that serve as a relay between the drones.

4   Tackling C2 (Approach) Agility

Once a C2 System is deployed, the drones start the tasks they are assigned to, and communicate to the leaders/PoCs when they eventually complete them. As defined by [3], *change* certainly occurs in a C2 System during mission at three different levels (*self, mission* and *environment*). In the context of Save-And-Rescue missions, the drones themselves may encounter difficulties due to battery or flight issues, damage or system failures (e.g. hitting a high-voltage line). Similarly, the mission may evolve over time when new information is acquired, triggering new tasks to perform. For example, detecting a distress signal may require to reallocate the drones in a specific place; and locating someone in a location difficult to access may require to carry special material near the rescue location. Finally, operating conditions may rapidly change in some locations (e.g. in mountains) that prevent drone flights, or require special equipment like anti-wind or anti-lightning prevention measures.

Our proposal for tackling C2 Approaches Agility in the context of Save-And-Rescue missions consists of defining a *communication protocol* aimed at organising when, where and how decisions for agility are taken, and how communication for supporting these decisions are transmitted. This protocol is based on two major choices: we define *roles* associated with specific entities on a Team, that confer specific tasks in the decision process; and we rely on *events* to detect and carry information throughout a Team to support agility decisions.

4.1 C2 Roles

Resources in a C2System need to find a balance between two crucial tasks: on the one hand, performing the tasks in order to complete the mission as soon and as well as possible; and on the other hand, monitoring the fleet to detect changes, and eventually react by redistributing the tasks, or reconfiguring the entire system. We identify three roles to achieve this balance:

(Task Performing) Entities execute tasks that are assigned to them by the *Task Allocator*, performing them in the order they are transmitted. A task execution may complete successfully, or fail. Both situations are reported back to the Task Allocator for providing a chance to reallocating failed tasks to another entity. Furthermore, during the course of the mission, an entity maintains a set of *live* sensors (corresponding to features), starting from the full list of sensors the drone is launched with; and sensors may stop functioning properly. Finally, a drone may stop functioning entirely.

A **Task Allocator** (Entity) keeps track of the tasks constituting a mission, and tries to allocate them to entities for performing them. It also collects sensor failures in order to appropriately dispatch tasks to drones that are able to handle them. Periodically, the Task Allocator attempts to reassign the tasks that were reported to have failed, trying to ensure an overall progress on the mission.

The **C2A Selector** (Entity) is the central communication point responsible for a team and centralises communication with the Command Base. When the drone fleet is deployed, it communicates the task list constituting the mission to the Task Allocator for enabling dispatch, and it may receive updates with new tasks to handle from the Base. The C2A Selector also has the capability to react to new situations and changes by enforcing a new C2 Approach over the team it is leading.

Table 2. List of Events Definitions, together with their *Producer* and *Consumer*.

Producer	Event	Consumer	Description
Entity	Completed()	*self*	The current task completed successfully
	Failed()	*self*	The current task failed
	SensorFailed(Feature)	*self*	The sensor realising feature f is out of service
	TaskCompleted(Id, Task)	TA	Entity Id has completed Task
	TaskFailed(Id, Task)	TA	Entity Id has failed Task
	SensorFailed(Id, F)	TA	Entity Id lost the ability to use sensor F
TA	Allocate(Id, Task)	Entity	Allocate Task to Entity Id
	Reschedule()	*self*	The Task rescheduling period is reached
	Evaluate()	*self*	The C2 System evaluation period is reached
	Manœuver(T)	C2AS	Trigger C2A Manœuver with pending Tasks T
C2AS	NewTask(T)	TA	Update Task list with T
	addTask(T)	C2AS	Updated Mission with new Task T

Note that roles may be freely distributed among team entities: a single drone may fulfil several roles (e.g. being a Task Allocator and C2A Selector); and depending on the team's size, task allocation may be distributed over several entities, depending on the C2 Approach at hand.

4.2   Event Communication

To enable intra- (i.e. among team's entities) and inter- (i.e. between teams) communication, we specify a set of events that capture what may happen in a C2 System that needs to be reported. These events are presented according to the role they refer to. At a first level, we have three *auto-diagnostic* events each drone is able to produce while executing tasks. These events are closely related to the way tasks are implemented, including which languages are used for describing these tasks. Two events notify when the current executing Task has Completed() or Failed(); and an extra event informs of a SensorFailed().

Each Entity can communicate with an associated Task Allocator to report internal events: the corresponding events simply report what happened at the first level with events TaskCompleted, TaskFailed, and SensorFailed (with appropriate parameters indicating the Entity, the Task and the sensor).

A Task Allocator may Allocate() a Task to an Entity (assuming it has adequate equipment for the Task), which is triggered when the periodic event Reschedule is issued. The Task Allocator also periodically Evaluate the C2 System since it collects the information about successful and failed Tasks as well as each Entity status regarding its sensors. When critical conditions are reached, the Task Allocator notifies the C2A Selector a deeper evaluation needs to be performed.

Table 2 classifies those events according to the Entity or role that produces and consumes it. Note that many events are produced and consumed by the same Entity (noted *self*); and that exactly one event (addTask) comes from the C2 System's environment (i.e. from *outside* the defined C2 System).

The event Evaluate triggers a special safety function embedded in the drone swarm software that periodically scans the overall system, through the appropriate communication channels, and reports the necessity of change. This function evaluates the current state of the C2 System (which drones are alive, with which capabilities), and gathers some information about the environment, to assess the feasibility of the mission with the current C2 Approach. If necessary (and eventually after reporting back to the Mission Officer), a manœuver is issued, changing the current C2 Approach into a new one.

4.3   C2 Approaches Manœuvering

C2 Approaches Agility is performed through *manœuvering*, i.e. the ability to adapt a C2 System to the changes occurring in the endeavour space (cf. Sect. 2.3). According to Table 1, manœuvering requires two pieces of information. First, **defining new leader(s)/PoC(s)**. This can automatically be inferred from the C2 System's current state, or recommended *a priori* when the mission is launched, using an election system inside teams, thus defining a candidate leader/PoC and possible replacements in case the candidate is not available. Second, **changing the Topology.** With our definition of topology (cf. Table 1), we only need to define an (communication) order among members, or a subset of members reachable from a common entity. This may easily be preprogrammed, or defined on the fly with more elaborated mechanisms taking into account the C2 System dynamic state. This process works at any level of Team decomposition, allowing to select C2 Approaches appropriate for any Team.

5   A C2 System Simulator

We built a prototype implementation based on a pipeline of tools that exchange informations in order to provide the ability to (i) specify C2 Systems; and (ii) simulate them. Thanks to our metamodel, we automatically generate a visual editor that allows to create and configure a C2 System based on the available sensors (e.g. vision or thermal cameras, GPS, etc.), and to define C2 Approaches for teams, that are enforced using a simple communication protocol. Once the C2 System is ready, it is automatically transfered to a multi-agent simulation engine [7] (based on Repast Symphony) that visually demonstrates how drones handle mission's tasks. The Officer may trigger changes (limited for now to predefined use cases where drones lose one particular sensor, or become unavailable, or force an environment change), or alter the mission with new tasks (cf. Fig. 4).

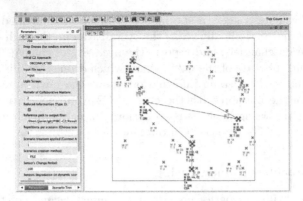

Fig. 4. Prototype simulator for building C2 System and simulating C2A Agility.

6 Conclusion

In this paper, we precisely captured, and made operational, the NATO notion of Command & Control (C2), for structuring the organisation and communication of Unmanned Aerial Systems deployed on missions such as Save-And-Rescue. We provided a metamodel that enables creating and editing C2 Systems using an arbitrary number of drone teams operating under C2 Approaches. We provided a simulator for deploying a C2 System that performs predefined tasks. The simulator allows to observe changes resulting from C2 Agility and the influence of C2 Approaches on mission completion.

We are currently putting an effort to formalise the behavioural semantics of C2 Systems, based on the choices described in this paper. Our goal is to provide empirical proof that a C2 System should, under reasonable expectations from the environment, enable to complete the mission [4].

Many challenges remain open. First, specifying mission's tasks need to be refined for measuring their progress, and allowing to resume tasks [11,15,19]. Second, when and how reconfiguring a C2 System after change detection is crucial, and still under investigation (in particular, clarifying the three-step mechanism explained in Sect. 2.3), possibly using Machine Learning [14] techniques in each phase (cf. among others, [1,5]).

References

1. Agrawal, A., Cleland-Huang, J.: Explaining autonomous decisions in swarms of human-on-the-loop small unmanned aerial systems. In: AAAI Conference on Human Computation and Crowdsourcing (2021)
2. Alberts, D.S., Hayes, R.E.: Power To the Edge. Command & Control in the Information Age. Command and Control Research Program Publications (2003)
3. Alberts, D.S., Hayes, R.E.: Understanding Command and Control. Command and Control Research Program Publications (2011)

4. Amorim, J.C., et al.: Providing command and control agility: a software product line approach. Expert Syst. Appl. **216**, 119473 (2023)
5. Cleland-Huang, J., Agrawal, A.: Human-drone interactions with semi-autonomous cohorts of collaborating drones. In: Interdisciplinary Workshop on Human-Drone Interaction (2020)
6. Clements, P., Northrop, L.M.: Software Product Lines: Practices and Patterns. Addison-Wesley (2001)
7. Dorri, A., Kanhere, S.S., Jurdak, R.: Multi-agent systems: a survey. IEEE Access **6**, 28573–28593 (2018)
8. Fernandes, R., Hieb, M., Costa, P.: Levels of autonomy: command and control of hybrid forces. In: International C2 Research and Technology Symposium (2016)
9. Galindo, J.A., Benavides, D., Trinidad, P., Gutiérrez-Fernández, A.M., Ruiz-Cortés, A.: Automated analysis of feature models: quo vadis? J. Comput. **101**, 387–433 (2019)
10. Gao, X., Yu, J.: Public governance mechanism in the prevention and control of the COVID-19. J. Chin. Govern. **5**(2), 178–197 (2020)
11. Garcia, S., Pelliccione, P., Menghi, C., Berger, T., Bures, T.: High-level mission specification for multiple robots. In: SLE, pp. 127–140 (2019)
12. Jonson, C., Nilsson, H., Lundin, R., Rüter, A.: Regional medical command and control management of influenza A (H1N1) mass-vaccination in the County of Östergötland, Sweden. Prehospit. Disast. Med. **26**(S1) (2011)
13. Leal, G.M., Zacarias, I., Stocchero, J.M., Freitas, E.P.D.: Empowering command and control through a combination of information-centric networking and software defined networking. IEEE Commun. Mag. **57**(8), 48–55 (2019)
14. Mitchell, T.M.: Machine Learning. McGraw Hill Education (1997)
15. Molina, M., Sanchez-Lopez, J.L., Campoy, P.: TML: a language to specify aerial robotic missions for the framework aerostack. Int. J. Intell. Comput. Cybern. **10**(4), 491–512 (2017)
16. Pigeau, R., McCann, C.: Re-conceptualising command and control. Can. Milit. J. **5**(1), 53–63 (2002)
17. Research and Technology Organisation: Exploring New Command and Control Concepts and Capabilities. Technical report TR-SAS-050, NATO (2007)
18. Research and Technology Organisation: Command and Control (C2) Agility. Technical report TR-SAS-085, NATO (2014)
19. Stadler, M., Vierhauser, M., Garmendia, A., Wimmer, M., Cleland-Huang, J.: Flexible model-driven runtime monitoring support for cyber-physical systems. In: International Conference on Software Engineering, pp. 350–351 (2022)
20. Vassiliou, M.S., Alberts, D.S., Agre, J.R.: C2 Re-envisioned: The Future of the Enterprise. CRC Press (2015)
21. Voelter, M.: DSL Engineering: Designing, Implementing and Using Domain-Specific Languages. CreateSpace (2013)

Author Index

B. Ben Hedia et al. (Eds.): VECoS 2023, LNCS 14368, p. 179, 2024.
https://doi.org/10.1007/978-3-031-49737-7

Printed in the United States
by Baker & Taylor Publisher Services